FOR WHAT TOMORROW . . .

Cultural Memory
in
the
Present

Mieke Bal and Hent de Vries, Editors

FOR WHAT TOMORROW . . .

A Dialogue

Jacques Derrida
and Elisabeth Roudinesco

Translated by Jeff Fort

STANFORD UNIVERSITY PRESS

STANFORD, CALIFORNIA

2004

Stanford University Press
Stanford, California

This book has been published with the assistance of the
French Ministry of Culture—National Center for the Book.

For What Tomorrow . . . by Jacques Derrida and Elisabeth
Roudinesco was originally published in French in 2001 under
the title *De Quoi Demain . . .* © Librairie Arthème Fayard
and Éditions Galilée, 2001.

Printed in the United States of America
on acid-free, archival-quality paper

Library of Congress Cataloging-in-Publication Data

Derrida, Jacques.
  [De quoi demain— English]
  For what tomorrow : a dialogue / Jacques Derrida and Elisabeth Roudinesco ;
translated by Jeff Fort.
    p. cm. — (Cultural memory in the present)
  Includes bibliographical references.
  ISBN 0-8047-4607-9 (cloth : alk. paper) —
  ISBN 0-8047-4627-3 (pbk. : alk. paper)
    1. Derrida, Jacques—Interviews.   2. Philosophers—France—Interviews.
3. Philosophy. I. Roudinesco, Elisabeth, 1944– II. Title. III. Series.
B2430.D484A5 2004
194—DC22

                                    2004007585

Typeset by Tim Roberts in 11 / 13.5 Adobe Garamond

Original Printing 2004

Last figure below indicates year of this printing:

13   12   11   10   09   08   07   06   05   04

Contents

Foreword

"For what tomorrow will be, no one knows," writes Victor Hugo in one of the poems in his *Twilight Songs*. And in his introduction to this work, he proclaims: "Everything today, whether in ideas or in things, in society or in the individual, is in a twilight state. What is the nature of this twilight? What will come after it [de quoi sera-t-il suivi]?"[1] This was our point of departure.

This dialogue, the product of a long history that began thirty years ago, corresponds to the classic definition of the genre in philosophy and in the humanities in general: an exchange whose logic is constructed from two unfolding discourses that intersect without ever fusing and that respond to each other without really opposing each other. Thus differences are stated, points of convergence, discoveries on both sides, surprises, interrogations; in short, a complicity without complacency.

The spoken word was first captured by a microphone, then transcribed; this gave us a preliminary transition from an oral to a written form.[2] Each of us then reworked the transcription in order to recast it as a veritable text, a text in *two hands*, in which two "idioms," two singular manners of expression within the same language, would cohabitate.

When I proposed this dialogue to Jacques Derrida, I worried that my admiration for him might be an obstacle to the completion of our work. His gifts as a speaker, the power of his arguments, his boldness regarding certain problems of our times—as well as the practical wisdom acquired from countless lectures given in every part of the world—threatened to take my voice away. But soon I understood that "the exercise would be beneficial," according to the well-known English expression from the so-called literature of "initiation."[3]

I selected nine themes. Each one of them seems to me to be the locus of one or several of the great questions that mark our age. We respond to them by way of a reflection that combines several approaches: philosophical, historical, literary, political, psychoanalytic.

In the first chapter, we recall the intellectual legacy of the 1970's, which has since been so maligned. In the second chapter, we treat the multiple uses, on both sides of the Atlantic, of the notion of difference (sexual, "ethnic," cultural, etc.) In the third chapter, we address the problem of the transformations of the Western family.

We then pass, in the fourth chapter, to a reflection on human freedom, before interrogating, in the fifth chapter, the rights of animals and the duties that bind humans in relation to them. In the sixth chapter, we call on the spirit of the Revolution after the failure of communism. The next two chapters are devoted, on the one hand, to the modern forms of an anti-Semitism that is present and to come, and, on the other hand, to the current situation regarding the death penalty and its necessary abolition.

The book closes with a chapter in praise of psychoanalysis, our common reference throughout this dialogue.

E.R.

FOR WHAT TOMORROW . . .

1

Choosing One's Heritage

Elisabeth Roudinesco: I would like first of all to evoke the past, our common history. It has become respectable today to express disapproval of the thinkers of the 1970's and to demand a "necessary accounting" or, even worse, a "repentance" from those who claim them as an inspiration. The works of the period, marked as they are by very peculiar intersections with "structuralism," are the targets of an incoherent jumble of reproaches: they excessively valorize the spirit of revolt; they indulge in the cult of aestheticism; they are too attached to a certain linguistic formalism; they reject democratic freedoms; and they are profoundly skeptical of humanism. I think this ostracism is utterly sterile; it seems better to approach our age in a completely different way, one that involves, in your words, "choosing one's heritage":[1] neither accepting everything nor erasing everything.

You are the heir to the major works of the second half of the century. A number of these came out of systems of thought that are being challenged today. You have "deconstructed"[2] these works, notably those of Claude Lévi-Strauss, Michel Foucault, Louis Althusser, and Jacques Lacan.[3] During their lifetimes, and taking their works as your starting point, you "explicated" yourself (you like this verb) in relation to them; you engaged in a work of textual commentary, while also insisting on the importance, for your own teaching practices, of Edmund Husserl, Martin Heidegger, and Emmanuel Levinas.

It was at that time, around 1967, that I began reading your works, especially *Of Grammatology* and *Writing and Difference*,[4] as did all the students of literature of my generation interested in avant-garde literature and in the structural linguistics coming out of the work of Ferdinand de Saussure and Roman Jakobson. The subversive gesture then consisted in affirming that the human subject is determined by language, by symbolic functions, by the destiny of a "letter" or a signifier, or again by a writing prior to speech, and finally by the existence of the unconscious in the Freudian sense. While we respected Jean-Paul Sartre's political engagement, our generation was critical of his reluctance to confront directly the question of the unconscious in the formation of the subject, and we were skeptical of his humanism, with its "full" and self-transparent subject.[5]

Later, specifically at the second Cluny conference organized in spring 1970 by *La Nouvelle Critique*,[6] the journal of the French Communist Party, I criticized you for what I saw as your "infidelity" to this heritage you were deconstructing. For my part, I wanted to be faithful, but not dogmatic. Later, I felt much closer to you, and I thought that you had been right in your attempt to make works speak from within themselves, through their fault lines, their blanks, their margins, their contradictions, but without trying to kill them. Hence the idea that the best way to be faithful to a heritage is to be unfaithful, that is, not to accept it literally, as a totality, but rather to take it as something in default, to grasp its "dogmatic moment": "I feel that I am also an heir: faithful as far as possible," you said in an interview from 1983.[7] Likewise, of Levinas you say that "his relation to ontology is one of both infidelity and fidelity."[8]

The true adversaries of the thought of the period appeared later, in 1986, when Luc Ferry and Alain Renaut published a book that received a lot of attention: *La pensée 68 (French Philosophy of the Sixties).*[9]

Today, you are in a way the last heir to this thought, which has proven to be so fruitful. You are even, if I dare say so, its survivor, since with the exception of Claude Lévi-Strauss, all the other protagonists of this scene are dead. And everything happens as if, through deconstruction, you managed to make them live and speak, not like idols but like the bearers of a living speech.

In addition, and this is no doubt because you are a faithful and an unfaithful heir, you have taken up the position of a universal intellectual in today's world, a position once occupied by someone like Zola or, more recently, Sartre. In this respect you embody a new form of dissidence, which your spoken words and your works (translated into more than forty languages) carry from one end of the world to the other. In short, I am inclined to say that you have triumphed.[10]

In this respect, I sometimes have the impression that the world today resembles you and resembles your concepts, that our world is deconstructed and that it has become Derridian to the point of reflecting, like an image in a mirror, the processes that decenter thought, psychology, and historicity and that you helped to set in motion.

Jacques Derrida: Faithful and unfaithful, how right you are! I often see myself pass very quickly before the mirror of life, like the silhouette of a madman (at once comic and tragic) who is dying to be unfaithful in a spirit of fidelity. I am therefore ready to go along with you, except in your allusion to triumph. I do not at all have the same feeling as you—and I'm not saying this out of politeness or modesty. No doubt the landscape has changed. No doubt we are seeing a diminution (but let's not exaggerate) of the compulsive and often pathetic efforts, desperate or fearful, to *discredit* at any cost—and not only my work, of course, but an entire configuration to which it belongs (although I am obliged to claim an unfortunate privilege here: I seem to attract a more stubborn and relentless aggression). No doubt we can discern the signs, at times equally disturbing, of a certain legitimacy. But can we really speak of triumph? No, and perhaps it is not desirable. To return to your point of departure, and to accompany you in this dialogue, I will hazard a few generalities on the notion of heritage.

It is true, whether it's a question of life or work or thought, that I have always recognized myself in the figure of the heir—and more and more so, in a way that is more and more deliberate, and often happy. By insistently confronting this concept or this figure of the legatee, I came to think that, far from the secure comfort that we rather too quickly associate with this word, the heir must always respond to a sort of double injunction, a contradictory assignation: It is necessary first of all to know and to know how to *reaffirm* what comes "before us," which we therefore receive even before choosing, and to behave in this respect as a free subject. Yes, *it is necessary* [*il faut*] (and this *it is necessary* is inscribed directly on and within the received heritage), it is necessary to do everything to appropriate a past even though we know that it remains fundamentally inappropriable, whether it is a question of philosophical memory or the precedence of a language, a culture, and a filiation in general. What does it mean to reaffirm? It means not simply accepting this heritage but relaunching it otherwise and keeping it alive. Not choosing it (since what characterizes a heritage is first of all that one does not choose it; it is what violently elects us), but choosing to keep it alive. Life—being-alive—is perhaps defined at bottom by this tension internal to a heritage, by this reinterpretation of what is given in the gift, and even what is given in filiation. This reaffirmation, which both continues and interrupts, resembles (at least) an election, a selection, a decision. One's own *as* that of the other: signature against signature. But I will not use any of these words without placing quotation marks and precautions around them. Beginning with the word "life." It would be necessary to think life on the basis of heritage, and not the other way around. It would be necessary therefore to begin from this formal and apparent contradiction between the passivity of reception and the decision to say "yes," then to select, to filter, to interpret, and therefore to transform; not to leave intact or unharmed, not to leave *safe* the very thing one claims to respect before all else. And after all. Not to leave it safe: to save it, perhaps, yet again, for a time, but without the illusion of a final salvation.

So you see very well why I am sensitive to what you say about the absence of or the refraining from all killing or putting to death. I have always forbidden myself—as far as possible, of course, and however "radical" or inflexible an act of deconstruction ought to be—to injure or to put to death. It is always by reaffirming the heritage that one can avoid this putting to death. Even at the moment—and this is the other side of the double injunction—when this very heritage, in order to save its life (within its finite time), demands reinterpretation, critique, displacement, that is, an active intervention, so that a transformation worthy of the name might take place: so that something might happen, an event, *some* history [*de l'histoire*], an unforeseeable future-to-come.[11]

My desire resembles that of a lover of the tradition who would like to free himself from conservatism. Imagine someone who is mad for the past, mad for an absolute past, a past that would no longer be a past present, a past whose measure or immeasure would be that of a bottomless memory—but a madman who dreads fixation on the past, nostalgia, the cult of remembrance. A contradictory and uncomfortable double injunction, therefore, bears on this heir who is certainly not what we call an "heir." But nothing is possible, nothing is of any interest, nothing seems desirable to me without this injunction. It demands two gestures at once: both to leave life in life and to make it live again, to save life and to "let live" in the most poetic sense of this phrase, which has unfortunately been turned into a cliché. To know how to "leave" and to "let" [*laisser*], and to know the meaning of "leaving" and "letting"—that is one of the most beautiful, most hazardous, most necessary things I know of. It is in close proximity with giving up and giving over, the gift, and forgiveness. The experience of a "deconstruction" is never without this, without this love, if you prefer that word. It begins by paying homage to that which, to those whom, it "takes on," I would say. "To take on [*s'en prendre*]"[12] is a very seductive, very untranslatable *figure* of the French language, don't you think?

This "figure" or style is well suited to a deconstruction that gets caught, that makes and lets itself be taken, in what it takes up and takes into consideration, even as it is "taken with it" and enamored by it.[13] In Latin, French, and English, as in German, the concept (*Begriff*) names the gesture of *taking hold*; it is a grasping. Deconstruction is seen as hyperconceptual, and indeed it is; it carries out a large-scale consumption of concepts that it produces as much as it inherits—but only to the point where a certain writing, a writing that thinks, exceeds the conceptual "take" and its mastery. It therefore attempts to think the limit of the concept; it even endures the experience of this excess; it lovingly lets itself be exceeded. It is like an ecstasy of the concept: a *jouissance* of the concept to the point of overflowing.

In the apparently rather fierce "deconstructive" texts that I wrote on the authors you mentioned, there is always a moment when, in all sincerity, I declare my admiration, my debt, my gratitude—as well as the necessity to be faithful to the heritage for the purpose of reinterpreting it and endlessly reaffirming it. Which is to say, at my own risk and peril, in a selective fashion. I never speak of what I do not admire, unless I am forced to do so by some sort of polemic (which I never initiate), and then in my reply I try to limit myself to issues that are impersonal and of common interest. If our heritage assigns contradictory tasks to us (to receive and yet to choose, to welcome what comes before us and yet to reinterpret it, etc.), this is because it is a testimony to our finitude. Only a finite being inherits, and his finitude *obliges* him. It obliges him to receive what is larger and older and more powerful and more durable than he. But the same finitude obliges one to choose, to prefer, to sacrifice, to exclude, to let go and leave behind. Precisely in order to respond to the call that preceded him, to answer it and to answer for it—in one's name as in the name of the other. The concept of responsibility has no sense at all outside of an experience of inheritance. Even before saying that one is responsible for a particular inheritance, it is necessary to know that responsibility in general ("answering for," "answering to," "answering in one's name") is first assigned to us, and that it is assigned to us through and through, as an inheritance. One is responsible before what comes before one but also before what is to come, and therefore *before oneself.* A double *before,* one that is also a debt, as when we say *devant ce qu'il doit: before* what he *ought to do* and *owing* what he *owes,* once and for all, the heir is doubly indebted.[14] It is always a question of a sort of anachronism: to come before [*devancer*] in the name of what came before us, and to come before the name itself![15] To invent one's name, to sign otherwise, uniquely in each case but in the name of the name passed down, if that's possible!

When it comes to the period of the 1970's that you referred to, this double law is verified. We could find other examples, of course, in the philosophical thought of earlier periods, whether in Plato, Descartes, Kant, Hegel, or Heidegger. But since you have decided to privilege what is common to us, I am happy that the conversation is beginning this way. Let us follow, like a dotted line, a few moments in our respective itineraries, at the points where they crossed in time.

At the end of the 1960's, indeed, for me it was a question of inheriting, I mean of responding to a heritage, to a moment in history in which a number of great works were already elaborated and present within the field of philosophy. I'm referring not only to Husserl and Heidegger but, closer to us, in France, to Levinas, Lacan, Lévi-Strauss, and, even closer, to Foucault, to Althusser, to Deleuze of course, to Lyotard. Even if this might look like eclecticism (but there was no hint of eclecticism in all this, precisely not; it has to do rather with another site of affinity, a common "belonging" that remains to be defined and that people are more aware of— even a little too much so—outside of France), I felt that at the deepest level I was in agreement with the gestures made by each one of them, however different they were. This is why, if one really wishes to follow my texts from the beginning, there is always a moment when I mark an alliance. I did so for *all* those we just named.

But this was also the moment of what you have called the "system." I began to write between 1962 and 1966, when structuralism was not only a systematic thought but a new thinking of the system, of the systematic form, with the prevalence of the linguistic model in Lévi-Strauss and Lacan, whatever the complications that each one brought to this model. I certainly sensed the fruitfulness and legitimacy of this gesture, at that moment, in response to various forms of empiricism and positivism, or to other epistemological "obstacles," as one often said. But I also saw the price there was to pay, namely a certain naïveté, the somewhat jubilatory repetition of old philosophical gestures, the rather somnambulist submission to a history of metaphysics that I was driven to decipher in terms of its program, its combinatorial procedures, all the possibilities that in my eyes had become tired and exhausted. I believed I could discern the sterilizing, precipitous, even dogmatic elements of this program—despite or even within the "subversion" you mentioned a moment ago. I'm thinking especially of the misrecognition or the *practical* denial of a certain number of motifs, for example, the notion of rupture in history, of interruption, the passage from one systematic force to another, etc. At the time, and with precaution, I insisted a great deal on this motif of *force*, which structuralism was in danger of neutralizing. And this link between force and history was, it seemed to me, something that had to be taken into account.

In each case, the deconstructive response to works like Foucault's, Lévi-Strauss's, or Lacan's was different. And different with each text. I almost never wrote on this or that author *in general*, nor did I treat the *totality* of a corpus as if it were homogeneous. What is important to me is rather the distribution of forces and motifs in a given work, and to recognize what is hegemonic in it or what is given secondary importance or is even denied. There, too, I tried—and I strive to do this in every case—to respect the idiom[16] or the singularity of the signature. While it was common to these authors, the structuralist axiomatic was put to work each time in a different style, on sites and corpuses that were heterogeneous. For each one, I wanted to uncover what you called the "dogmatic moment"— the residue of credulity—in order to "deconstruct" it while also respecting the structuralist exigency. I never said anything against structuralism.

E.R.: On the contrary, in 1963 you wrote a beautiful sentence in "Force and Signification": "If it recedes one day, leaving behind its works and signs on the shores of our civilization, the structuralist invasion will become a question for the historian of ideas."[17] This is an homage: the day when structuralism will have disappeared as a creative force, it will be necessary to mourn it, but also to judge its place in the history of civilization.

J.D.: I have the weakness of being attached to this gesture. That is why I come back to the question of putting to death: in no case do I want deconstruction to be used to denigrate, injure, or diminish the force or the necessity of a movement—and if it is necessary to do that here or there in polemical moments, I regret it in advance. Hence the situation you described before: at certain moments within a process, alliances shift, and I find myself again allied with Lacan and Foucault, as I have explicitly said in certain contexts. One thing that the sinister grimace of the grotesque book *French Philosophy of the Sixties* did at the time (must we really speak of it again? do you insist?) was, indeed, to distinguish the camps. It may happen that I point out my reservations with regard to some specific moment in the thought of Lacan or Foucault, knowing all the while that, despite everything, when faced for example with such obscurantist attacks, I remain on their side in the general movement of what one calls the experience or the exigency of thought.

That is why the idea of heritage implies not only a reaffirmation and a double injunction, but at every moment, in a different context, a filtering, a choice, a strategy. An heir is not only someone who receives, he or she is someone who chooses, and who takes the risk of deciding. This is very explicit in *Specters of Marx*.[18] Every text is heterogeneous. The heritage, too, is a "text," in the broad but precise sense I give to this word. The heir's affirmation consists, of course, in his interpretation; it consists in choosing. He discerns in a critical fashion, he differentiates, and this is what explains the mobility of alliances. In certain situations, I am Lacan's ally against others; in other situations, I object to Lacan. I see no opportunism or relativism in this.

E.R.: You have dealt with the theme of the enemy, the friend, the adversary, particularly in a seminar in which you deconstruct the work of Carl Schmitt.[19] You point out that, according to Schmitt, political difference proceeds from a discrimination between the friend and the enemy. Without this discrimination, there is no politics. You oppose to this a more Freudian conception of politics in which "hatred would be inscribed in the very mourning of our friends."[20] And you cite the famous story of the hedgehogs that Freud took from Schopenhauer. Some porcupines give up cuddling each other to ward off the cold: they hurt each other with their quills. Obliged one winter day to huddle together, they end up finding a mean distance between attraction and repulsion, friendship and hostility.

It seems to me that we must make a certain distinction. Those with whom you "explicate yourself" through deconstruction are close to you; the "others" are not. They seek to destroy and not to choose a heritage.

I admire both the great systems of thought and the subversive—and therefore deconstructive—value they bring into play. That's why, when I was a student of literature at the Sorbonne before 1968, I read your texts at the same time as those of the "others." Later I was in perfect agreement with Lacan's statement in response to Lucien Goldmann, who had stressed that it is men who make history, and not structures. Goldmann made this comment in reference to the slogan written on a blackboard at the Sorbonne in May 1968: "Structures don't hit the streets." Lacan answered: "If the events of May demonstrate anything, it is precisely structures hitting the streets."[21]

Your texts and those of the "structuralists" (Lacan, Foucault, Barthes, Althusser, Lévi-Strauss) functioned at the time as critiques of "political enemies," those who upheld the old Sorbonne, who didn't want to talk about modern literature, or about linguistics, and even less about psychoanalysis. For example, I remember (and I recounted this in *Généalogies*) that the chair of linguistics, André Martinet, forbade the name of his "enemy," Roman Jakobson, to be uttered, and his assistants, our "masters," obeyed him. You—you and the others—were the incarnation of Revolution, a revolution that affirmed the importance of structures (and of their deconstruction), but that was in every way a political engagement: the freedom to speak forbidden names before these mandarins and their servants. These are things that our conservatives forget today when they dream of restoring the old Republican-style school. It is no doubt necessary to maintain its spirit to the extent that it was progressive. But it must not be forgotten how openly reactionary it could be at certain moments.

It was later that I was able to grasp the way you deconstructed systems of thought within a critical space that did not destroy them but made them live otherwise. I'm thinking especially of two very important interventions.

The first concerns a chapter in part seven of *Tristes Tropiques* entitled "A Writing Lesson." Describing the life and customs of the Nambikwara Indians, a seminomadic people of western Brazil with whom he stayed for a while,[22] Lévi-Strauss shows how writing irrupts among a group of Indians who, however, don't know its rules, when the chief uses the traces drawn on a sheet of paper as a way to make the members of his tribe believe that he possesses the power to communicate with the whites. Lévi-Strauss concludes from this that writing is thus an instrument of colonization, violence, and exploitation that puts an end to a state of nature founded on the prevalence of a full speech not suspected of inauthenticity. For my part, I consider *Tristes Tropiques* one of the most beautiful books of the second half of the century, both because of its style, the melancholy that animates it, and for the way it mixes autobiography, theoretical reflection, and an adventure story. I discovered it and grew to love it when I was very young, and for me it was a moment of political awakening with regard to colonization in general.

It's obvious that this book touched and fascinated you, since you devote some magnificent pages to it. But concerning this "writing lesson," you relate Lévi-Strauss's anticolonialist position—according to which the appearance of writing is a violence exercised on the subject—to that of Rousseau. In his *Essay on the Origin of Languages*, Rousseau in fact condemns writing for being a destruction of the "plenitude of presence" and a veritable sickness of speech: a "dangerous supplement." You oppose to Lévi-Strauss, in his continuation of Rousseau, the idea that this protest against the written word is only the lure of an inverted ethnocentrism pray to the illusion of some possible origin of full speech as the source of a naturalist or libertarian ethics. The civilization of writing would therefore be wrongly suspected by ethnology of having contributed to the extinction of so-called peoples "without writing." According to you, this attitude is the mark of a repression of the trace and of the letter—in the Freudian sense of the term—whose mechanism would have to be deconstructed for its meaning to be understood.

Your second intervention[23] concerns Foucault's commentary on Descartes's famous passage on the origin of madness in the *Meditations*.[24] In *L'histoire de la folie*, Foucault separates, in Descartes's text, the exercise of madness from that of dreams. In the first, madness is excluded, and this decree of philosophical exclusion announces the political decree of the "great confinement" in 1656. In the second, madness is part of the subject's virtual possibilities, such that the subject's sensible images become deceitful under the assault of the "Evil Genius."

Whereas Foucault has Descartes say that "man can indeed be mad if the *cogito* is not," you stress, on the contrary, that with the act of the *cogito*, thought no longer has to fear madness because "the *cogito* is valid even if I am mad." You therefore reproach Foucault for constituting an event as a structure since for you the division between madness and reason, that is, the ostracism of madness, begins not with Descartes but with Socrates' victory over the pre-Socratics.

These debates today might seem rather hairsplitting, but they had a powerful effect on the social and political engagements of an entire generation of students. Just as with Heideggerian thought in the 1930's, then with Sartre's reflections on being, the other, and nothingness, these debates made it possible to enter a modernity that sought to reconcile aesthetics and politics, the unconscious and freedom, humanism and antihumanism, progress and the critique of the illusions of progress, in short, to understand the phenomena of exclusion, the construction of the subject and of identity, the status of madness, the problems of racism, and the struggles of the colonial period.

J.D.: Indeed, there is nothing serious in politics without this apparent "hairsplitting" that sharpens the analyses without being intimidated even by the impatience of the media. Within this complex field, so difficult to delimit, there is room for differences that appear to be microscopic. All these authors *seem* to use the same language. In other countries, they are quite often cited in a series. And this is irritating, for as soon as you look at the texts with any precision, it becomes clear that the most radical demarcations sometimes hang, precisely, by a hair. Obviously, by chance and by necessity, it was a happy moment in which everyone crossed paths, all those who were interested in micrological differences and very refined textual analyses. There's an enormous nostalgia. You see, I remain inconsolable . . .

It was possible then to be opposed and to make decisions concerning issues of great importance for thought, on the basis of arguments that today might be judged much too sophisticated or uselessly subtle. My relation with each author was different. To return to the word "deconstruction," for example, Foucault seems to me more of a "deconstructor" than Lévi-Strauss, to the extent that he was more impatient and more rebellious, less politically conservative and more engaged in "subversive" actions and "ideological" struggles. Which is not the case with Lévi-Strauss or Lacan. But from another point of view, it seems to me that Lacan was more daring as a "deconstructor" than Foucault. I have therefore felt—and still feel today—closer to Lacan than to Foucault. Lévi-Strauss is yet another matter. My critique had to do at first with a very particular point, a passage in *Tristes Tropiques* (in "A Writing Lesson") which, in my opinion, revealed a philosophy and an "ideology" whose limits I tried to articulate and other signs of which can be found elsewhere.

But after *Of Grammatology*, in a second text on Lévi-Strauss that I wrote a little later ("Structure, Sign and Play in the Discourse of the Human Sciences"),[25] I tried, on the contrary, in an analysis of his introduction to the work of Marcel Mauss,[26] to accompany Lévi-Strauss's demonstrations and concerns, in my way, by subscribing to them up to a certain point. A double relation, therefore, and once again a divided one.

What has always left me a little perplexed with Foucault, beyond the debate on the *cogito*, is that while I understand very well the necessity of marking divisions, ruptures, and passages from one *episteme* to another, at the same time I have always had the impression that this risked making him less attentive to long sequences, in which one might find differences at work beyond even the Cartesian moment. We can find other examples, even in texts like *Discipline and Punish*[27] or in other more recent works. Foucault's typical gesture consists in hardening into an opposition a more complicated play of differences that stretches along a more extended time. To schematize in the extreme, I would say that Foucault sets up as ruptures and binary oppositions a range of more complex differences. For example, the couple visibility/invisibility in *Discipline and Punish*. Contrary to what Foucault says, I don't believe that there is a shift from the visible to the invisible in the administration of penalties beginning in the eighteenth century. While I recognize the relative legitimacy of this analysis, according to certain limited criteria, I would be tempted to say that in the evolution of punishments, we shift not from the visible to the invisible but rather from one visibility to another, more virtual, one. In a seminar on capital punishment, I am trying to demonstrate that the same process is oriented toward another modality, another distribution of the visible (and therefore of the invisible) that can even, on the contrary, extend the virtual field of the spectacular and the theatrical, with decisive consequences.

The same goes for the *cogito*. I understand the correctness of what Foucault says about Descartes, except that at a certain moment one can read the event of the *cogito*, in the demonstration laid out by Descartes, as an inclusion (and not as an exclusion) of madness. Thus the gesture of Descartes can be understood differently. And, of course, the consequences of this are unlimited, not only for the interpretation of Descartes, which is certainly important, but also for the protocols of reading and the methodological or epistemological apparatus in *L'histoire de la folie*.

What interested me was not simply a political opposition (conservative/nonconservative) but the price to be paid, in each case, whenever any progress is made. Each time, the theoretical gains and the advancement of knowledge were made possible by a presupposition. I looked for this presupposition that, by putting on the breaks—if I can say it this way—made it possible both to accelerate and to absorb the shock of acceleration.

E.R.: We'll come back to this question later. All these thinkers of the 1970's are *also* writers. That is their strength. Like you, I have a nostalgia for this period, but it is necessary to move forward. Now, there are intersections different from those of our generation. Lévi-Strauss's writing is classic. A naturalist thinker, he wanted to show the existence of a continuum between the biological and the cultural. Foucault, in my opinion, is more an heir to German romanticism. As for Lacan, indeed, even though he belongs to the same generation as Lévi-Strauss, he is closer to you in terms of style.

In *French Philosophy of the Sixties*, Ferry and Renaut trumpet a return to French philosophy via Kant, that is, to a neo-Kantian philosophy of professors, and they reproach the period—which they fuse into a single amalgam—for being too Nietzschean-Heideggerian. Now what would be so shameful about being Nietzschean-Heideggerian? There is something very political in their alleged theorizing. If France were not deeply influenced by German philosophy, and, conversely, if Germany were not inspired by the philosophy of the Enlightenment, it would be a disaster for the two countries and for Europe. One characteristic common to the thinkers we are discussing is that they reintroduced German philosophy into France. Even Lévi-Strauss claims a debt to Freud and Marx.

Lacan reintroduced Hegelian philosophy into Freudian thought by way of Alexandre Kojève's teaching, and he did this at a time when French psychoanalysts wanted to banish from their ranks the entire German legacy of Freud. In your case, the legacy of Husserl, Heidegger, Nietzsche, and Levinas is central. You speak of this in "Violence and Metaphysics."[28]

J.D.: Writing and France! In my attempt to respond to you, I will link the two motifs of "writing" (of the idiom in writing, in the *manner* of writing) and "nationality." A first lateral remark: even those you just designated as figures from whom I have received a visible inheritance—Heidegger, Levinas, Husserl—are thinkers about whom I have never really ceased posing many questions. Very serious, central questions. Always with a radical disquiet, restless and bottomless, especially when it comes to Heidegger and Husserl. I'll speak more of this later.

To return to the question of writing and nationality: whether we are talking about Foucault, Lévi-Strauss, Deleuze, Althusser, or Lyotard, I have always had the feeling that, despite the differences in style, they maintained a common relation to the French language, one that is at bottom very placid, very sedentary. They all write "a certain French"; they have the respect not of an academic or conventional attitude, but of a certain classicism. Their writing does not make the French language tremble; it does not shake up the most traditional French rhetoric. In that regard, I have the feeling that everything I'm trying to do involves a hand-to-hand struggle with the French language, a turbulent but *primal* hand-to-hand struggle; I mean one in which the entire stakes are set, in which the essential is at stake.

As you know, I have for this language an anxious, jealous, and tormented love. That is one thing I have in common with Lacan, although we write in very different ways. He, too, has a way of *touching* and *mistreating* [*toucher à*] the French language, or of *letting himself be touched and mistreated* by it, which it seems to me, and if this is not too unfair, I do not sense in the others. I share with him a constant attention to a certain movement of the sentence, to a work not of the signifier but of the letter, of rhetoric, composition, address, destination, mise-en-scène. So in this respect I feel myself closer to Lacan than to any of the others. Although, from another point of view, Lacan is so French—my God—so much more French than I am! One should be able to say and to think all these things at once: "they" are all more "French" than I am, and some of them are more French than others; and yet I would dare to claim that between the French language and me there will be, there will have been, more love. More mad love, if you like. And more jealousy, reciprocal jealousy, if that doesn't seem too senseless and insane!

It is a matter here of a relation to the Frenchness of the language, of the letter, of rhetoric, composition, the scene of writing. That said, and since you brought it up again, the authors of *French Philosophy of the Sixties*, who were never capable of reading all those people, wrote a book full of oafish blunders and crude gestures, a null book, but a symptomatic one. Interesting because symptomatic! By mixing everything together, they end up ignoring the critiques, directed at Nietzsche and especially at Heidegger, that were contained in this "Nietzschean-Heideggerian" filiation. They acted without looking closely, as if the choice of a heritage could be confused with a blind incorporation. They did not see the differences manifested, in each one, in relation to Nietzsche or Heidegger. As for me, while my relation to Heidegger was explicit, my "explication" in relation to his thought was rather stormy, as I show not only in *Of Spirit*,[29] where this confrontation is best displayed, but beginning with my first texts and my first references to Heidegger. Even if I owe a great deal to Heidegger, as do many others, he inspired me from the start with an intense political disquiet. This was also the case, in a completely different way, with Levinas.

E.R.: The authors of *French Philosophy of the Sixties* wanted to prove that this entire philosophical generation was hostile to democracy. Their arguments are stunningly simpleminded. They set out to show that Pierre Bourdieu is a "French Marx," Lacan is a "French Freud," Foucault is a "French Nietzsche," and you are a "French Heidegger." Such a legacy would be dishonorable because in their eyes Marx is responsible for the gulag, Nietzsche is a poor nihilist aesthete incapable of understanding the progress of Western reason, and Heidegger is simply a Nazi. As for Freud, he is no more than an obscurantist emerging from the depths of German romanticism and a proponent of an irrational vision of the unconscious.

Consequently, the heirs of this so-called "German" thought are simply antidemocrats who are hostile to humanism because they critique the ideal of progressivist humanism and are all supporters, each in his own way, of the great totalitarian regimes of the century. But the worst, according to Ferry and Renaut, is that Foucault, Lacan, and Derrida are all three Heideggerian, plus something else: Foucault = Heidegger + Nietzsche, Lacan = Heidegger + Freud, Derrida = Heidegger + Heidegger.[30] In other words, all three not only are antidemocratic but are suspected of having sympathies for a philosopher of whom it is clearly said throughout the book that he was nothing but a lackey in the service of Nazism. And it is for this reason, still according to Ferry and Renaut, that the young people involved in May 1968 followed these thinkers: out of hatred for man and adherence to a criminal communism, a suspect antihumanism, or a dubious aestheticism.

Along the way, Ferry and Renaut forget about Althusser; they turn Bourdieu into a Marxist, even though he never was one; and they bungle through a particularly ridiculous exegesis of the works of Lacan and Foucault. Moreover, they neglect the fact that every important moment of French thought of the twentieth century, every writer who left a mark on the century, in philosophy or in literature—from Georges Bataille to Emmanuel Levinas, passing through André Breton and Alexandre Koyré—was traversed by the double legacy of Nietzsche and Heidegger, by infinitely varied and contradictory readings of these two philosophers' works. As for Freud's thought, it is truly perilous to say that it is obscurantist or that it is linked on one side to Nazism and on the other to the gulag.[31]

But what strikes me about this book is that it is inscribed within a pro-French nationalist tradition. And this detestation of Germany and of German philosophy is in my opinion all the more suspect in that it is manifest at the very moment when the political construction of Europe is being played out, a Europe in which the reconciliation between Germany and France is necessary in order to exorcise the demons of the past, especially in their nationalist forms.

J.D.: That's true, but I don't know whether this point of view is pro-French or anti-German. It is after all in the name of a certain Kant and of Kantian philosophy that they often claim to speak. The object of their attack is what they call a style, what they try to reduce—referring to "me"—to an "ingenuousness" or a "lexical" "fecundity." In my case (the case of "French Heideggerianism," the title of their chapter on me!), I recall this formula, in which they discover that "Derrida = Heidegger + Derrida's style." In short, just a way of writing.[32] Many conflicts and oppositions have been motivated less by questions concerning explicit arguments or philosophical content than by gestures of writing. Very often, authors define themselves through their allergy to a way of writing, to a manner of dealing with language, to a scene of writing—one which, in addition, is translated and "exported," as they remark with some impatience.[33] It is not at all by chance that they attacked me in terms of writing, saying "he has nothing to say," or "he writes differently," or that somehow "people are interested in him." Confusing writing with style and style with aestheticism, they claim that "Derrida" is Heidegger with a different aesthetic. But if they had taken the time and trouble to *read* what I wrote, they would have seen that the stakes were very serious in a different way. That said, I believe as you do—and this is how I will sum up the matter—that the Franco-German question not only was decisive for that period but remains so today. In my book on the work of Jean-Luc Nancy,[34] I return to this history of the Franco-German border. And let us not forget that the thinkers of the Enlightenment both were and were not German. The *Aufklärung* is not exactly the same as *les Lumières* or as *Illuminismo*, etc. There are many very complex interweavings. But I agree, there are political stakes in this affair, both avowed and hidden, having to do with the question of the nation, the nationalist tradition, in philosophy and in theory. It has to do with the national specificity of the institution of the university, and all the professional stakes involved in the institutional field.[35]

E.R.: It seems to me that every time France and Germany have been divided by intensified nationalism, it was, as I said, a disaster for Europe. But when, on the contrary, Germany and France were bound together in the Enlightenment—and I include in this program the critique of the Enlightenment, the deconstruction of the philosophy of progress, for example—this rapprochement was in fact a powerful ferment for the construction of Europe. You also say that the true greatness of Europe consists in "not closing itself in its own identity and in advancing itself in an exemplary way toward what it is not, toward the other heading or the heading of the other."[36]

When I wrote a history of psychoanalysis in France, I realized that nothing was worse than the French chauvinism that led to the notion that psychoanalysis was "Kraut science," and therefore to the claim that Freud—that is, German culture—wanted to reduce man to the savagery of his sexual drives. Critics in France said that Freud's supposed "pansexualism" was the manifestation of a "Teutonic" spirit, forgetting all the while the specificity of the Viennese spirit at the turn of the century.[37]

J.D.: The resistance was not reciprocal. After the Second World War, the resistance to French thought was—and still is—stronger and more intense in Germany than the other way around.

E.R.: Are you thinking of how Heidegger's work was reintroduced into France by Jean Beaufret,[38] whereas the reading of Heidegger was, in a way, banished from Germany because of his collaboration with Nazism?

J.D.: I'm thinking of the reaction of Jürgen Habermas.[39] First, with a great lack of understanding and even violence, he took on what he interpreted as a French neoconservatism (Foucault, Lyotard, myself). The *Philosophical Discourse of Modernity*[40] abundantly develops its critiques of my work, especially with reference to certain American readings of it. I found these critiques more than unjust, and I responded to them a little in various places, especially in *Limited Inc.*[41] But that lies in the past, and we have even moved beyond it; we were able to explain our positions to each other, to a certain extent, fortunately in a very friendly way. We met at a seminar in Frankfurt last June, then during a gathering in Paris. Our political choices, especially concerning Europe, are often very similar, allied, if not deeply identical; and they have appeared as such on a number of public occasions.

E.R.: You say that there is neither relativism nor nationalism in philosophy. In its original existence, philosophy is Greek. It is therefore not Western or European but universal, insofar as it took hold of the Greek world and then deployed foundational concepts belonging to no nation or ethnicity in particular. In other words, anyone can appropriate the conceptual apparatus of philosophy as something universal that cannot be contained within any border.

On a number of occasions, you have stressed that we must think the contemporary world on the basis of concepts provided by philosophy insofar as it is never identical to itself, like culture in fact, of which you say also that its basic characteristic is not to have an identity but to be the bearer of a difference.[42] The heritage is therefore already inscribed within a modernity that consists precisely in not retreating into the "self-identical." This seems to me to be a fundamental issue.

J.D.: Indeed, it is a question of nothing less than this: the signification of philosophy [la *philosophie*]. The "idea," the institution, of philosophy is inscribed first in a particular language and in a culture, in Greek language and culture. Thus what we can rigorously call "philosophy" exists nowhere other than in Greece. While there are certainly very powerful bodies of thought elsewhere, which are other than philosophy, philosophy as a specific project of the thinking of being was born in Greece.

But it was born—and we can follow Husserl and Heidegger in this—as the universal project of a will to deracination. If philosophy has a root (Greece), its project consists at the same time in pulling up the roots and in making it such that what is thought in Greek—and later in German, according to Heidegger—is delivered into "more than one language." Philosophy, then, is delivered; it tends at least toward liberating itself, from the start, from its linguistic, territorial, ethnic, and cultural limitations.

The universal projected in this way is not a given, the way an essence would be; rather, it announces an infinite process of *universalization*. For twenty-five centuries this project of universalization of philosophy has never ceased to mutate, to be displaced, to break with itself, to extend itself. Today it must be deployed further in order to be delivered all the more from its ethnic, geographic, and political limits. The paradox is indeed that we are liberating ourselves from ethnocentrism, and eventually from Eurocentrism, in the name of philosophy and its European filiation. There is a living contradiction there, that of Europe itself, yesterday and today: not

only does it give itself weapons to use against itself and against its own limitations, but it gives political weapons to all the peoples and all the cultures
that European colonialism itself has subjugated. Once again, it resembles
a process of autoimmunization.

And often those who gave their lives in struggles for independence
did so after first taking up philosophemes from Enlightenment Europe.
The most striking example is Nelson Mandela, who has taken up a discourse that is not only European but British. He often borrows its logic
and arguments.[43]

Let's take the example of international law [*droit*]. In its concepts it is
substantially European, but it bears within it a transformation of the law
that remains always perfectible, and therefore incomplete. We must be very
careful not to let the European element of international law come to limit
this law, so that we can liberate the law from its own Eurocentric limits,
and yet without destroying the memory of this law, which makes possible
and also prescribes transformation, infinite perfectibility.

So here, too, there is an infinite task of deconstruction: it is necessary
to draw on the heritage and its memory for the conceptual tools that allow
one to challenge the limits that this heritage has imposed up to now. At the
heart of international law, there are sites where it is necessary to pass beyond or to displace limits. Human rights [*droits*] are perfectible; they are
ceaselessly transformed. So it is better to define these rights by pulling
them out of their limits: to recognize the rights of women, the right to
work, the rights of children, etc. But this gesture must be carried out in the
name of an idea of right already present in the project of the Universal Declaration of Human Rights, itself based on the declaration of 1789.

In the same way, if Greek philosophy is European at its point of departure, but if its vocation is indeed universal, this means that it must ceaselessly liberate itself from relativism. Philosophical work consists in a constant movement of liberation: to do everything to recognize but also to pass,
without necessarily betraying, its own ethnocentric or geographic limit.

2

Politics of Difference

E.R.: The debate on ethnocentrism can be framed in terms of the question of difference. You wrote this term with an "a" (differance) for the first time in 1965, in an article on Antonin Artaud, "La parole soufflée,"[1] and then in a long paper entitled "Différance," presented January 27, 1968, to the Société Française de Philosophie.[2] I would tend to say that in the beginning, even if you do not say this explicitly, the term recalls both the Nietzsche of *The Birth of Tragedy* and the notion of the heterogeneous put forward by Georges Bataille. It is a matter of defining a sort of "accursed share,"[3] a difference in the sense of the absolute or of duplicity, something that cannot be symbolized or that exceeds representation. You find the traces of this in Artaud's theater of cruelty, where no distinctions are posited among the apparatuses of the theater, the author, the actor, and the director. In short, "differance" would be "improvisational anarchy." It would be a bearer of negativity but also of an alterity that would ceaselessly escape from the same and the identical.[4]

Once again, by way of these extremely complex and refined concepts, you pose a problem that is essential to our modernity. How can we think difference as a universal without yielding to communitarianism or to the narcissistic cult of minor differences? How is it possible to escape from the psychology of peoples, rebaptized as ethno-psychology—with all its variants (ethnopsychiatry, ethnopedagogy, ethnopediatrics, ethnopsychoanalysis, etc.)—or from theories of the "archetype" that refuse the very idea of a possible universality of the human subject, beyond all cultural, social, and other differences?

J.D.: So, republic or democracy? First, if you don't mind, a few abstract remarks on differ*a*nce (with an "a") and differences (with an "e"). What is universalizable about differ*a*nce with regard to differences is that it allows one to think the process of differentiation beyond every kind of limit: whether it is a matter of cultural, national, linguistic, or even human limits. There is differ*a*nce (with an "a") as soon as there is a living trace, a relation of life/death or presence/absence. This became linked for me very early on with the immense problematic of animality.[5] There is differ*a*nce (with an "a") as soon as there is something living [*du vivant*], as soon as there is something of a trace [*de la trace*], across and despite all the limits that the strongest philosophical or cultural tradition thought it could recognize between "man" and "animal."

So there is indeed a universalizing potential here. But differ*a*nce is not a distinction, an essence, or an opposition, but a movement of spacing, a "becoming-space" of time, a "becoming-time" of space, a reference to alterity, to a heterogeneity that is not first a matter of opposition. Hence a certain inscription of the same, which is not the identical, *as* differ*a*nce. At once economy and aneconomy. All this was also a meditation on the question concerning the relation of the signified to the signifier (and therefore of a certain Saussurian linguistics that dominated many discourses of the period, often in a schematic and simplified form).

After that, my work developed as a lengthy interrogation of all the differences held to be simple oppositions. I insist on this: differ*a*nce is not an opposition, not even a dialectical opposition; it is a reaffirmation of the same, an economy of the same in its relation to the other, which does not require that the same, in order to exist, be frozen or fixed in a distinction or in a system of dual oppositions. One can, of course, draw from this apparently abstract proposition all the means necessary for problematizing the ethics and politics that you include under the label of communitarianism.

In a general way, and for a great many reasons that I deal with elsewhere—particularly in *Monolingualism of the Other*[6]—I have always mistrusted the cult of the identitarian, as well as that of the communitarian discourse often associated with it. I am always seeking to recall the more and more necessary dissociation between the political and the territorial. So I share your anxiety concerning the communitarian logic, the identitarian compulsion, and like you I resist this movement that tends toward a narcissism of minorities that is developing everywhere—including within feminist movements. In certain situations, it is nonetheless necessary to take on the political responsibilities that demand from us a certain solidarity with those who are struggling against this or that discrimination, and to gain recognition for a threatened, marginalized, minoritized, delegitimized national identity or language, or else when a religious community is subjected to oppression.

This in no way prevents me from mistrusting the identitarian or communitarian demand *as such*. And yet I must make it my own, at least provisionally, whenever I recognize a discrimination or a threat. In that case, whether we're talking about women, homosexuals, or other groups, I can understand the vital urgency of the identitarian reflex. I can then accept a momentary and prudent alliance, while also stressing its limits, and making them as explicit and intelligible as possible. I therefore do not hesitate to support, however modestly, causes such as those of feminists, homosexuals, colonized peoples, up to the moment when I become mistrustful, when the logic of the demand seems to me potentially perverse or dangerous. Communitarianism or state nationalism are the most obvious figures of this risk, and therefore of this limit to solidarity. The risk must be reevaluated at every moment, in shifting contexts giving rise to exchanges that are in each case original. There is no relativism in this; on the contrary, it is the condition of an effective responsibility, if such a thing exists.

Political responsibility regarding situations that are always complex, contradictory, and overdetermined (as people used to say) means attempting to calculate the space, the time, and the limit of the alliance. That is why I feel divided between the two motifs of the *republic* and the *democracy*. The two terms are close, but they are becoming more and more opposed, in a way that is somewhat artificial, in France, where this polarity is becoming more and more an object of accusation. I, however, would like to be *both* a republican *and* a democrat. According to the situation, according to the context or the addressees, I accentuate the movement toward one pole or the other. As you know, political choices are often determined by gradations rather than by clearly defined oppositions of the type: I am this *or* that. No, I am this *and* that; and I am this rather than that, according to the situations and the urgencies at hand.

E.R.: What do you think about the debate on parity, from this perspective?[7]

J.D.: I was very wary of the discourse, the logic, and the rhetoric of what is strangely called "parity," no doubt partly for the same reasons as you. The introduction of sexual difference into the constitution is something that troubles me.

E.R.: There is a risk of instating quotas.

J.D.: Yes, for example. But from the moment when someone says: "There is only a binary choice. You must vote yes or no to parity thus determined," I can see that if I vote against it, I risk ratifying a catastrophic situation. France is the most backward country when it comes to the presence, and especially the representation, of women in political life. If I were given official notice that I had to vote either "for" or "against," I would, at that moment and despite all my reservations, vote in favor of parity, because if I voted "against," I would be confirming a massive and intolerable fact: the underrepresentation of women in politics to a degree unheard of in Europe, and with the most serious consequences and implications. Particularly those consequences and implications that from the beginning, more than thirty-five years ago, called for the most insistent and explicit deconstruction of all the effects of phallogocentrism,[8] a deconstruction that was meant to be not only "theoretical" or "speculative" but concrete, effective, political.

E.R.: It seems to me that there are other ways to fight against this underrepresentation; and I wonder why it has reached such extremes in France's political sphere, while in other areas of social life there are as many women as men in certain professions, if not more: this is the case particularly with students and professionals in psychology. According to certain sociologists and statisticians, the feminization of a profession is a sign of its devalorization. To tell the truth, I'm not so sure.

In any case, I spoke out against parity because I think that quotas do nothing to advance the struggle for women. It even seems humiliating. Moreover, certain supporters of parity, especially some women, claimed that they should place the opponents of parity in the category of misogynists or reactionaries, accusing them of wanting to "erase the difference between the sexes" and targeting Simone de Beauvoir, who was reproached for not fully realizing herself as a woman because she was never a mother. Hence the renewal of a "matricentrist" conception of femininity among these supporters of parity: a woman cannot flourish outside maternity. This is such a tired, outmoded idea.[9]

In other European countries, in Sweden for example, it wasn't necessary to pass such a law for women to be more present in political life. It would be necessary perhaps to reflect on how the struggle against inequality moves forward, and why, in certain sectors, there exists such a disparity between men and women.

J.D.: I explained my position in an article published in the newspaper *L'Humanité*.[10] I note why, in my view, the recourse to law in this affair, to a constitutional transformation, confirmed a symptom: the French political parties and personnel, unlike those of other European countries, have had recourse to a *formal* juridico-political *decision*, whenever they were unable and unwilling to change the situation, precisely because of the resistance within their own ranks. A paralyzing, paralyzed resistance. Against a phallocentrism that could no longer be publicly assumed, and thus faced with an asymmetry that is already spectacular and ridiculous in Europe, it finally became necessary for one part of the parties to do violence to the other.

E.R.: If I understand you, then, you are affirming the necessity always to be in the forefront of the struggles against the most threatening obstacles to freedom, even if it also means critiquing the excesses created by the struggles.

J.D.: It is indeed necessary to take the context into account in the most refined way possible without yielding to relativism. There is no pure and simple "communitarianism" that I support as such. But in certain situations, which must be analyzed in each case in a singular way, I may be led to take positions that, for someone in a hurry, might resemble the very thing that I am challenging: both relativism and communitarianism. And let's not ever forget something that is massively obvious, which people often try to conceal (or to conceal from themselves), especially those who assume the role of eloquent advocates of universalism over and against communitarianism or against differentialism, those who defend the "republican" principle against the "democratic" one, etc. Let's never forget that the examples of "communities" associated with the idea "communitarianism" are always minority (or minoritized) communities who are underrepresented and even reduced to silence. Now, what is defended under the banner of secular and republican universalism (and this is what they want neither to say nor to see) is also a *communitarian* constellation: the *French* republic, the *French* citizenry, the *French* language, the indivisible unity of a *national territory*, in short, an ensemble of cultural traits bound up in the history of a nation-state, embodied in it, in its tradition, and in a dominant part of its history, etc.

In what I just said, I privileged "nationality," the idea of nation-state sovereignty linked with this "republicanism"; but I could have spoken of the heterosexual phallocentrism that denounces the supposed communitarianism of "women" and "Gays and Lesbians" [English in original], etc. Since this "community" is the strongest, since it is largely hegemonic in the context of this debate, one can easily deny its character as a "community" along with all the communitarian interests it defends. And the protest against "democratic" communitarianism in the name of "republican" universality is almost always voiced by the strongest community, or else the community that still thinks it's the strongest and intends, perhaps, to remain so by resisting the threats from communities that are diverse and are still in the minority.

E.R.: On a related topic, and since you have taught for such a long time in a number of American universities, I would like to ask you about the notion of "political correctness" (which in French is called *correction politique* or *politiquement correct*). This term was invented by conservatives as a way to designate, pejoratively, a politics of teaching seen as "leftist and radical" that involves rereading classic literary and philosophical works or works of art history with reference to multiculturalist criteria. It is supposedly necessary to "correct" these works by removing what is "incorrect" in them with regard to oppressed minorities (women, blacks, Hispanics, homosexuals, colonized peoples, etc.). Hence the idea of "censoring" all the texts of Western culture (from Plato to Freud, without forgetting Sade) that include passages considered "incorrect" with regard to minorities. This revision in teaching supposedly developed in English, French, and Comparative Literature departments.[11] It is related to another movement called "affirmative action" (referred to in French as *discrimination positive*), which involves instituting, through legislation, a preferential treatment favoring these same groups who have been victims of injustice. This policy rests on the idea that, in order to repair an inequality, it is appropriate to valorize one difference against another difference.

In 1995, I began a petition with Philippe Garnier to denounce the puritanism that had led to the cancellation of a large exhibition on Freud at the Library of Congress in Washington because the exhibition—clearly orthodox and perfectly debatable—excluded the work of a certain number of "revisionist" historians who were challenging this orthodoxy.[12] Seeing themselves as victims of ostracism, these latter had succeeded in preventing the exhibition from being installed. In our petition, we used the phrase "politically correct" to designate those who attacked the orthodoxy, and because of that you refused to sign it, even though you completely agreed with the initiative itself.[13] I would very much like for you to specify your position today. Don't you think there is a real danger that this politically correct thinking in the United States might extend further?

J.D.: An imported product, the mode of thinking and speaking called "politically correct" [English in original] is also a double-edged sword, or, if you prefer, a two-sided trap. You escape from the first side only to fall into the second. It is therefore the site of a high-risk debate. So I will try to proceed slowly and prudently. My irritation at the use, and especially the abuse, of this pseudoargument is first of all a French response. We have to leave this expression, "politically correct," in its original language. I regret that this American catchword has been imported to denounce everything that certain people don't like (for this is indeed what's happening) or to level the accusation of suspect and rigid orthodoxy, or even of leftist neoconformism, at every critical discourse that invokes a norm or recalls an ethical or political prescription. Take the example of the Renaud Camus affair.[14] As soon as anyone is rightly outraged at the contents of such a book (as astonishing for its naive blindness as for its compulsive literary tics straight from the "Old-France Right"—not to mention the "sociological" inanity it displays on every page), he is immediately accused, by this or that self-authorized voice, of wanting to institute a thought, or in fact a policing mechanism, called "politically correct." I therefore protest, and have done so for a long time, against the mechanical abuse (especially in France) and against the rhetorical or polemical effects of this loaded expression, which, by browbeating people with stock formulas and wooden language[15] (for this is truly a *langue de bois*), tries to put an end to all critical thought, all protest, all rebellion. As soon as anyone stands up to denounce a discourse or a practice, he or she is accused of wanting to reestablish a dogmatism or a "political correctness." This other conformism, this counterconformism, seems just as grave. It can become a facile technique for silencing all those who speak in the name of a just cause. Imagine the scene: someone protests against a particular perversion (whether racism, anti-Semitism, political corruption, domestic violence, or, who knows, delinquency or crime), and in response people point their fingers and say: "Enough with this political correctness!" We know that this scene is repeated everywhere, and precisely in the order you suggested: those who rose up against certain sentences in Renaud Camus were *also* accused of being "politically correct"!

It is always dangerous to translate or to import a term blindly or, in certain cases, to instrumentalize it, without recalling its use in the present context of American society. There the denunciation of "political correctness" [English in original here and below] is massively conservative in its origins and is organized, we should say manipulated, by conservative political groups in the Congress and the Senate.

E.R.: Let's try to understand what this denunciation is aimed at.

J.D.: Certain works—I'm thinking particularly of Dinesh D'Souza[16] —have presented the American university in general as a place entirely dominated by censors who want to dictate everything in the name of "political correctness" and who frantically defend the dogmas of communitarianism, feminism, antiracism, etc.—and sometimes postmodernism, poststructuralism, or even, and sometimes especially, that diabolical deconstruction. It is often quite a caricature, and the symptom is its own denunciation.

E.R.: Is this version really exaggerated?

J.D.: Yes, it is. Certain people have an interest in circulating imaginary statistics. There are some fanatics in American universities, of course, and, as here in France, there are doctrinaire pundits who, with their rigid judgments, would like to censor or exclude anything that doesn't conform to this "political correctness." But this is not a massive phenomenon, as some would believe or have others believe.

E.R.: But all the same, it can go as far as expurgating philosophical texts of the past, for example, taking out words considered insulting to this or that community.

J.D.: Independently of such terroristic forms of censorship, it's true that there is, in a much more widespread fashion, a vigilance—which I believe is necessary, both over there and here—with regard to all the signals that, in teaching, in language, can recall phallocentrism, racism, racist segregation. I'm not referring here to the caricatural aspects of this politics. The caricature exists, but it is in the minority.

E.R.: A caricature that would nonetheless aim to expurgate the texts of the past.

J.D.: These excesses sometimes appear, and in those cases the conservatives have a right to complain. Along with others, who are therefore right to do so. I myself have not refrained from doing so. But, beyond the caricature, which is in the minority and relatively rare, a general ethics of vigilance seems necessary with regard to all the signals that, here or there, in language, in advertising, in political life, teaching, the writing of texts, etc., might encourage, for example, phallocentric, ethnocentric, or racist violence.

It is important to remember that in the United States, despite the progress in civil rights, racism is a massive phenomenon. Right now I'm working on the death penalty,[17] and there is no doubt that almost all of the executed prisoners are black. And blacks (African Americans!) who are poor. To recall this or to teach it, to analyze this phenomenon with insistence—does this mean giving in to "political correctness"? In the United States, it is unquestionable that there is racial oppression, perfectly visible but often denied. As for the situation of women, although the symptoms of inequality are different, this situation calls for legitimate struggles, and it helps to explain this figure of American feminism that is often wrongly and too hastily criticized in France. The history of "affirmative action" [English in original] is complex, and you know that right now, even among blacks, its perverse and negative effects are being denounced. And yet it is true that, in many respects, whether we're talking about the situation for women or for blacks, the United States is also, in part, a country in the process of development, a country where the inequalities are massive.

E.R.: Much more than in Europe?

J.D.: Of course! Or in any case, distributed differently than in Europe. That is why there must be constant vigilance.

As for homosexuals, no one can deny the phenomena of exclusion. The ostracism (whether avowed or denied) of which they are still the victims—in Europe, too—derives from the same logic. Using a term like "political correctness" as a catchword to shoot down every call for vigilance seems dangerous to me. And suspect. When the term is not pressed into service by embattled conservatives, it is imprudently taken up by people on the left who may be quite refined but who are sheltered from these harsh and dangerous "sites" (oppression, repression, exclusion, marginalization).

In short, even as I rebel against the "French" abuse of this new "catchword," I remind people that in the United States—where this movement ("political correctness") is much less widespread and powerful than it is said to be, at least in its caricatural form—well, yes, vigilance is no doubt very necessary, provided that under the pretext of being vigilant one does not lapse into sleep or close one's eyes to all the "American" ills that engendered, as a response, such abuses of "political correctness." These ills came first and are very grave in another way.

E.R.: But don't you think that when one has the pedagogical authority that you have and is capable of elaborating very refined concepts, one has a duty to go further and to think *also* about the danger of reversal or the perverse effects produced by movements of emancipation and by what is called postmodernism?

J.D.: Isn't that what I'm trying to do by attempting to avoid or to dismantle what I just called the double trap?

E.R.: I don't know the United States as well as you do, and this is no doubt why I am less able to accustom myself to these ways of thinking; but every time I go there I feel a terrible violence. Allow me to relate an anecdote. I saw our friend Yosef Yerushalmi[18] leave a room full of professors, during a small party where we were gathered, simply because he wanted to smoke, and it had become impossible to smoke where we were. The exclusion of smokers seems downright horrific to me, this marking of "difference" (and not differ*a*nce) in public places, with smokers on one side and nonsmokers on the other, amounts in my eyes to an unacceptable compartmentalization.

J.D.: Don't forget that a similar law was passed here in France.

E.R.: Yes, but fortunately it's not enforced here with the same rigidity, and I believe we owe it to the Revolution and to our republican ideals,
which valorize the integration of the other as he is, not as we would wish
for him to be. This principle rests on the idea that integration would produce a change in oneself. I see this way of marking difference negatively
also in the puritanism that obliges professors to keep the door open when
they meet with students, to avoid being accused of attempting to manipu-
late or seduce someone. I agree with you in insisting on the necessity to
fight ceaselessly for emancipation, but when it comes to women, for example, I have the feeling that the fight is on the right track, even though a
lot of inequalities still exist, whereas men are threatened with being the
next victims in turn—victims, in this case, of a certain matricentrism.

J.D.: In the text I referred to earlier,[19] it was precisely the problem of
the *mater* that I raised, this new argumentation or this old-new argument
for maternitarian authority.

As for the accusations of "sexual harassment" that invaded certain
American universities, I also find it troubling. Some of the laws and regu-
lations are as comic as they are terrifying: a professor cannot meet with a
student in his office without leaving his door open. Sometimes he risks being accused because he smiled, gave a female student a "compliment," invited her to have coffee, etc. In some cases he can be prosecuted by the
law—the law internal to the university or the law in general. It sets up a
microclimate of terror, and sometimes gives rise to plots as perverse as the
evil that one claims to be attacking, or to machinations that instrumentalize the law for implacable ends. That said, sexual harassment exists, let's
never forget that, and not only in the university, and not only in the
United States!

E.R.: I'll go much further than you. The interdictions on sexuality,
when it's a matter of a student and a professor, seem insane to me, even if
one of them has a more obvious transferential power over the other.

J.D.: It is always a question of what is called "power." In principle, in
the legislation on "sexual harassment" [English in original], consensual relations are considered less serious. The problem takes the form of an abuse
of authority outside its supposedly normal field of influence. In the spirit
and in the precise letter of the law, it is necessary to condemn the teacher

(sometimes, but very rarely, a woman) who abuses a relation of virtual power in order to seduce someone who, in fact, depends on him (or her) for, let's say, a curriculum vitae or a recommendation.

E.R.: It strikes me as aberrant.

J.D.: Yes and no.

E.R.: In the passions of love, there is always some kind of power and dominance of one over the other, of one and the other.

J.D.: That's undeniable.

E.R.: How can one decide the question? What does "consensual" mean? Lovers always fight, and no one will ever be able to regulate sexual passions and passions of love before the courts. It seems dangerous to want to do that. It involves an interference in private life that seems both alarming and pointless. In other words, I think that our democratic societies should be extremely vigilant when it comes to the question of the free exercise of sexuality and the passions of love between adults.

J.D.: The difficulty is always to distinguish between, on the one hand, a sexual violence that is "tolerable," in a way, because it is "structural," the violence that inhabits relations of passion and love—which always include, indeed, a form of violent asymmetry or even double asymmetry, sometimes very refined, subtle, sublime, platonic or romantic, and sometimes brutal and massive—and, on the other hand, types of aggression for which the distinction is difficult to delineate. That's why there are laws against rape, or at least what everyone agrees to call "rape," even if the most widely shared passion never excludes some kind of asymmetry from which the scene of rape is never completely erased—and even informs the lovers' desires.

E.R.: I agree in condemning all physical violence; the difficulties arise when it becomes a question of psychic violence.

J.D.: What is called "psychic violence" can reach levels and take on forms of *cruelty*, as we say, which must never be underestimated. Regarding all these types of violence, a confused and perverse game brings the category of "sexual harassment," as it operates in the United States, into a climate of dramatization—in which, however, it is not the case that everyone is losing their head. Where is the border between a violence that is legitimate, in some way irreducible, which we were just speaking of, and the violence that is called abnormal or abusive?

E.R.: This brings up the question of the normal and the pathological. I would say that the border separates, on one side, the excess and abuse of power, the exploitation of the body, or the transformation of the subject into a commodity, and, on the other, transference, passion, dominance, voluntary servitude.

J.D.: Let's take the case of psychoanalysis and homosexuality. You emphasize in your book and in the questions you wrote for the States General of Psychoanalysis that the exclusion of homosexuality has to stop because it is based on a dubious concept of perversion.[20]

E.R.: Indeed, I addressed the problem in a radical way. I think that we must abandon the famous unwritten rule instituted in 1921 by the directors of the International Psychoanalytic Association (IPA)[21] (Ernest Jones, Sandor Ferenczi) that barred homosexuals from the psychoanalytic profession on the grounds of perversion. As if the category of the "perverse" applied only to homosexuals. In addition, like you, I am in favor of the PaCS.[22] I supported not only the PaCS but also the abolition of all forms of classification that would make homosexuality a "vice," an "anomaly," or a form of deviance, in short, against any discriminatory terminology. Freud was in any case very cautious on the subject,[23] and Lacan accepted homosexual practitioners into the Ecole Freudienne de Paris (EFP, 1964–81).

Disordered Families

E.R.: I would like to continue with the question of homosexuality and to discuss with you the ways in which it is being normalized in democratic societies. As for myself, I defend the idea that we must accept homosexual couples' having children: by adoption, same-sex parenting, coparenting,[1] or artificial insemination with a donor (AID). It is said that, in these situations, one is giving up on transmitting the sacrosanct existence of the "anatomical difference between the sexes,"[2] which is supposedly necessary for the elaboration of all imaginary and symbolic differences. This claim seems inaccurate to me. There is so far no indication that the children of gay parents or *enfants d'homos*, as they refer to themselves, are more perturbed than others, or more ignorant about this famous difference.[3] This difference will still be transmitted to the child, since what remains invariant is the biological reality of making a human being. It remains to be seen whether this difference is the major component of the other differences. At any rate, no discipline (psychoanalysis or anthropology) can really resist this kind of social reality, although we know that every human society is based on the existence of prohibitions, symbolic functions, laws, limits, etc.

J.D.: I would be tempted to say, in a somewhat abstract and negative way, that this experiment *must not be forbidden*. Once it has become lawful, whatever has to happen will happen. Even in the most normal cases, what happens happens: there are families considered normal in which the legitimate children are very unhappy. The adaptation to new parental structures is under way, and it will continue. Irreversibly, I think, even if we can foresee, here or there, certain reactions, resistances, and frictions, unequal rhythms. In "our" societies, this mutation will be more difficult for children adopted by homosexual couples. But a repressive law would change nothing. Everything must be done to create the legal conditions that allow for practices in which desire is expressed, or in any case where, as with heterosexual marriage, such desire is now assumed to be present in the majority of cases. After that there will of course be failures (and even psychoanalytic treatments that will attempt to "cure" them!), as there are in families considered normal and legitimate. Emerging on the horizon is the more general question concerning the *model* of the typical Western family cell, the heterosexual couple with two or three children. The dominant model, which, let us not forget, is that of the "couple"—well, it encompasses, includes, or implies other couples, an entire combinatorial of couples, provided (and this is the only condition required by the model) that they remain couples, "bicephalic" units. The homosexual couple is yet another "couple" that in its turn also demands legitimate children. And why not? Is it so far from the dominant norm? Can it not reconstitute, I mean conserve, sometimes in a very conservative way, the most traditional functions (the figure of the father, the mother, etc.)? A number of mutations are under way, among which the adoption of children by homosexual couples is only a particular case. I'm not sure it's the most profound or the most transgressive.

E.R.: For example, take the case of artificial insemination with a donor. It is chosen mostly by homosexual women, much more than by men, who, if they're homosexual, must have recourse to a surrogate mother. In one case, there is a continuity between the biological order and sexual orientation, in the other there is a split, since a man cannot be inseminated but can donate his sperm. It seems to me that this asymmetry reemerges in the distribution of roles and in unconscious psychic structures: in relation to the children in their care, men in a couple act rather as teachers, uncles, or guardians, whereas women more easily imitate the heterosexual parenting model. I wonder if the danger in general—with both homosexuals and heterosexuals—doesn't come from the excessive place given to maternal omnipotence. We know that when a woman becomes a mother, she necessarily finds herself in a position of all-powerfulness in relation to the infant in its state of dependence. During the first months of life, this fusional power of the mother with the child may be necessary for the future socialization of the child, but the mother must then renounce it herself so that the child can open up to the world of alterity, to what is called "the third party"—first incarnated in the father, and therefore, in principle, by whoever symbolically occupies the place of the father, a place that can be that of the other or of one who is "different" (whatever his or her sex).

At the same time, I notice that homosexual couples often want to appear just as "normal" as traditional couples, to the point of imitating them sometimes in a caricatured way. I wonder then whether this desire for normality will cease with the end of social discrimination or whether, on the contrary, it will be more pronounced.

J.D.: Does a couple of homosexual men propose or impose two fathers on their child? I'm not so sure. Does a couple of homosexual women engender two mothers? Is there not always in all these situations, "in our homes," a father and a mother, or something of a father and something of a mother [*du père et de la mère*]? not to mention grandparents, uncles, and aunts, all sorts of relays and substitutes, as always, among friends, etc.? Beyond any juridical interpretation, I wonder above all how (and whether) the familial model, a very stable and foundational reference for psychoanalytic theory, might be able, in transforming itself, to transform psychoanalysis.

With Freud and his successors, including Lacan, the oedipal theory assumes a fixed model: the stable identity of the father and the mother. And especially of a mother *supposed* to be irreplaceable. We will have to come back to this point, which I regard as decisive. In the end, it is the psychoanalytic approach to this culture that should be affected by everything now displacing the familial model. This mutation of psychoanalysis itself should correspond in any case to what it regards as its primary mission: to engage above all with what, directly or otherwise, touches on the familial model and its norms. Psychoanalysis has always wanted to be a psychoanalysis of families.

E.R.: I think that now there are already two positions: that of the dogmatists, attached to a fixed model that is disappearing more and more from social reality—if only with recomposed families—and that of the modern thinkers who are more "deconstructive" and sensitive to the transformations brought about by the subjects themselves. I situate myself on the same side as you: from the moment when a new reality takes shape, when it exists, psychoanalysis—like any other discipline—must think it, interpret it, take it into account, and not condemn it. That would amount to excluding or denying it, and therefore to transforming a discipline into a deontological code and turning its practitioners into censors or prosecutors.

J.D.: Since you have brought up the word "deconstruction," we could show that deconstruction has always been "of the family," "deconstruction of the family" (with a few small "revolutionary" consequences for civil society and the state, which I will leave it to you to imagine). As it happens, I also say that deconstruction is "what happens" or "what arrives" [*ce qui arrive*], what happens as the im-possible. Well, it becomes "what happens to the family," but as the im-possible. We can follow the trajectory of these propositions in the direction of the problems we have just been discussing (PaCS, coparenting, same-sex parenting, artificial insemination, etc.). The transformation of the psychoanalytic milieu that you discuss in your most recent book[4]—this new generation of analysts and patients—is not unrelated to the transformation of family structures.

What we are dealing with here is a transformation of society itself, a transformation of the very model we've been talking about: whether it's a matter of sexuality, the single-parent family, illegitimate or legitimate children. This social turbulence will produce effects on the psychoanalytic scene: on the side of the patients and on the side of the training of clinicians. It's an indissociable set of relations: transformation of the social field—or of the symbolic field—on one side; transformation of the analytic profession on the other.

E.R.: Don't you think that the Freudian thesis regarding the revalorization of the paternal function by way of phallocentrism is the only one that thinks both the deconstruction of the family and its destiny to come within a changing world? In other words, I have the impression that the family is eternal, that it is not in danger, that its richness comes both from its being anchored in a symbolic function and from the multiplicity of its possible recompositions.

J.D.: What is called "the family"? I would not say without hesitation that the family is eternal. What is inalterable, what will continue to traverse History, is that there is, or that there *be, something of* a family, some social bond organized around procreation. What are called "animal" families should also be analyzed in their complexity, as primatologists do. But it would be necessary to introduce the issues involved in their work into the field of psychoanalysis, philosophy, anthropology. There has been very little interest, it seems to me, in the symbolic, social, and familial structures proper to what is called the "animal" world.

As you know, even supposing that the prohibition of incest is the essential trait constituting what is "proper to man" or to anthropological "culture" (an enormous problem that I will leave in the background here), there exists a modality of incest avoidance among certain primates that could be taken into account, that could shake up quite a few things.

I would therefore speak not of an "eternity" of any family model but of a transhistoricity of the family bond. And the model referred to by Freud—and by so many others—is only that of a limited sequence. At once very long and very brief, according to the chosen scale. Very long because it covers millennia, and very brief because, as we see quite clearly, it was *instituted*, and the moment will come, indeed is already being announced, when it will be if not deinstituted, at least diabolically complicated. It is already terribly overdetermined, and has been for a long time. As for the current microreflection on the single-parent family or on the adoption of children by homosexual couples, I don't know if we can foresee how long it will last. Its future is uncertain. Certainly, there will always be "something of a family," but what will its organization look like centuries or millennia from now? It is difficult to say. By using the word "organization" here, I'm referring to what institutes a normative, dominant, or even legal model in a given society. But whether one rejoices over it or deplores it, the effective experience, in each case singular, does not conform and has never submitted to this statutory "organization." That, too, is the unconscious! Within and without a family!

So many things can be done with a man and a woman! With sexual difference (and homosexuality is not sexual indifference), we can imagine so many "familial" configurations! And even in what we consider "our" most stable and familiar model, there are so many subspecies! The "progress" made by genetics liberates or accelerates our imagination—jubilant, terrified, or both at the same time, before all sorts of things that I would not call unknown (especially not by the unconscious), but not yet "registered" by what we could call, in the widest sense, a person's civil state.

E.R.: What are you thinking of?

J.D.: I'm thinking of families that have not only two or three mothers, without counting the fathers, but also families with 3 + *n* parents. This already exists.[5] It exists in the unconscious structures of the most "orderly" families. If you seriously take account of the complexity that is *already* at work in family relations in Western societies, you have a first idea of how much more complicated things will be in the future.

Thus we can imagine a recomposition, an extremely complicated combinatorial, produced not only from an internal logic of transformation but also from techno-genetic transformations, and from reactions to cloning, to organ transplants, to artificial insemination. We will always invent new ways to "normalize"—and I don't mean "naturalize"—the effects that are most unexpected, the apparently unassimilable and monstrous effects of these new techno-genetic powers. Already, with regard to the prospects of cloning, people are fortunately beginning to relativize, to differentiate, to complicate the first reactions, the first reactive delirium, whose ideological patterns and metaphysical presuppositions became the object of critical analyses, not to say deconstructions, already so long ago. As if cloning[6] began with cloning! As if there weren't cloning and then more cloning! As if there weren't a clonelike way of reproducing the discourse against cloning.

Wherever there is repetition and duplication, even resemblance, there is cloning—that is, wherever there is "nature" and "culture," which are never without some kind of cloning. The question concerning cloning will therefore never be "Yes or no?" but "How?": how to deal with difference or with the reproduction of the identical, and first of all: "What is duplication?" Can one pose the question "What is . . . ?" without there being a virtual duplication, and therefore without some kind of cloning that has made this language possible? I am not saying this to evade the issue or to evacuate an important question. I am recalling a few things that should be, and are in fact becoming, obvious: before thinking of monstrous generations of clones armed to the teeth and ready to invade Europe, we know that certain therapeutic cloning techniques will soon be at our disposal, will be useful, and will therefore soon be considered indispensable. The distinction between therapeutic cloning and reproductive cloning does not hold, as long as one has not answered some apparently philosophical questions: for example, what is a re-production (whether "natural" or not, "artificial" or not; what, then, is "nature"? etc.)?

What is the integrity of a person? At what moment and according to what criteria can one define the origin of a person? What is a birth? What, in "nature" or in "culture," is foreign to all "cloning," etc.? These old questions remain or become brand new, thanks in particular to the techno-genetic mutations occurring now. This is why there will always be, not THE family, but *something of* a family, some attachments, some sexual differences,[7] some "sexual relation" (even when there is none, as Lacan would say), some social bond around childbearing in all its forms, some effects of proximity and of the organization of survival—and some law [*du droit*]. But this persistence of an order produces no *a priori* determinable figure of any particular familial model.

E.R.: Fundamentally, some people think that every form of psychical organization is only a cultural or social construction, while others, on the contrary, maintain the "naturalist" notion according to which society—and therefore psychic life—has a determining biological foundation. In this perspective, some people think that homosexuality is a culture—a constructed identity—the way a gender is,[8] while others claim that it is innate, even genetic, and instinctual. Certain homosexuals even dream of a day when scientists will discover the homosexual gene, which would then make it possible to deny that homosexuality results from a particular environment or an unconscious psychical organization.

In this debate, one encounters the idea of a possible biological foundation of human societies.[9]

J.D.: I would prefer not to let myself get trapped in an alternative between naturalism and constructivism. And I do not consider legitimate any of the numerous conceptual oppositions evoked, presupposed, or taken as firmly established in such an alternative. I try to be neither a naturalist nor a constructivist—particularly if the latter refers to some sort of totally deracinated artifactual confection, outside of all biological premises. Between the two, you inscribe the concept of "psychic life" [*psychisme*]. Here, too, we would need to know what is meant by *psyché*. In Freud, the relation of the psychical to the biological is, as you know, always suspended, set aside to be worked out later, in future generations, and it is therefore in truth very complicated.[10]

In all these problems, which are considerable, I would not want to renounce either side. I would like to find a way to take into account biological and genetic determinisms, which are themselves complex and not simply "natural." In the phenomena of biology and genetics there are encodings, directed bifurcations, "languages," and modes of "writing." Put another way, there is a sort of "culture," even a "technics" of genetics that makes possible all sorts of constructions. So I don't want to renounce biological and genetic knowledge insofar as it has something open about it, something progressive and perfectible.

However, the *psyché*—or culture, or the symbolic, to take up, without accrediting them, these equivalences so often taken for granted—the *psyché*, then, takes over where the so-called genetico-biological laws leave off, precisely in a way involving differ*a*nce. At certain "moments," this differ*a*nce can interrupt these laws; at other moments, it can introduce the economy of a new configuration into the immanence of the living being. The interruption itself belongs to the field of what is genetically or biologically possible. These are not only different "moments" of differ*a*nce. Differ*a*nce means at once *the same* (the living being, but deferred, relayed, replaced by a substitutive supplement, by a prosthesis, by a supplementation in which "technology" emerges) and *the other* (absolutely heterogeneous, radically different, irreducible and untranslatable, the aneconomic, the wholly-other or death). An interruption involving differ*a*nce is both reinscribed into the economy of the same and opened to an excess of the wholly other. To return to this word, there is some *psyché*, that is, there is some "life," as soon as this differ*a*nce appears, or more precisely (for it may not appear *as such*; no doubt it never does) as soon as it leaves a *trace* (neither a sign nor a signifier, nor anything whatever that one might call "present" or "absent," but a *trace*).

To return to the question of the family, there will always be something of a familial bond around *birth*. It would be impossible therefore to erase birth—and consequently, among other things, a certain genetic inheritance. But what is it "to be born"? If we distinguish it rigorously from the origin, the beginning, provenance, etc., "birth" is perhaps a question of the future and of arrival, a newly arrived question. Philosophy is much more prepared to work on questions of the origin and the end, of life and death. But philosophy (and no doubt science too, most often, and in any case psychoanalysis) has given little "thinking" attention to what, in birth, does not fall under these categories.

You are familiar with the supposed certainty with which one always knows who the mother of a child is, while one does not know, with the same type of assurance, who the father is. Paternity is induced from a judgment; maternity is observed in a perception. This "evident" fact (what is indeed *supposed* to be evident in maternity but not in paternity) is blithely invoked by Freud in the "Rat Man" case history, where he cites Lichtenberg.[11] From this he deduces that patriarchy was a step forward for reason and rational judgment, a step beyond sense perception.

But this schema, even and especially in Freud, seems more fragile than ever. Today less than ever can we be sure that the mother herself is the woman we believe we saw giving birth. The mother is not only the genetrix since, as psychoanalysis (and not only psychoanalysis) has always taught us, another person can become or can have been "the" mother, one of the mothers. Now the most difficult thing to think, and first of all to desire, then to accept otherwise than as a monstrosity, is precisely this: more than one mother. Supplements of mothers, in an irreducible plurality. Today, the surrogate mother and the one who, properly speaking (as we improperly say), becomes the mother—that makes two people. Not to mention all the other mothers who step in to take over at different times. In other words, the identity of the mother (like her possible juridical identification) depends on a judgment that is just as derived, and on an inference that is just as divorced from all immediate perception, as this "legal fiction" of a paternity conjectured through reason (to use a phrase from Joyce's *Ulysses* referring to paternity).

Techno-scientific capabilities (artificial insemination, surrogate mothers, cloning, etc.) will no doubt accelerate a mutation in the father/mother relation in the future. But this will only be an acceleration, a differ*a*nce, however spectacular or dreadful their effects may appear: the "mother," too, has always been a "symbolic" or "substitutable" mother, like the father, and the certainty acquired at the moment of giving birth was in my opinion an illusion. A very self-interested one, certainly, and the projection of a powerful desire, but an illusion. It remains one, for ever and more than ever.

E.R.: Can you explain that a little more?

J.D.: Consider something else that is "evident": before the possibility of surrogate mothers, we know that, in certain social milieus, the mother "gave birth." But another woman, the nurse, raised the child. The father, for his part, could become the true mother, and the "symbolic" or "fantasmatic" mother could be different from—but more "real" than—the "real" mother. The position of the mother is never reducible to that of the genetrix. In the *Confessions* Rousseau calls Mme. de Warens "Maman," and how many other examples are there of mothers who are not "mamans" and of "mamans" who will never be mothers.

E.R.: Particularly in the eighteenth century.

J.D.: Today less than ever. (No doubt it would be necessary to sharpen the distinction between mother and maternity, the desire of the mother and the desire for maternity. I have tried to do this elsewhere.)[12] The possibilities are now multiplying for having semen carried by another woman who is simply a "rented belly" (*utero in affitto*), as they say in Italian; a "carrier mother" (*mère porteuse*), as we say in French; or, in English, a "surrogate mother." The mother is therefore not the woman who carried the child, nor even the one who gives birth to it. From the point of view of the relation between nature and reason, the opposition between legal fiction and natural maternity will necessarily be displaced. Nevertheless, there will be *some* birth and *some* familial bond around the child. This invariant will remain, but the organization of the respective positions is becoming more mobile. It has never been "natural" for any "living being" ("human" or "animal"), but it will come to seem less and less so. Since the "social," "symbolic," or "fantasmatic" bond around birth will always remain, it will be necessary to delineate an irreducible relation between what one calls, on the one hand, genetics, biology, the "natural," and on the other, the symbolic or the "cultural." The thread [*fil*] of this first filiation exists; one can no longer deny it scientifically (even where it consists in its being interrupted and in differing/deferring).

Even in what seem to be the most spiritual or intellectual spheres, the genetic figure of "life" survives, however enigmatic the apparently figural link remains between what is called natural life and spiritual or mental life.[13] We will have to learn how to learn, all over again, to take it more and more into account. I don't want to choose between genetics, the symbolic function, and constructivism. What is constructed is not constructed just anyhow. It remains true nonetheless that we mustn't mix everything together. We mustn't crush the various dimensions of the living being into each other, a living being that always consists in, and survives by, *knowing* and *knowing how to discern*. There is no life ("animal" or "human") that does not suppose some aptitude for discerning, analyzing, distinguishing: between the forms of life as well as between the "living" and the "dead." Let us begin then by applying this aptitude for discerning to life itself, in general; let us distinguish its structures and levels.

E.R.: I agree with you, but what has changed in relation to the classic model of the legal fiction and the supposed certainty of maternity is that now we can identify the biological father using genetic testing. That, in my opinion, is a radical change.

J.D.: Identifying a genitor is not the same as designating a father. The genitor is not the father! The father is someone who *recognizes* his child; the mother recognizes her child. And not only in a legal sense. The obscurity of the question lies entirely in this "experience" that is so hastily called "recognition." Beyond or on this side of the law, its modalities can be diverse, complex, convoluted; they can spread, become stabilized or destabilized in the course of a history whose end is never determinable. It is this "experience" that will give rise to a very complex interweaving of symbolic possibilities—and that will found a bond (always more or less stable or fragile, never assured) between the "moment of the genitor" and the "symbolic moment." Not only can this phenomenon of "recognition" never be reduced to its legal dimension or to some "paternal" or "maternal" privilege, but it would be very unwise to reserve it exclusively for the *human* "family." Many species of what we brutishly call "the animal" have a very refined, concrete, complex experience of this, with all sorts of "substitutive" resources and "prosthetic" relays, "step-fathers" and "step-mothers," uncles, etc. And not only among the "higher apes," and not only among mammals!

E.R.: You don't believe that the ability to identify with certainty the "trace" of this or that specific individual (a genitor, a criminal, etc.) brings about a change in our representations of origins and filiation?

J.D.: Yes, in our representations. And this is important especially in judicial procedures, for inheritance laws and criminology, and thus for the law and the techniques used by police in the service of the law. But this has little impact on the issues we're discussing, which are prejuridical and even prepolitical. From the point of view of symbolic organization, fantasmatic investments are absolutely necessary (and the history of law is folded into this, in its often dubious concepts). Look at what happens with the substitutions of children in maternity wards. In the order of the fantasy, parents absolutely want to have their own child. But if someone substitutes another child for theirs without their knowing it, if the secret is well kept, kept even from the unconscious, the parental bond will be established in the very same way. No one is any the wiser.

Whether paternal or maternal, the desire or the fantasy of appropriation is not of a purely genetic order, but it comes to be grafted—and to be nurtured like a parasite—on a fantasy of genetics: "my flesh and blood!"; "I love my child because he is my flesh and blood, because he comes (a little) from me myself (a little, a little more), as another." Well, I'm not so sure.

E.R.: All the same, the systematic recourse to the trace, to proof, that is, to the absolute archive, only fosters this narcissistic fantasy of a paternity that has finally been "proven"?

J.D.: A "narcissistic fantasy," certainly, but that doesn't establish any paternity. There is no absolute archive, and the trace is not a proof. The fantasy is set into motion, it imparts motion, from the moment when the father and/or the mother *believes* [*croit*] in effect that he or she is the *authentic* "parent" of what thus *grows* [*croît*] with them. We have to dig further and further into the meaning of "believe." And "grow." And the growth of a belief [*la croissance d'une croyance*]. In this case and in others. There is a fantasy *of* the genetic: one loves one's children more than those of other people because one projects onto them a narcissistic identification: this is my flesh and blood, this is me. And the fantasy can be nearly the same, or can resemble it, with adopted children.

E.R.: But in our societies, the anonymity concerning the origin of children born under an X or conceived through artificial insemination will no doubt be lifted. Some people want this; others do not.[14] I am rather in favor of it, but what is certain is that a child ought absolutely to be able, if he or she wants, to have access to his or her history, since we know after all that truth is inscribed in the unconscious. Besides that, I think that parents ought to tell the truth to their children about their origins, in the case of adoption as well as in cases of artificial insemination with a donor.

J.D.: What can I say to a friend who tells me that "parents ought to tell the truth to their children"? Of course, it is better for the child to believe that he or she knows. I do believe that I know who my father and my mother were. And I can never know, with what is called certain knowledge, what happened between my presumed father and mother "around" my birth. What is important for my equilibrium, for my "mental health," is that I feel sufficiently sure that my father is my father, and my mother my mother. Even if I have been effectively deceived until the end of my days, the belief can work.

E.R.: Honestly, I don't think so. As I see it, there is no effective deception in this domain. The truth always ends up emerging, and children who are deceived about their origin almost always show symptoms indicating that their unconscious knows the truth even while deforming it. You who argued, against Lacan, that a letter does not necessarily arrive at its destination—in other words, that there is no imperialism of the signifier[15]—how can you believe in the effectiveness of an act of deception?

J.D.: Precisely, that's a good example. It's because a letter can always not arrive at its destination that acts of deception (and other similar things—distraction and errors, multiple paths, complete misunderstandings, etc.) can suspend and hold at bay what you are calling the truth, what we desperately hope to maintain as the truth.

The notion of effectiveness ought indeed to pass by way of the unconscious. If something is effective for consciousness, and if, unconsciously, there are symptoms that come through, there is in fact no effectiveness. But if I am absolutely certain, consciously *and* unconsciously, that my mother is my mother and that my father is my father, that will work just as well.

E.R.: On condition that it's true and that the parents aren't hiding a secret about one's filiation.

J.D.: If they keep the secret while showing symptoms of the secret, it won't work, you're right. Otherwise, it does work, even if it's "false." It becomes "true."

E.R.: But when you keep a secret of this order about the origin of a filiation, you can't suppress the symptoms. Of course, if the parents themselves are unaware of the child's origin, they aren't lying when they transmit the truth of their ignorance. But in fact, the secret you want to conceal always returns in the form of symptoms.

J.D.: Often, but not always, not necessarily. When I speak, as I just did so hastily, of an "effectiveness" that passes through the unconscious, I would like for this to be understood very carefully. I'm not offering cynical praise for a lie that works thanks to the unconscious or even that works with it (even though this often has to be considered; but here, improvising as we are, there isn't time enough to lay out, as one would have to do, the enormous question of truth, of veracity and the symptom, within a logic that takes psychoanalysis more or less seriously).

No, I'm only suggesting that we take into account a specific causality (a psychic or symbolic causality, if you like) that cannot be reduced to a pure and simple genetic process, assuming this "pure and simple" ever exists. Consider—purely hypothetically—that if Mme. de Warens had really been able to persuade Jean-Jacques that she was authentically "Maman," then she would have been. This would not have been a lie or a dissimulation, even if—according to "objective" criteria and a concept of truth that have no relevance to what we're talking about, namely filiation, paternity, maternity—even if "Maman" was not his mother.

4

Unforeseeable Freedom

E.R.: Now that we have spoken of the genetic or biological trace, we can logically address the question of contemporary scientism, that is, the ideology originating in scientific discourse, and linked to the real progress of the sciences, that attempts to reduce human behavior to experimentally verifiable physiological processes.[1]

In order to combat the growing influence of this point of view, which goes hand in hand with the transformation of the human into a machine, I have wondered if it isn't necessary to restore the ideal of an almost Sartrean conception of freedom—one that, however, would not be emptied of unconscious determinations.

J.D.: Of course scientism isn't science. And the men and women who are scientists recognize each other by the fact that they are never, almost never, adherents of scientism. If scientism consists in illegitimately extending the field of scientific knowledge or in giving scientific theorems a philosophical or metaphysical status that doesn't belong to them, it begins at the point where science ends and where a theory is exported beyond its field of pertinence. Scientism disfigures what is most respectable in science.

However, I would be more hesitant than you to use the word "experimentalism" or "experimentation." The experimental gesture is not necessarily dictated by scientism. But it is true that when experimentalism is pushed as far as possible, it has to be adjusted to the rational specificity in which it is being deployed. There can be experimentation in the natural sciences, in biology, in research on the genome, but also in a different way in psychology.

Do "neurons" think? This is a very old question and one that is in general posed very poorly by the official representatives of "neurological" science, who lack any philosophical culture. This is well known. However competent they may be in their respective domains (although the delimi- tation of such a "domain" is sometimes difficult, and does not fall entirely within the competence of the "specialist" as such; as for the institutional evaluation of such a competence, that too is problematic), "scientists" sometimes say just anything at all when they try to involve themselves in philosophy or ethics. So in fact it is in the name of science that we must be vigilant against scientism and scientistic positivism.

As for confusing (I would rather say "articulating") thought (as it is called—but what is called thinking?), "human behavior," or "psychic life" with mechanical phenomena, this would trouble me if we were dealing with a systematically reductive and simplifying approach. I even think it is necessary to have an interest—and I share this interest—in machines and in the complexity of their functions. What bothers me about some of the people who identify with scientism is that their mechanical models often fall far short of the hypercomplexity of the machines, real or virtual, pro- duced by humans (and to which, for example, all the aporias or the "im- possibles" taken up by deconstruction bear witness, precisely there where it puts the most powerful formalizing machines to the test, in language; and it does this not in order to disqualify the "machine" in general, quite the contrary, but in order to "think" it differently, to think differently the event and the historicity of the machine). In my opinion, the most "free" thought is one that is constantly coming to terms with the effects of the machine. That's why I rarely use the word "freedom" as I know you do.

On certain occasions, however, I will defend freedom as an excess of complexity in relation to a determinate machinelike state; I will fight for specific freedoms, but I will not calmly speak of Freedom [la *liberté*]. Did- n't Lacan say somewhere that he never uses this word?[2]

If I am cautious about the word "freedom," it is not because I sub- scribe to some mechanistic determinism. But this word often seems to me to be loaded with metaphysical presuppositions that confer on the subject or on consciousness—that is, on an egological subject[3]—a sovereign inde- pendence in relation to drives, calculation, economy, the machine. If free- dom is an excess of play in the machine, an excess of every determinate machine, then I would militate for a recognition of and a respect for this freedom, but I prefer to avoid speaking of the subject's freedom or the freedom of man.

E.R.: But which machines are you referring to?

J.D.: There is *some* machine everywhere, and notably in language. Thus Freud, our common and privileged reference, speaks of economy, of unconscious calculation, of principles of calculation (reality principle, pleasure principle), of repetition and repetition compulsion. I would define the machine as a system [*dispositif*] of calculation and repetition. As soon as there is any calculation, calculability, and repetition, there is something of a machine. Freud took into account the machine of economy and the product of the machine.[4] But in the machine there is an excess in relation to the machine itself: at once the effect of a machination and something that eludes machinelike calculation.

Between the machinelike and the non-machinelike, then, there is a complex relation at work that is not a simple opposition. We can call it freedom, but only beginning at the moment when there is something incalculable. And I would also distinguish between an incalculable that remains homogeneous with calculation (and which escapes it for contingent reasons, such as finitude, a limited power, etc.) and a noncalculable that in essence would no longer belong to the order of calculation. The event—which in essence should remain unforeseeable and therefore not programmable—would be that which exceeds the machine. What it would be necessary to try to think, and this is extremely difficult, is the event *with* the machine. But to accede, if this is possible, to the event beyond all calculation, and therefore also beyond all technics and all economy, it is necessary to take programming, the machine, repetition, and calculation into account—as far as possible, and in places where we are not prepared or disposed to expect it.

It is necessary to track the effects of economic calculation everywhere, if only in order to know where we are affected by *the other*, that is, by the unforeseeable, by the event that, for its part, is incalculable: *the other* always responds, by definition, to the name and the figure of the *incalculable*. No brain, no neurological analysis, however exhaustive it's supposed to be, can render the encounter with the other. The coming of the other, *l'arrivance de l'arrivant*—the "arriving-ness" of the arrival—this is *what happens*, this is the one *who or which arrives*[5] as an unforeseeable event. Knowing how to "take into account" what defies accounting, what defies or inflects otherwise the principle of reason, insofar as reason is limited to "giving an account" (*reddere rationem, logon didonai*), and not simply denying or ignoring this unforeseeable and incalculable coming of the other—that too is knowledge, and scientific responsibility.

E.R.: Today, the notion of unconscious determination and the Freudian thesis of the three narcissistic wounds[6] are a part of our discourse. They have been accepted. Everyone today knows that he or she has an unconscious, and in this sense psychoanalysis has taken up where the philosophy of consciousness, the philosophy of the subject, left off. It became the philosophy of the "decentered" subject. It succeeded in bringing together two antagonistic traditions, by modifying both of them, each through the other: the neurophysiological model and the "spiritual" model (introspection, self-invention, exploration of inwardness). It added to this a clinical heritage coming, on the one hand, from psychiatry (classification of illnesses) and, on the other, from the old therapeutics of the soul (treatment through transference).

But what is even newer today, it seems to me, is that this modern, decentered subject doesn't want to know anything about this unconscious whose existence he's aware of. He prefers to fall back on machines, neurons, organic processes, over which he has no hold. Hence my idea to restore a space of freedom to this subject who is determined or closed in on all sides by machines (social, economic, biological). For if we are really determined in every way, and no breach is possible, we risk replacing the psychical by the cultural and establishing something that, far from universal, would resemble not difference or exile but "roots," some origin anchored in a territorial sovereignty, however imaginary it might be. Not to mention that in the political domain scientism is always quite sinister.

I would recall, with regard to a domain I know well, that it was always in the name of an alleged scientific neutrality—and therefore of a form of scientism—that the directors of the World Psychiatric Association refused, twenty years ago, to denounce the abuses of their discipline in the former Soviet Union. It is in the name of this same alleged scientificity, in their practice and in their theory, that psychoanalysts made themselves complicit with the Latin American dictatorships by claiming that their ethics required them to remain neutral regarding the torture and human rights abuses that were occurring. Under the Nazi regime, the argument of scientific neutrality was abundantly exploited in this way.[7] And today we're seeing a "softer" version of this attitude. In psychiatry, for example, one often evokes the supposed scientificity of its approach to mental illness, which amounts to nothing more than the psychic exploitation of its subjects.

As for the current return to a purely traumatic or organic causality, or to a trace, to explain neurosis—even though Freud abandoned this thesis in 1897[8]—I see this as a regressive attitude. Without denying economic, biological, or social determinations, one can leave a certain space for psychic life and for the idea of subjective freedom.

J.D.: Of course, but it is less clear to me what you are calling "a certain space," and what it is we would indeed want to save. The difficulty we have to confront lies in the words "subject" and "freedom." I would call what resists or ought to resist this determinism—or this imperialism of the determinist discourse—neither subject, nor ego, nor consciousness, nor even unconscious; rather I would make it one of the sites of the other, the incalculable, the event. Singularity is indeed exposed to *what comes*, as other and as incalculable. Singularity as such (whether it appears as such or not) can never be reduced, in its very existence, to the rules of a machine-like calculation, nor even to the most incontestable laws of any determinism. What to call it? It's a very difficult problem. In calling it *freedom*, I am always afraid of reconstituting a philosophical discourse that has already been exposed to a certain deconstruction (freedom as sovereign power of the subject or as independence of the conscious self, will of the "cogito," and even the freedom of *Dasein*, etc.).

The only attempt, the most convincing effort to open a passage by which the word or concept of "freedom" might be given a postdeconstructive virtue—and this often seems to me indispensable, in particular for welcoming or giving rise to what is coming, to what will come, under the name of another ethics, a repoliticization capable of approaching another concept of the political, a progressive transformation of international law, etc.—I believe I perceive this, at least perceive it, in certain passages of *The Experience of Freedom*, by Jean-Luc Nancy.[9]

It has often happened, in recent years, when I had to give a name to things of this order—the "free," the incalculable, the unforeseeable, the undecidable, the event, the arrival, the other—that I speak of "what comes."

E.R.: What comes?

J.D.: Yes, what arises unforeseeably, what both calls upon and over-whelms my responsibility (my responsibility *before* my freedom—which it nonetheless seems to presuppose, my responsibility in heteronomy, my freedom without autonomy), the event, the coming of the one who or which comes but does not yet have a recognizable figure—and who there-fore is not necessarily another man, my likeness, my brother, my neighbor (you see all the discourses that would thus be called back into question again by the one who or which comes in this way). It can also be a "life" or even a "specter" in animal or divine form, without being "the animal" or "God," and not only a man or a woman, nor a figure sexually definable ac-cording to the binary assurances of homo- or heterosexuality.

That is what an event worthy of the name can and ought to be, an *ar-rivance* that would surprise me absolutely and to whom or for whom, to which or for which I could not, and may no longer, *not respond*—in a way that is as responsible as possible: what happens, what arrives and comes down upon me, that to which I am exposed, beyond all mastery. Heteron-omy, then—the other is my law. What thus comes down upon me does not necessarily come to me in order to elect me, as me, by presenting itself be-fore me, in such a way that I *see it coming* horizontally, like an object or a subject that can be anticipated against the background of a horizon or a foreseeable future. There is no *horizon* for the other, any more than there is for death. The other who or which comes upon me does not necessarily *present* itself before me in a horizontal perspective; it can fall upon me, ver-tically (not from the Most High, and yet from so high!) or surprise me by coming at my back, from behind or from below, from the underground of my past, and in such a way that I don't see it coming, or even such that I never see it, having to content myself with feeling or hearing it.[10] But barely.

E.R.: Something like the dimension of the tragic?

J.D.: We can call it tragic with a few precautions. "The one who or which comes" exceeds any determinism but exceeds also the calculations and strategies of my mastery, my sovereignty, or my autonomy. This is why, even if no one is simply a "free subject," there is in this place some-thing "free," a certain space of freedom is opened, or in any case is pre-sumed open by the one who or which comes, a *spacing* that is liberated, *dis-engaged* (before and for the pledge [*le gage*], the engagement, the response, the promise, etc.). That is why this figure is linked to all the political questions of sovereignty. It is there that I am exposed and, I dare say, happily vulnerable. Whenever something other [*de l'autre*] can arrive, there is a "to come," there is something of a "future-to-come." With the determinism you spoke of, there is no future.

E.R.: Because everything would be closed down?

J.D.: Everything is already past or present, and there is no future. But whenever the one who or which remains to come does come, I am exposed, destined to be free and to decide, to the extent that I cannot foresee, predetermine, prognosticate. This can be called freedom, but with the reservations I just indicated. The condition for decision (the decision that *it is necessary* [*il faut*], which it is necessary to presuppose everywhere) is the experience of the undecidable I just spoke of in terms of "the one who or which comes." If I know what it is necessary to decide, I do not decide.

Between knowledge and decision, a leap is required, even if it is necessary to know as much and as well as possible before deciding. But if decision is not only under the authority of my knowledge but also *in my power*, if it is something "possible" for me, if it is only the predicate of what I am and can be, I don't decide then either. That is why I often say, and try to demonstrate, how "my" decision is and ought to be the *decision of the other* in me, a "passive" decision, a decision of the other that does not exonerate me from any of my responsibility. This is a scandalous proposition for common sense and for philosophy, but I believe I can rationally demonstrate (though I can't do it here) its ineluctable necessity and its implications. When I say "rationally," I am obviously appealing to a history of reason, and therefore also to its future, its "future-to-come." To the one who or which comes under the name of reason.

E.R.: For you, then, the possibility of freedom would be what comes, what would be unknowable: the unforeseeable, incalculable event.

We could then think of the question of the advances made in biological science not as a determinism preventing the exercise of subjective freedom but as something that ought to be included in this incalculable moment. I'm thinking of cloning in particular, which we've already discussed. I don't share the opinion of those who demonize science without understanding that it is scientism, and not science, that is so violently attacking humanism, philosophy, Freud and psychoanalysis. I think that the fantasy of fabricating a human being (reproductive cloning) is a product of scientism, a scientific imaginary that, in the current circumstances, there is little need to fear.[11] Even if such reproduction is technically possible, the status of the clone will not be what we imagine today, precisely because in order to exist, a clone will have to be a subject and find a singular identity. In this regard, I think that Freud would have found the current problems very exciting.

J.D.: It's very complicated, of course; we must begin by recognizing that. Given a certain imagery, a certain theatricality of the identical, serial reproduction of human individuals, I understand why people would be terrified, and it's in this light that I explain to myself the immediate and passionate reactions of certain individuals and political leaders at the highest level, the official so-called "sages" of the Comité d'éthique, for example.[12] The philosophical, ethical, political, or juridical "competence" of these "sages," their supposed knowledge (and we should recall that wisdom is, precisely, not simply a form of knowledge, a knowledge supposed by others, here less than ever)—that is precisely where the problem is located. Even if (just as a hypothesis) we did not question the scientific competence or the supposed lucidity of these "sages," we are here entering zones of decision in which the very idea of competence, knowledge, or wisdom has—for reasons I gave a moment ago—a pertinence that is rigorously insufficient and essentially inadequate. But from the point of view of the imagination, I understand their terror, and I can also share it. Upon reflection, I believe that in any case there has been, is, and will be *some* cloning. Legislation will not prevent cloning.

And then, if we examine closely the concept of cloning—the reproduction of two identical individuals, two identical structures of living beings—this has always existed; it occurs all the time in reproduction in general. Reproduction in general cannot be controlled or forbidden; we cannot deny that something identical is always returning and multiplying. The identical returns all the time. In one way or another, whether in the family, in language, in the nation, in culture and in education, in tradition, one seeks to reproduce by giving oneself alibis. Without an identifying reproduction, there wouldn't be any culture either.

Finally, we must acknowledge—and here we are approaching more realistic, more effective, concrete and practical considerations—that the possibility of cloning will not necessarily be exploited for terrifying ends.

E.R.: Nonreproductive cloning, designed to cure certain genetic illnesses, obviously signals an incontestable scientific advance.

J.D.: Absolutely. For all these reasons, we should not let ourselves be too impressed by images when we address such a problem. We must also analyze this imaginative compulsion to expect the worst, the monstrous (of which we have had many examples in the history of science and technology), and not to treat the question as if it were monolithic. There are different problems that fall under the name of *cloning*. One cannot speak out for or against cloning in general. Here, too, it is better to prepare a differentiated, progressive approach, without letting oneself be paralyzed, without giving in to a fearful legislative reaction, to a reactive political response in the form of "all or nothing."

E.R.: It seems that this is what people did.

J.D.: The important decisions are still to come. Who does what, and with what? From a concrete and legislative point of view, it is necessary to address with great care, case by case and sector by sector, the problems related to this or that possibility. Who does what with this considerable power? I am not against cloning *in general*, but if the threat of reproducing human beings emerges, I mean an effective, massive *threat*, etc., according to criteria to be determined, it will be necessary to wage a political war, as people have done in other situations. It would not be the first time. There has always been *some* reproduction.

Let's consider, for example, the notion of training. I'm thinking of the training not only of animals but also of certain political militants. One tries to "reproduce" individuals who think the same thing, who conduct themselves in the same way with respect to the leader and within the group, according to well-known patterns. There, too, it is a question of cloning. Not to mention all the techniques, all the prostheses, all the grafting, for example, and not only in military matters and in the classic and modern methods of conducting warfare.

E.R.: But today we are dealing with something different, the introduction of a mechanism of identical reproduction in the biological order!

J.D.: But where does the biological begin? How is it delimited? What is going to be reproduced?

E.R.: In the current debate, I think it is necessary to distinguish scientism from true scientific activity, without ever forgetting that scientists are perfectly capable of conceiving, in the name of science, the most delirious projects.[13] I see certain manifestations of scientism—in the behaviorist or cognitivist aberrations, for example—as barbarous, to the extent that in each case it is fundamentally a question of reducing the human being to a body with no subject. On this point I think it's useful to reread the famous lecture by Georges Canguilhem, "Le cerveau et la pensée" [The Brain and Thought],[14] in which he denounces the barbarity of every form of psychology that would claim to base itself on biology and physiology in order to affirm that thought is merely the effect of cerebral secretion. As I see it, we must combat the mythologies of scientism that claim, for example, that one day a well-programmed computer will be able to write *In Search of Lost Time* even better than Proust. I also think that the recent deciphering of the genome, which clearly shows that science provides no "readymade" solution to the organization of human life, will allow scientists themselves to critique the irresponsible aberrations of scientism.

And yet I am still struck by the mixing of genres that occurs today between the domain of the "rational" and that of the "irrational." Recently, with regard to cloning, the United States Congress quite seriously consulted the guru of the Rael sect (Claude Vorilhon) for his opinion on the question of reproductive cloning. The guru in question, an advocate of reproductive cloning, is the exact replica of these mad scientists depicted in French literature. But he is also a charlatan who exploits his followers financially and sexually.

He brought together fifty women from his sect who agreed to receive an egg identically reproduced fifty times, and he claims that, thanks to them, he can "duplicate" a child who died at ten years of age whose parents want to bring him back to life. And he has actually carried out the implantations with his team of "scientists." What is disturbing about all this is not that such fantasies have been taken up by a sect—such things have always existed—but the fact that a delusional discourse of this type could be placed on the same level as science by an authority as important as the United States Congress: here scientism and occultism come together.[15]

J.D.: Ethico-juridical reactions should not be modeled on this scientistic caricature, nor should they let themselves be trapped in a simple alternative: a mechanistic, physicalistic, physiologistic determinism, on the one hand, and, on the other—safe and sound—the beautiful freedom of human thought.

The responsibility that must be taken, by whomever it may be, but particularly by legislators and politicians, ought to respond, or attempt to correspond, to what we can know scientifically about the reality of the mechanisms of reproduction, and not to the compulsions that "scientism" would invest in these mechanisms. There have always been phenomena of reproduction, of the articulation between the machine and the living being. The history of literature, since you referred to that, is constituted by that kind of thing, by quasi-mechanical and automatic functions, always on the border of plagiarism (a notion as obscure and problematic as cloning). We must not forget this, even if the example of Proust's book is indeed a caricature.

E.R.: It seems to me that today scientism is even more barbaric than in the past. The supporters of what is called cognitive behaviorism really believe that one day we will be able to do completely without the concepts of the subject, the unconscious, and consciousness. In a debate I recently had on this subject, Dan Sperber claimed that soon we would effectively be able to do without the subject, saving only the subject of the law, a subject with no affect, no desire, and especially no unconscious (in the Freudian sense).[16]

J.D.: Western law is the very site, or in any case a privileged site, of the emergence and the authority of the subject, the concept of the subject. If it is maintained in law, it is maintained everywhere. How would one save the subject of law?

E.R.: As a remnant necessary for the survival of the social bond. From this perspective, it would be a question of maintaining the existence of a subject of ethics or of responsibility, with no basis in any psychic or affective reality, devoid of any drives or impulses. This has nothing to do, of course, with the subject of ethics of which Foucault speaks, which is a subject in the process of inventing itself by letting go of itself.[17] In what I am referring to, there would be, on one side, the computer that would replace thought and, on the other, behaviors and cognition as purely physiological or biological processes. There would then be no place for the autonomy of any psychic life in relation to a world constituted as symbolic, signifying, or passionate. Man would thus be regarded as a machine in the body of a chimpanzee, and his subjectivity would be only the fruit of an "incorrigible" illusion leading him to see himself as endowed with free will.

J.D.: The difficulty, it seems to me, is to take into account the possibility of this extreme, extended, and extendable mechanization, and to forget that there is a point where calculation reaches its limit: play, the possibility of play within calculating machines. And what you call affect, that is, the relation of the living being to the other—the relation to oneself as a relation to another—this affect remains, by definition, incalculable, something foreign to all machines.

E.R.: That's my opinion. There is something undecidable, or *some* undecidable, as you say.

J.D.: Undecidable, incalculable—or rather, as I suggested a moment ago, noncalculable.

E.R.: And therefore unanalyzable.

J.D.: Well, in any case, something that resists analysis and thus always remains to be analyzed. It is no doubt through this irreducibility of affect, that is, of the other and the relation to the other, that what we still call freedom or the unconscious should be reintroduced, but without falling into a reactionary ideology.

E.R.: Passion and conflict . . .

J.D.: The other, the arrival of the other is always incalculable. This does not fail to produce effects in the machine, but it cannot be calculated by the machine. It is necessary *to think*, that is, *to invent* what is necessary so that we do not close our eyes to the machine and to the extraordinary progress of calculation, while still understanding, within and outside the machine, this play of the other, this play with the other. Once one accepts its principle and gives oneself over to this exposure to the other—to the event that comes to affect us, and therefore to the affectivity by which life is defined—at that moment, it is necessary to be prepared to invent the coming of a discourse capable of taking this into account.

E.R.: What you call "hospitality."[18]

J.D.: For example. That may well be one of the names for what is in question here: to welcome, in an inventive way—with some genuine effort and good will—the one who or which comes into one's home, and comes to oneself, inevitably, without invitation.

E.R.: At the time of the affair of the undocumented immigrants,[19] you intervened in a remarkable way in what you called a "crime of hospitality."[20]

J.D.: "Crime of hospitality" was a citation. A terrible phrase from Jacques Toubon,[21] I think. A family in Brittany had taken in some Basque friends who were in the country illegally; they did this out of friendship. Now, according to the law invoked by Toubon, the state can prosecute anyone who welcomes into their house or at their table, even on a personal and private basis, persons whose presence in the country is illegal. In this case, they were Basque.[22] To me this expression seemed *striking*, shall we say. And in one blow, for it was also a blow, the offer of hospitality was associated with a criminal act.

A certain political rhetoric was able to couple these two words together, and this ugly blow risked legitimating the worst. To go back to the debate you began with, I regularly oppose unconditional hospitality—*pure hospitality* or a *hospitality of visitation*, which consists in letting the visitor come, the unexpected arrival, without asking for any account, without demanding his passport—to a *hospitality of invitation*.

Pure or *unconditional* hospitality assumes that the one arriving has not been invited to the place where I remain master of my domain and where I control my house, my territory, my language, where (according, on the contrary, to the rules of *conditional* hospitality) he should in some way conform to the accepted rules of the place that welcomes him. Pure hospitality consists in leaving one's house open to the unforeseeable arrival, which can be an intrusion, even a dangerous intrusion, liable eventually to cause harm. This pure or unconditional hospitality is not a political or juridical concept. Indeed, for an organized society that upholds its laws and wants to maintain the sovereign mastery of its territory, its culture, its language, its nation, for a family or for a nation concerned with controlling its practices of hospitality, it is indeed necessary to limit and to condition hospitality. This can be done with the best intentions in the world, since unconditional hospitality can also have perverse effects.

However, these two modalities of hospitality remain irreducible to one another. This distinction requires a reference to that hospitality which at times we anxiously dream of and desire, one involving exposure to the one *who* or which comes. This pure hospitality, without which there is no concept of hospitality, applies to the crossing of a country's borders, but it also has a role in ordinary life: when someone arrives, when love arrives, for example, one takes a risk, one is exposed. To understand these situations, it is necessary to maintain this horizon without horizon, this unlimitedness of unconditional hospitality, even while knowing that one cannot make it a political or juridical concept. There is no place for this type of hospitality in law and politics.

E.R.: In the situation I mentioned, your intervention can be described as deconstructive. On the one hand, you accept completely the idea that there would be an immigration policy, that is, a control over the flows of migration, and on the other hand, within a very elaborate engagement with words and language, you indicate the limits and the illusions of a political attitude that would consist in wanting to master, through technology, the question of hospitality in general.

On this point, I follow you completely. I have never thought it was necessary to open all the borders and stop controlling the flows of migration. And yet for all that, I have not been satisfied with the policies of the Left on this score, although I find them better than those of the Right. I especially did not appreciate it when certain Far Left intellectuals, no doubt in the minority but supported by others, compared Patrick Weil to a proponent of the final solution and imputed things to him that he never said.[23] At that point, I refused to sign any petition whatsoever on this question. I have always been very wary of those who claim to fight for a just cause with extreme arguments.

J.D.: Once the field of conditional hospitality has been circumscribed, it becomes possible to discuss a policy. Within this field, it is still possible not to agree—as was the case with me—with the political decisions made by Chevènement and by the government he belonged to. Like others, I argued that there was much more space to welcome foreigners than people were saying, and that immigration had not increased, contrary to the claims about the dreaded "threshold of tolerance." It was imperative not to give in, because of electoral or other concerns, to the fearful fantasies of those who saw themselves "invaded" by North African immigration. Therefore, once the necessity—and the virtues—of a conditional hospitality were recognized, debate became possible and something could be changed by a relative struggle, located on a specific front.

That's why I found Jean-Pierre Chevènement's declarations excessive when he felt it necessary to decry the "irresponsibility" of intellectuals who supposedly wanted to open all the gates.[24] No one was demanding the effacement of the borders or the elimination of visas. To denounce as irresponsible those who were fighting for a more generous—and no less calculated—hospitality was a shocking gesture that expressed the political weakness of someone getting carried away by his rhetoric.

5

Violence Against Animals

E.R.: Among the aberrations of contemporary scientism, there is a particularly striking one that mixes a utilitarian and cognitivist perspective, a juridical ideal, and an ecological (or "deep ecological") goal. I'm thinking of the "Darwinian" project conceived by Peter Singer and Paola Cavalieri[1] that would involve not protecting animals against violence by instituting animal rights, but rather granting human rights to "nonhuman great apes." Their reasoning, which seems aberrant to me, is based on the idea that, on the one hand, great apes are endowed with cognitive structures enabling them to learn language in the same way as humans, and on the other hand, they are more "human" than those humans suffering from madness, senility, or organic illnesses that would deprive them of their reason.

The authors of this project thus trace a dubious border between the human and the nonhuman by relegating the mentally handicapped to a biological species no longer belonging to the human kingdom, while also placing the great apes within another biological species integrated into the human but superior to that of felines, for example, or to other animals, whether they're mammals or not. Consequently, the two authors condemn article 3 of the Nuremberg tribunal code demanding that every new therapeutic or experimental treatment be preceded by tests on animals. You have been interested in the question of animality for a long time; I'd like to hear your opinion on these questions.

J.D.: The "question of animality" is not one question among others, of course. I have long considered it to be decisive (as one says), in itself and for its strategic value; and that's because, while it is difficult and enigmatic in itself, it also represents the limit upon which all the great questions are formed and determined, as well as all the concepts that attempt to delimit what is "proper to man," the essence and future of humanity, ethics, politics, law, "human rights," "crimes against humanity," "genocide," etc.

Wherever something like "the animal" is named, the gravest, most resistant, also the most naive and the most self-interested presuppositions dominate what is called human culture (and not only Western culture); in any case they dominate the philosophical discourse that has been prevalent for centuries. In all my texts one finds explicit indications of the active conviction that I have always held in this regard. Beginning with *Of Grammatology*, the elaboration of a new concept of the *trace* had to be extended to the entire field of the living, or rather to the life/death relation, beyond the anthropological limits of "spoken" language (or "written" language, in the ordinary sense), beyond the phonocentrism or the logocentrism that always trusts in a simple and oppositional limit between Man and the Animal. At the time I stressed that the "concepts of writing, trace, gramma or grapheme" exceeded the opposition "human/nonhuman."[2] All the deconstructive gestures I have attempted to perform on philosophical texts, Heidegger's in particular, consist in questioning the self-interested misrecognition of what is called the Animal in general, and the way in which these texts interpret the border between Man and the Animal.[3] In the most recent texts I have published on this subject, I am suspicious of the appellation "Animal" in the singular, as if there were simply Man *and* the Animal, as if the homogeneous concept THE Animal could be extended universally to all nonhuman forms of living beings.

Without being able to go into great detail here, it seems to me that the way in which philosophy, on the whole but particularly since Descartes, has treated the question of THE (so-called) animal is a major sign of its logocentrism and of a deconstructible limitation. We are dealing here with a tradition that was not homogeneous, to be sure, but hegemonic, and that in fact proffered the discourse *of* hegemony, of mastery itself. But what resists this prevalent tradition is quite simply the fact that there is a multiplicity of living beings, a multiplicity of animals, some of which do not fall within what this grand discourse on the Animal claims to attribute to them or recognize in them. Man is one of them, and an irreducibly singular one, of course, as we know, but it is not the case that it is Man *versus* THE Animal.

On the other hand, even though great violence has forever been practiced against animals—we already find traces of it in biblical texts that I have studied elsewhere from this point of view—I try to show what is specifically modern in this violence, and the "philosophical" axiom—or symptom—of the discourse that supports it and attempts to legitimate it. This industrial, scientific, technical violence will not be tolerated for very much longer, neither de facto nor de jure. It will find itself more and more discredited. The relations between humans and animals *must* change. They *must*, both in the sense of an "ontological" necessity and of an "ethical" duty. I place these words in quotation marks because this change will have to affect the very sense and value of these concepts (the ontological and the ethical). That is why, although their discourse often seems to me poorly articulated or philosophically inconsistent, I am on principle sympathetic with those who, it seems to me, are in the right and have good reasons to rise up against the way animals are treated: in industrial production, in slaughter, in consumption, in experimentation.

To characterize this treatment, I would not use the word "cruelty," despite the temptation. It's a confused, obscure, overdetermined word. At bottom, whether it's a matter of blood (*cruor*) or not (*Grausamkeit*), cruelty, "making suffer" or "letting suffer" for pleasure—this too, as a relation to the law, would be what is proper to man. (Regarding the right to punish or the death penalty, this word is used in an extremely confused way. Elsewhere I study the history and the "logic" of the lexicon of "cruelty." A psychoanalytic reading would be useful here, and a reading of the psychoanalytic use of the word, in Freud in particular.)[4] However one characterizes it, the violence inflicted on animals will not fail to have profound reverberations (conscious and unconscious) on the image humans have of themselves. This violence, I believe, will become less and less tolerable. I will also not use the word "rights," but that is where the question becomes complicated. There have been, before the arguments you mentioned, numerous declarations of animal rights.

E.R.: What are the terms used in thinking about animal rights?

J.D.: It is too often the case—and I believe this is a fault or a weakness—that a certain concept of the juridical, that of human rights, is reproduced or extended to animals. This leads to naive positions that one can sympathize with but that are untenable. A certain concept of the human subject, of post-Cartesian human subjectivity, is for the moment at the foundation of the concept of human rights—for which I have the greatest respect but which, as the product of a history and of a complex set of performatives, must be relentlessly analyzed, reelaborated, developed, and enriched (historicity and perfectibility are in fact essential to it).

Now, when it comes to the relation to "the Animal," this Cartesian legacy determines all of modernity. The Cartesian theory assumes, for animal language, a system of signs without response: *reactions* but no *response*. Kant, Levinas, Lacan, Heidegger (much like the cognitivists) hold a position in this regard almost identical to Descartes's. They distinguish *reaction* from *response*, with everything that depends on this distinction, which is almost limitless. With regard to the essential and to what counts on a practical level, this legacy, whatever the differences may be, governs modern thought concerning the relation of humans to animals. The modern concept of right depends massively on this Cartesian moment of the *cogito*, of subjectivity, freedom, sovereignty, etc. Descartes's "text" is of course not the cause of this large structure, but it "represents" it in a powerful systematicity of the symptom. Consequently, to confer or to recognize rights for "animals" is a surreptitious or implicit way of confirming a certain interpretation of the human subject, which itself will have been the very lever of the worst violence carried out against nonhuman living beings.

The axiom of the repressive gesture against animals, in its philosophical form, remains Cartesian, from Kant to Heidegger, Levinas, or Lacan, whatever the differences between these discourses. A certain philosophy of right and of human rights depends on this axiom. Consequently, to want absolutely to grant, not to animals but to a certain category of animals, rights equivalent to human rights would be a disastrous contradiction. It would reproduce the philosophical and juridical machine thanks to which the exploitation of animal material for food, work, experimentation, etc., has been practiced (and tyrannically so, that is, through an abuse of power).

A transformation is therefore necessary and inevitable, for reasons that are both conscious and unconscious. Slow, laborious, sometimes gradual, sometimes accelerated, the mutation of relations between humans and animals will not necessarily or solely take the form of a charter, a declaration of rights, or a tribunal governed by a legislator. I do not believe in the miracle of legislation. Besides, there is already a law, more or less empirical, and that's better than nothing. But it does not prevent the slaughtering, or the "techno-scientific" pathologies of the market or of industrial production.

Of course there are irreducible differences, uncrossable borders between so many species of living beings. Who can deny this without push-
ing blindness to the point of stupidity [*bêtise*]? But there is not only one
border, unified and indivisible, between Man and the Animal.

E.R.: But where and how would you cross the limit? Would it not be
necessary to look again at the notion of a divide between nature and culture, on which anthropology is based?

J.D.: That's the least that can be said. There are a great number of
different structures in the animal world. Between the protozoon, the fly,
the bee, the dog, the horse, the limits multiply, particularly in terms of
"symbolic" organization, encoding or the practice of signs. If I am unsatis-
fied with the notion of a border between two homogeneous species, man
on one side and the animal on the other, it is not in order to claim, stu-
pidly, that there is no limit between "animals" and "man"; it is because I
maintain that there is more than one limit, that there are many limits.
There is not *one* opposition between man and non-man; there are, between
different organizational structures of the living being, many fractures, heterogeneities, differential structures.

The gap between the "higher primates" and man is in any case
abyssal, but this is also true for the gap between the "higher primates" and
other animals. This is something undeniably obvious to common sense—
but while tremendous progress is being made in primatology, this progress
is not receiving the attention it deserves. It describes, in a direct and sometimes astounding way, extremely refined forms of symbolic organization:
work of mourning and of burial, family structures, avoidance if not prohibition of incest, etc. (But "prohibition" itself, for man, forbids without always preventing, such that the opposition between avoidance and inter-
diction still remains problematic.)

All this is very complicated—it is co-implication itself. I do not say
that we must renounce identifying a "proper of man," but one could
demonstrate (I am working on this elsewhere, particularly in my teaching)
that none of the traits by which the most authorized philosophy or culture
has thought it possible to recognize this "proper of man"—none of them
is, in all rigor, the exclusive reserve of what we humans call human. Either
because some animals also possess such traits, or because man does not
possess them as surely as is claimed (an argument I used against Heidegger,

particularly in *Aporias*,[5] with regard to the experience of death, of language, or of the relation to being *as such*). That said, once again, I have *sympathy* (and I insist on this word) for those who revolt: against the war declared on so many animals, against the genocidal torture inflicted on them often in a way that is fundamentally perverse, that is, by raising en masse, in a hyperindustrialized fashion, herds that are to be massively exterminated for alleged human needs; not to mention the hundreds of species that disappear each year from the face of the earth through the fault of humans who, when they don't kill enough, let them die—supposing that the law could ever be assured of any reliable difference between *killing* and *letting die!*

My sympathy therefore goes out, certainly, to those who themselves feel a sympathy, who feel themselves in compassionate and living sympathy with these living beings. But I will never renounce, and I don't believe it is necessary to renounce, *analyzing* (I mean this in all its senses, including the psychoanalytic sense) the two fundamental attitudes. I cannot provide such an analysis here in a brief improvisation. But I do not believe in absolute "vegetarianism," nor in the ethical purity of its intentions—nor even that it is rigorously tenable, without a compromise or without a symbolic substitution. I would go so far as to claim that, in a more or less refined, subtle, sublime form, a certain cannibalism remains unsurpassable. And of course, to respond to your question, I regard it as ridiculous and heinous to place certain animals above handicapped humans in some new hierarchy.

E.R.: What strikes me about such an excessive claim is that it would establish a sort of division between what would be human and what would be nonhuman. To bring great apes into the order of human rights, it would be necessary to exclude the mentally ill.

J.D.: Do they really say that?

E.R.: Yes, even if the word "exclusion" is never pronounced. But the reasoning that aims to extend human rights to include great apes presupposes this notion of separation, limit, division, which leads in the end to a rejection.[6] The entire rhetoric depends on a claim, both "cognitive" and "utilitarian," of an alleged passage from the human to the nonhuman that would be linked to the existence of neurological or cerebrally degenerative illnesses.

J.D.: It amounts to reintroducing, in effect, a properly racial and "geneticist" hierarchy. This is precisely the sort of thing that our vigilance must never overlook.

E.R.: But how do you reconcile a concern for being compassionate toward animals with the necessity for humans to eat meat?

J.D.: It is not enough to stop eating meat in order to become a non-carnivore. The unconscious carnivorous process has many other resources, and I do not believe in the existence of the non-carnivore in general. Even in the case of someone who believes he can limit himself to bread and wine. (I confront this question more effectively, I believe, when I speak of the necessary deconstruction of "carno-phallogocentrism.")[7] Even if we didn't already know this since long ago, at least for two thousand years, psychoanalysis would teach us that "vegetarians," like everyone else, can also incorporate, symbolically, something living, something of flesh and blood—of man and of God. Atheists, too, still like to "eat the other." At least if they love, for it is the very temptation of love. A thought here for Kleist's *Penthesilea*.[8] She was one of the major figures of a seminar I gave a few years ago on that very subject: "Eating the other."

E.R.: Just as, from a psychoanalytic point of view, the terror of ingesting animality can be the symptom of a hatred for the living taken to the point of murder. Hitler was a vegetarian.

J.D.: Some people have dared to base some of their arguments on this famous vegetarianism of Hitler—arguments against vegetarianism and against those who are friends to animals. Luc Ferry,[9] for example. This caricature of an indictment goes more or less like this: "Oh, you're forgetting that the Nazis, and Hitler in particular, were in a way zoophiles![10] So loving animals means hating or humiliating humans! Compassion for animals doesn't exclude Nazi cruelty; it's even its first symptom!" The argument strikes me as crudely fallacious. Who can take this parody of a syllogism seriously even for a second? And where would it lead us? To redouble our cruelty to animals in order to prove our irreproachable humanism? Elisabeth de Fontenay recalled that among the philosophers of the time who called for a reconsideration of our treatment of the "animal question," quite a number of them were Jews. In her rich and beautiful preface to

Plutarch's *Trois traités pour les animaux* (in Amyot's translation),[11] she is not content to recall, after Hannah Arendt, that Kant was Eichmann's favorite author. She gives a direct response to those who denounce any questioning of the humanist axiomatics on animals as an "irresponsible deconstructionist aberration."[12]

For my part, in the still unpublished part of my lecture at Cérisy ("L'animal que je suis") ["The Animal That I Am"], I closely analyze a text by Adorno[13] (without necessarily subscribing to every part of it) that claims to decipher in the Kantian notions of human autonomy, dignity (*Würde*), and self-destination or moral self-determination (*Selbstbestimmung*) not only a project of mastery and sovereignty (*Herrschaft*) over nature but a veritable hostility, a cruel hatred "directed against animals" (*Sie richtet sich gegen die Tiere*). The "insult" (*schimpfen*) against animals ("Animal!"), or against man as an animal, would thus be a distinctive trait of "authentic idealism."

Adorno goes very far in this direction. He dares to compare the virtual role played by animals in an idealist system to the role played by the Jews in a fascist system. According to this logic, now well known, and which often does seem to impose itself very convincingly, we would associate the figures of the animal and the Jew with those of woman and the child, or even of the handicapped in general.

E.R.: One of the major features of racism, sexism, and anti-Semitism has always been to assign an inferior status to someone in order to exclude him (or her) from the human, to stigmatize him by virtue of physical traits that would place him within the world of animality. Hence, indeed, the idea that Jews are more "feminine" than non-Jews, that women are more "animal" than men, and finally that blacks are even more "beastly" than all the others. The idea that the handicapped person is "inferior" to animals falls directly into these sorts of considerations.

It seems to me that there will never be an end to the destructive drive, because, as Freud stresses, it is inherent to man. Certainly, we must have prohibitions, without them no civilization is possible. But even as we fight against violence, it is necessary to acknowledge that there will never be an end to it. The prohibition against killing animals seems to me impossible to put into practice in our societies, and in any case it's not desirable. Generally speaking, it seems to me that the excess of prohibitions of every kind often generates forms of violence no one expected.

J.D.: No doubt it will always be necessary to kill animals. And probably humans too! Even after the universal abolition of the death penalty, if we ever get there!

E.R.: But it's not the same thing. Can one put someone who kills animals on the same level as someone who murders humans? And more generally, can one consider that a zoophile (in the sexological sense) ought to be punished by the law in the same way as a pedophile or a rapist? There is a law that punishes the mistreatment of animals, and French law even recognizes the notion of a "juridical personality" for domestic animals or animals held in captivity, which means that they could have rights and be defended in cases of abandonment.[14] But I'm not sure one can punish a human for sexual acts committed against animals. Is there mistreatment of animals in *all* cases of zoophilia? How can the animal express the violence done to it in such cases?

J.D.: Kant insists that we find a means of applying the *lex talionis* (a categorical imperative of the right to punish, according to him, and of any right to punish that is rational and intelligible *a priori*) to those guilty of "bestiality," no less than to those who rape or practice pederasty. We are studying these texts very closely in my seminar on the death penalty. This doesn't mean that one ought to consider the animal a victim. The animal, for its part, is not wronged, even if human dignity is not unscathed by sexual commerce with such an "animal." The latter is not a subject of law (nor therefore of power) who could protest against a "wrong" done to it and occupy the place of a plaintiff in a trial.

There is however a sentence from Jeremy Bentham that I like to cite, which is something like: "The question is not: can they speak? but can they suffer?"[15] Because, yes, we know this, and no one would dare to doubt it. Animals suffer; they manifest their suffering. We cannot imagine that an animal doesn't suffer when it is subjected to laboratory experimentation or even to circus training. When one sees an incalculable number of calves, raised on hormones and stuffed into a truck, on their way from the stable straight to the slaughterhouse, how can we not imagine that they suffer? We know what animal suffering is, we feel it ourselves. Moreover, with industrial slaughter, these animals are suffering in much larger numbers than before.

E.R.: You agree with Elisabeth de Fontenay. But how is it possible to reconcile this desire to reduce animal suffering with the necessity for industrial organization in raising and slaughtering animals, which makes it possible to prevent so many humans from starving?

J.D.: A large-scale disorganization-reorganization of the human earth is under way. One can expect the best and the worst from it, of course. But, without offering praise for some elementary vegetarianism, one can recall that the consumption of meat has never been a biological necessity. One eats meat not simply because one needs protein—and protein can be found elsewhere. In the consumption of meat, just as in the death penalty, in fact, there is a sacrificial structure, and therefore a "cultural" phenomenon linked to archaic structures that persist and that must be analyzed. No doubt we will never stop eating meat—or, as I suggested a moment ago, some equivalent, a substitute for some carnate thing. But perhaps qualitative conditions will be changed, together with quantity, the evaluation of quantity, as well as the general organization of the field of food and nourishment. On the scale of the centuries to come, I believe there will be veritable mutations in our experience of animality and in our social bond with other animals.

E.R.: Do you think there is an excess?

J.D.: You were saying that excessive and hyperbolic prohibition produces symptoms. Likewise, I believe that the spectacle man creates for himself in his treatment of animals will become intolerable. All the debates we are speaking of are telltale signs of this. It's no longer tolerable. If you were actually placed every day before the spectacle of this industrial slaughter, what would you do?

E.R.: I wouldn't eat meat anymore, or I would live somewhere else. But I prefer not to see it, even though I know that this intolerable thing exists. I don't think that the visibility of a situation allows one to know it better. Knowing is not the same as looking.

J.D.: But if, every day, there passed before your eyes, slowly, without giving you time to be distracted, a truck filled with calves leaving the stable on its way to the slaughterhouse, would you be unable to eat meat for a long time?

E.R.: I would move away. But really, sometimes I believe that, in order to understand a situation better and to have the necessary distance, it is best not to be an eyewitness to it. And then, let's not forget that gastronomy is an integral part of culture! Could the French culinary tradition do without meat?

J.D.: There are other resources available for our gastronomic refinement. Industrial meat is not the last word in gastronomy. Besides, more and more—you're aware of this debate—certain people prefer beasts raised in certain conditions said to be more "natural," on certain types of fields, etc. Therefore, it will indeed be necessary, in the name of the very gastronomy you're speaking of, to transform practices and "mentalities."

E.R.: José Bové's struggle against "bad American food," and against McDonald's in particular, is perhaps a first sign of this change.[16] Likewise, the problem of "mad cow disease"[17] will have to lead to some inevitable transformations.

J.D.: Don't ask me to subscribe unconditionally to what is being done or will be done in this domain, but the signs do count. They remind us that a mutation is under way.

E.R.: To return to the question of animality, I remain attached to the idea of a certain division between the animal and the human. Even if among the great apes there are symbolic practices, rituals, attitudes indicating the avoidance of incest—all of which is very fascinating—it seems to me that the discontinuity remains and that it has to do with language, conceptualization. All these differences, I think, ought to be recalled, even if, as Elisabeth de Fontenay argues, when it comes to animals, we can "assume that they have worlds that may intersect and overlap with the human world."[18] What do you think about this?

J.D.: I spoke not only of *one* division, but of several divisions in the major modes defining "animal" cultures. Far from erasing limits, I recalled them and insisted on differences and heterogeneities. There is a question of temporal and historical scale in the duration of these phenomena, and this must be taken into account. Like you, I believe that there is a radical discontinuity between what one calls animals—primates in particular—

and man. But this discontinuity cannot make us forget that between different animal species and types of social organizations of living beings there are other discontinuities.

In the current transformation of the law, even as the general axiomatics of human rights are retained, progress can be made in establishing relations between humans and animals that would move in the direction of maximum respect. In this regard, the evaluation can only be *economic* (strategy, dosage, measurement, the best compromise). I'm not saying that we must not in any way interfere with animal life; I'm saying that we must not invoke the violence among animals, in the jungle or elsewhere, as a pretext for giving ourselves over to the worst kinds of violence, that is, the purely instrumental, industrial, chemico-genetic treatment of living beings. Whether this treatment is carried out for the production of food or in the form of experimentation, it is necessary to set up rules so that one cannot do just whatever one pleases with nonhuman living beings.

It will therefore be necessary to reduce, little by little, the conditions of violence and cruelty toward animals, and, to that end, to modify, on a large historical scale, the conditions of breeding, slaughter, treatment en masse, and of what I hesitate (only in order not to abuse the inevitable associations) to call a *genocide*, in a situation where, in fact, the word would not be so inappropriate.

When I spoke on this question in the United States, at the law school of a Jewish university, I used this word *genocide* to designate the operation consisting, in certain cases, in gathering together hundreds of thousands of beasts every day, sending them to the slaughterhouse, and killing them en masse after having fattened them with hormones. This earned me an indignant reply. One person said that he did not accept my use of the word genocide: "We know what genocide is." Let's withdraw the word then. But you see very well what I'm talking about.

Over a more or less long term, it would be necessary to limit this violence as much as possible, if only because of the image of man that it reflects back to him. This is not the only or the best reason, but it will have to count as well. This transformation will no doubt take centuries, but, I repeat, I do not believe that we can continue to treat animals as we do today. All the current debates indicate a growing unease concerning this question within industrial European society.

For the moment, we ought to limit ourselves to working out the rules of law [*droit*]^{19} such as they exist. But it will eventually be necessary to reconsider the history of this law and to understand that although animals cannot be placed under concepts like citizen, consciousness linked with speech, subject, etc., they are not for all that without a "right." It's the very concept of right that will have to be "rethought." In general, in the European philosophical tradition, there is no conception of a (finite) subject of law [*droit*] who is not a subject of duty (Kant sees only two exceptions to this law [*loi*]: God, whose rights are without duty, and slaves, who have duties but no rights). It is once again a matter of the inherited concepts of the subject, the political subject, the citizen, the sovereign self-determination of the subject of law . . .

E.R.: And of consciousness.

J.D.: And of responsibility, speech, and freedom. All these concepts (which traditionally define what is "proper to man") are constitutive of juridical discourse.

E.R.: Therefore they cannot be applied to animals.

J.D.: One cannot expect "animals" to be able to enter into an expressly juridical contract in which they would have duties, in an exchange of recognized rights. It is within this philosophico-juridical space that the modern violence against animals is practiced, a violence that is at once contemporary with and indissociable from the discourse of human rights. I respect this discourse up to a certain point, but I want to reserve the right, precisely, to interrogate its history, its presuppositions, its evolution, its perfectibility. In this sense, it is preferable not to introduce this problematic concerning the relations between humans and animals into the *existing* juridical framework.

That is why, however much sympathy I may have for a declaration of animal rights that would protect them from human violence, I don't think this is a good solution. Rather, I believe in a slow and progressive approach. It is necessary to do what one can, today, to limit this violence, and it is in this sense that deconstruction is engaged: not to destroy the axiomatics of this (formal and juridical) solution, nor to discredit it, but to reconsider the history of law and of the concept of right.

E.R.: It seems to me that some progress is being made. I'm thinking in particular of the struggle against hunting and for the preservation of species.

J.D.: That struggle is a minor one. I have no taste for hunting, for that kind of hunting, nor for bullfighting, but I recognize that, from a quantitative point of view, it's nothing compared to the violence of the slaughterhouses and the poultry farms.

E.R.: You're against bullfighting?

J.D.: Yes, or very mistrustful in any case, in terms of the desires that play into it and the forms these desires take.

E.R.: And yet bullfighting inspired some very beautiful literary texts (those of Michel Leiris in particular). The bullfighter risks his life in the arena. The principle of bullfighting involves a struggle to the death, a contest, equal between man and animal, a sort of remainder from the age of chivalry. It's the opposite of hunting or slaughtering animals. I don't think one ought to forbid all violent and high-risk practices.

J.D.: I didn't say that I was against Leiris's texts, but that I am against the cult or the culture of bullfighting and other similar things. Besides, I can like or admire particular texts by Leiris without ceasing to ask questions about the desire or the experience of Leiris himself, etc. Following that logic, under the pretext that forbidding violence can lead, through a perverse effect, to the emergence of other more serious violence, one risks giving free rein to all kinds of violence and then folding one's arms. I could give you many very troubling examples. Should we refrain from condemning or denouncing racist, anti-Semitic, xenophobic, or sexist violence under the pretext that if they are "repressed" here or there, they risk a greater resurgence elsewhere? I'm not saying that your argument is without value, but one cannot use it in a systematic way without the risk of being paralyzed regarding any sort of prohibition.

E.R.: I am always worried that we are moving toward the construction of a sanitized society, without passions, without conflicts, without insults or verbal violence, without any risk of death, without cruelty. When one claims to be eradicating something on one side, there is the risk of its resurgence where it isn't expected.

J.D.: I think I can understand and share your worry. It leaves intact the responsibility that must be taken concerning the calculation of risks.

What sort of violence can or ought one tolerate, or even cultivate, in order to avoid what you call a "sanitized society," that is, if I understand correctly, a dead or sterilized society?

E.R.: It occurs to me for example that the right to verbal insult is fundamental, and that a difference must be maintained between what one can say, even publicly, and what one can write. On the other hand, although I think that laws against defamation, racism, anti-Semitism, violation of privacy, etc., are absolutely necessary—they exist in any case, and in France I find them to be good—it is always necessary to try to allow, to the greatest possible degree, the expression of insults and verbal violence. Think of blasphemy, for example, or pornography. It is necessary both to make sure that restrictive laws are respected and to guarantee the widest possible freedom of expression.[20]

J.D.: I agree. But it is necessary to limit as much as possible the censorship effect produced by legal prohibitions, and to prefer analysis, discussion, and counteroffensive critique. Public space ought to remain as open as possible to freedom of expression. I, too, dislike the image of an "organic," sanitized, antiseptic, sterilized society. That is why I have begun to say that, in any case, there is and will be cruelty, among living beings, among men.

E.R.: And you think that the more limits there are, the better?

J.D.: In this area as in others, the only response is *economic*: up to a certain point, there is always a measure, a better measure to take. I don't want to forbid everything, but I also don't want to forbid nothing. I certainly cannot eradicate or extirpate the roots of violence against animals, abuse and insults, racism, anti-Semitism, etc., but, under the pretext that I cannot eradicate them, I don't want to allow them to develop unchecked. Therefore, according to the historical situation, it is necessary to invent the least bad solution. The difficulty of ethical responsibility is that the response cannot be formulated as a "yes or no"; that would be too simple. It is necessary to give a singular response, within a given context, and to take the risk of a decision by enduring the undecidable. In every case, there are two contradictory imperatives.

The Spirit of the Revolution

E.R.: *Specters of Marx* is a book to which I am all the more sensitive in that you touch on an invariant in which I have a great interest: the melancholy of the Revolution. In 1989, I published a book, *Théroigne de Méricourt: A Melancholic Woman During the French Revolution,*[1] in which, referring to a woman who was a pioneer of feminism in 1789 and who ended her days locked up in the Salpêtrière, I tried to show how a subjective collapse, a plunge into madness, was related to a historical situation: the transition from the Revolution to the Terror. At the time, of course, I was thinking of Louis Althusser, to whom I was very close, and of the destiny of an entire generation of communists faced with the disaster of real socialism; seeing their ideal collapse, they were forced to mourn a certain political engagement,[2] or else they risked succumbing to melancholy. I came back to this question in *Why Psychoanalysis?*, where I spoke of a "depressive society."

In *Specters of Marx*, dedicated to Chris Hani, a hero in the struggle against apartheid who was assassinated as a communist,[3] you associate three great "scenes" of Western culture: Hamlet confronting the ghost of his father, who has returned so *inopportunely* [*à contretemps*] to demand vengeance and to entrust his son with the mission of setting right the "time out of joint"; the publication of the *Manifesto of the Communist Party*, whose famous sentence you comment on: "A specter is haunting Europe: the specter of Communism";[4] finally, the scene of our times, dominated by the specter of a defeated communism that has come to haunt the future of

a unified world under globalization and the triumph of the market economy, a world in a state of "catastrophe,"[5] a world caught up in a "manic
phase," incapable of mourning over what it claims to have put to death.

Much like the murdered king who disrupts Hamlet's life by walking
along the ramparts of Elsinore, Marx has become a specter for our depressive Western society, which never ceases to proclaim the death of the Revolution, without being able—very fortunately in my opinion—to eradicate the *spirit* of the Revolution. This spirit slumbers in each one of us, and
the more one proclaims its death, the more it returns to torment its adversaries (the high priests of free-market capitalism), obsessed by the loss of
their enemy. No matter how much we stage the death of communism or
rejoice over the definitive death of Marx, the corpse is still moving, and its
specter is disrupting the world. You describe the state of the world in terms
of a "geopolitical melancholy," and you propose to carry out a "psychoanalysis of the political field" in order to analyze the "wounds" and sufferings of the new economic order.

You choose Hamlet and not Oedipus, that is, the guilty rather than
the tragic conscience; you use psychoanalysis as an instrument for the political analysis of a world in ruins; and finally, you pay homage, without
saying so explicitly, to the last great Marxist philosopher, Louis Althusser,
who succumbed to melancholy.

J.D.: Once again, I don't know which angle to choose among all
those that you are proposing to me. I will take one on the fly; I'll take off
with your word *melancholy*. You were speaking of Althusser. *Specters of
Marx* is perhaps also, in fact, a book on melancholy *in politics*, on the politics of melancholy: politics and the work of mourning, when what one
thus calls "the work of mourning" succeeds or does not succeed, when it
succeeds poorly or appears impossible. For a long time now I myself have
been "working" at *mourning*—if I can put it this way—or have been letting myself be worked by the question of mourning, by the aporias of the
"work of mourning," on the resources and the limits of psychoanalytic discourse on this subject, and on a certain coextensivity between work in general and the work of mourning. The work of mourning is not one work
among others. All work involves this transformation, this appropriating
idealization, this internalization that characterizes "mourning."

I tried to draw a few consequences from this within the geopolitical
situation that followed the upheaval referred to as the "collapse" of the so-

viet model of communism and the so-called "death of Marx." But as for the "melancholy" in question, this interminable and irreducible "half-failure," this structurally defeatist behavior that marks the geopolitical unconscious of the age, I do not believe that it simply registers the decease of a certain communist model. It mourns—sometimes without tears, and without knowing it, but often in tears and blood—over the corpse of the political itself. It mourns over the very concept of the political in its essential traits, and even in the specific traits of its modernity (nation-state, sovereignty, party form, the most accredited parliamentary topology).

On the other hand—and I follow you here, too—without being able for one instant to explain the one by the other or to reduce the one to the other, this melancholy of the political and what you call Althusser's "melancholy" remain two inextricably intertwined histories. As you recalled, we were very close, Althusser and I, for almost forty years. We were bound in a certain way that for me, in this case as in that of other important and very dear friendships, is still enigmatic. Bonds of friendship that were faithful, certainly, and most often affectionate, even tender, but at times (on his side, I must say in all truthfulness) not free of aggression; the depth of these bonds went beyond any *political* concerns or positions, at least in terms of positions that were decipherable within the current code of the political; for I believe that, in what was most secret in it—and most easily misunderstood from the point of view of current or (as one says) "dominant" political language—our alliance was *also* political. Some of the texts published after his death seem to me to attest to this. At the time, I did not know most of these texts. They say all this much better than I can while improvising here. And we were also colleagues.[6] For some twenty years we inhabited, also in a very uncanny way—like patient and impatient passersby, like occasionally unwanted guests, like a spectral bad conscience—the same strange "rue d'Ulm," with its students and common spaces. (Who will ever write, without giving in to any sort of socio-academicism, the history of this "house" and its filiations? This would be an almost impossible but indispensable task for beginning to understand the various "logics" of French intellectual life in this century.) Not to mention what continued to bring us together, Althusser and me, during the last ten terrible years of his life. More than one book would be necessary for that . . . But to return to your suggestion, it is true that in *Specters of Marx* I was able to make a gesture from which I had previously thought I should refrain. For many years, for reasons that become more legible in this book (even though they already were in other ways), I could neither subscribe to the Althusserian gesture (a certain return to Marx) nor denounce or critique it from any position that would have been seen as anticommunist, anti-Marxist, or even as that of the communist party.

So for a long time I was virtually reduced to silence, a silence that was also assumed, almost chosen, but also somewhat painful with regard to what was happening right in front of me. I was no doubt the contemporary, and the very proximate witness, of this adventure—a witness whom it would be wrong to call "passive"—but I would not say that *Specters of Marx* was determined by the end of this series of events, and even less by the end of Louis Althusser. I try to account for the connections between these stories, these two "ends of stories" (if not these "ends-of-history"), in some long notes in *Specters of Marx* on deconstruction, on Marxism and psychoanalysis, on the motifs of the "end" ("end of philosophy," "end of history," etc.) that dominated an entire configuration during the 1950's and 60's, on a certain way of attempting a psychoanalytic approach to the work of mourning in politics.

Why the figure of Hamlet? First, what I privileged in *Hamlet* was the passage concerning his relation to the ghost and to time: *The time is out of joint.*

E.R.: In French: *Le temps est hors de ses gonds;* "time is off its hinges."[7]

J.D.: As if it were a matter of beginning—if we can put it this way—with the impossibility of thinking or rather of "conceiving" of the contemporary, of synchrony: (the) time is disjointed. There is at the same time more than one time in the time of the world ("time" here is also history, the world, society, the age, the current *times*, etc.). This motif of disjunction governs many things in this book, the idea of justice in particular. *Specters of Marx* is perhaps first of all a book on justice, on a justice that is not to be confused with harmony, proportion, order. In "Force of Law,"[8] I had insisted on the irreducibility of justice to law. There I propose a deconstruction of the Heideggerian concept of justice. This proposition occurs everywhere, even if it is not very visible in the foreground: a calling into question, then, of Heidegger's interpretation of *dikê*, of justice as harmony. Heidegger's gesture interests me insofar as it attempts (justly so, we might say) to think the just beyond or on this side of juridicism or Roman law. But what troubles me is that his interpretation determines or halts this thought of the just or of justice (*Dikê*) as the accord, the joining or the re-joining (*der fugend-fügende Fug*) of an injustice (*Adikia*) that for its part would be unjoined, disjointed, out of joint (*aus den Fugen, Un-Fug*). Such a rejoining, according to Heidegger, who insists precisely [*justement*] on this point, amounts to thinking justice on the basis of Being as presence (*als Anwesen*), that is, as always in Heidegger, on the basis of the *logos* or the *legein*, a force of gathering (*Versammlung*) and accord. It seems to me on the contrary that at the heart of justice, of the *experience of the just*, an in-finite disjunction demands its right, and the respect of an irreducible dis-sociation: no justice without interruption, without divorce, without a dis-located relation to the infinite alterity of the other, without a harsh experience of what remains forever *out of joint.*[9]

My interest in the figure of Hamlet, and in his "spectral" experience, also had to do with the privilege granted to the father/son relation, the masculine *installation* of sexual difference. The problematic of sexual dif-ference, the analysis of this powerful privilege, of this privilege of power it-self, of this privilege of the law as authority of the father—all this commu-nicates with the family scenes evoked throughout the book: the war of the brothers or the sons in relation to the father's legacy (Marx/Stirner, "the bad brother" or the "bad son" of Hegel for example),[10] the question of fetishism and of the "sex of the fetish."[11]

Hamlet is also the machine of repression in politics. Spectrality gov-erns not only the problematic of mourning but also that of technics, the media, virtual reality; it therefore also governs the problematic of any ac-count, in psychoanalytic and political reflection, of a general logic of spec-trality.

We cannot claim to do justice to a political reality without taking this virtual spectrality into account. I analyze all the *phantoms*, and in particu-lar the way in which Marx himself tried to chase (away) the phantom (to pursue it and to distance it *at the same time*), when he reminds European society how much it dreads the specter of communism. In his debate with Max Stirner,[12] he reproduces the panic fear of spectrality, and his critique of ideology is also a critique of the revenant.

I tried to be faithful not only to a complex concept of heritage but also to one of the "spirits of Marx," a spirit inspired by an idea of justice ir-reducible to all the failures of communism. This book was written shortly after the fall of the Berlin wall, but I constantly refused to posit a symme-try between Nazi totalitarianism and Soviet totalitarianism. And I did this even though I believe that the gulag, the figure of Soviet violence, is at least equal to the Nazi barbarity.

Recently, in the United States, I saw a sort of documentary about a group of Russians who had emigrated to France during the Revolution. Summoned by the Soviet regime (in the 1980's, I believe) under a false pretext, they were invited to move back to their country, where some fine promises had been made to them; and in any case, they wanted to go back. Then they were caught in a whole series of horrible traps. Victims of the worst police perversions, they all ended up in the gulag.

But if I believe it is necessary not to give in to this symmetry, it is not, therefore, in order to claim that the gulag is less "grave" than the Shoah. The comparison ceases to be accurate when we take into account an undeniable and massively obvious fact: the communist idea, the ideal of justice that guided and inspired so many communist men and women, all strangers to everything resembling a "gulag," this idea can never be made to correspond—as a parallel, an analogy, or an equivalent, or even as a comparable opposite—to the slightest Nazi "ideal" of "justice." Whether one does or does not respect, ethically or politically, what I am calling here somewhat hastily an "ideal of justice," one *must absolutely* recognize what, in essence, separates this "communist" "ideal" from what Nazism will have set into motion. Once one has assumed this absolute duty, a duty of thought that is itself "justice," then one can complicate matters and pose all the necessary questions on the meaning and the history of this "idea," of this "ideal," on history as the history of the idea, on the history of history and of communism, and other fundamental questions of this kind. That would be another phase and another side of the same absolute duty.

E.R.: I agree with you on all these points, and we must be vigilant regarding all the historians who claim to establish an equivalence between the two ideas by in fact reducing communism to Stalinism. At the outset, communism does not have the same project as Nazism, which aims from the very beginning at genocidal destruction.

J.D.: On the "communist" side, the totalitarian evil took the form, terrifying indeed, of a *corruption* of the project—or of the "ideal." But the corruption of a plan is not the plan, even in the hypothesis according to which the plan allowed itself to be perverted in its original form. Nazi totalitarianism, on the contrary, was the plan itself *as* perversion, perversion accomplished. Whatever questions I must continue to ask myself on this subject, my respect for the communist "idea" is therefore intact (I indicate this respect in *Specters of Marx* with the necessity of an untiring deconstructive critique of capitalistic logic). The questions that remain, even the most radical and disturbing, the most necessary, are of another order from those of the Nazi evil, the "Nazi" enigma. The asymmetry is not, alas, between the facts and the unleashings of cruelty; it is elsewhere, in the interpretation of an *elsewhere to come* (call this what you like, for the moment— ideology, ideal, idea, etc.).

Even during the period when I was extremely reserved regarding the Communist Party, and regarding some who were trying to break with it, I always respected, I would even say I shared, this ideal, in my way (troubled and reserved)—and this is what reduced me to silence.

But if we want to save the Revolution, it is necessary to transform the very idea of revolution. What is outdated, old, worn out, impracticable, for many reasons, is a certain theater of revolution, a certain process of seizing power with which the revolutions of 1789, 1848, and 1917 are generally associated. I believe in the Revolution, that is, in an interruption, a radical caesura in the ordinary course of History. In any case, there is no ethical responsibility, no decision worthy of the name, that is not, in its essence, revolutionary, that is not in a relation of rupture with a system of dominant norms, or even with the very idea of norm, and therefore of a knowledge of the norm that would dictate or program the decision. All responsibility is revolutionary, since it seeks to do the impossible, to interrupt the order of things on the basis of nonprogrammable events. A revolution cannot be programmed.[13] In a certain way, as the only event worthy of the name, it exceeds every possible horizon, every *horizon of the possible*—and therefore of potency and power.

E.R.: The fate of the revolutionaries of 1793 is fascinating. Everything happens in effect as if, gradually, in this nonprogrammable time, they were becoming aware, without being able to stop the machine, that the Terror would end up getting them in their turn. These men were heroes who, from the moment they committed regicide, knew that they were condemned to the same fate as the sovereign whose head they had cut off. They knew they were going to die this violent death that they had set into operation with the guillotine, in order to give birth to a new society that they imagined would be more just and less violent. But at the same time they were determined by a destiny that escaped them and of which they knew nothing.

The most representative image of this epic can be found in the juxtaposition of the Convention, as it votes on and passes the most modern laws—the very foundations of the Republic—and the guillotine, functioning simultaneously and at full capacity two steps away from the Assembly. There is indeed a logic in this history, but a noncalculable logic, the logic of a revolutionary project, a trace of which one finds for example in the famous statement of Bertrand Barrère, which I often quote in relation to the creation of the asylum (23 Messidor Year II): "Over the doors of the asylums, then, place inscriptions announcing their imminent disappearance, for if the Revolution is over and we still have unfortunates among us, then all our revolutionary work will have been in vain." It is thus a question of thinking the end of institutional confinement at the very moment when the asylum is being invented, but invented only as the anticipated project of its own end. The entire spirit of the Revolution is contained in these words. In this sense, contrary to what François Furet says, the Terror is not already contained in 1789, and 1793 is not, in anticipation, a sort of prefiguration of the October Revolution of 1917. There are, moreover, some very beautiful pages on this subject in Michelet.[14]

J.D.: Concerning the Terror, it would be necessary here to reread (otherwise) Maurice Blanchot's text in *The Work of Fire*, "Literature and the Right to Death."[15] This text is at one and the same time very forceful and extremely equivocal. It was written in 1947–48—a date heavily charged with significance—a century after Victor Hugo's outcry against the death penalty, and the very year when a new Universal Declaration of Human Rights proclaimed the right to life (without explicitly condemning the death penalty, in order not to encroach upon the sovereignty of states). In my seminar on the death penalty, I propose a double reading of this text, as detailed and demanding as possible. I cannot reconstitute it here in all its complexity; that would take hours. But in a word: within a logic whose principle belongs to a tradition that is both Kantian and Hegelian, Blanchot associates the very idea of right with the necessity or possibility of the death penalty, and even (this time in a non-Kantian way) of the Terror.[16] Without reducing the extreme singularity of this text, it is also necessary to recognize in it the intersecting legacies of Sade and Mallarmé, there where the question of literature is deployed in this revolutionary space. The essence of literature, its origin or its possibility, would also be this right to death; hence the properly revolutionary movement of literature, and hence the analogy between the literary act, "the Last Act," and revolutionary action.[17] Let us not forget that all this is accompanied by immense praise for Sade, "the writer par excellence," a man who combines "all the . . . contradictions," the one who felt more "acutely [*vivement*]" than any other that "sovereignty is in death," and the one whose work "revels in itself as absolute sovereignty." Blanchot here speaks of "cruelty," "madness," and "blood."[18] But let us not forget, either—and this remains to be thought—that Sade was nonetheless opposed to the death penalty. It was Lacan who recalled this, quite rightly, and saw in it, divined in it, I would say, in an ellipse, the refusal of a certain Christianity.[19]

E.R.: Robespierre, too, was hostile to the death penalty.[20]

J.D.: And Saint-Just. Blanchot is not interested in this mutation within the Revolution. Before the Revolution, and still at the beginning of the Constituent Assembly, Robespierre spoke out against the death penalty; then he voted for the death of the king. The question of the Terror therefore remains more open than ever. But at the beginning, all this was unforeseeable for the actors. Unlike Robespierre, Kant, for his part, criticized Beccaria[21] and remained an unconditional supporter of the death penalty—but precisely with an absolute exception in relation to the sovereign. We see a veritable chasm thus opening between these two figures, Kant and Robespierre, an almost symmetrical inversion of trajectories and logics (I am studying this in my seminar).

After he had written publicly, at the beginning of the Constituent Assembly, that he was hostile to the death penalty in general, Robespierre was converted to the death penalty—if we can put it that way—at the moment of condemning the monarch and having him "formally" executed (which is inadmissible to Kant, and more unjustifiable than an assassination of the sovereign). What happened after that was not only the Terror and the tumbrels but the postponement of abolition, until almost two centuries later (!), by the Convention in 1795 (October 26; 4 Brumaire Year IV): "Beginning on the day of the general peace proclamation, the death penalty will be abolished in the French Republic."

We find here again the great question of cruelty. At the beginning of the Constituent Assembly, it was possible to believe that abolitionism would triumph. It was supported by a majority in the Constitution Committee and the Committee on Criminal Legislation. The members of the Constituent Assemblies were quite familiar with the question; many of them were readers of Beccaria, including Robespierre, who was an eloquent abolitionist. He declares in effect that the death penalty is essentially unjust, that it is not the most repressive or the most effective penalty, and that it multiplies crimes far more than it prevents them.

This is a logic and a lesson that were learned from Beccaria. The reference to the *cruelty* of the death penalty is at times literal. After evoking judicial errors, "a sorry testimony to the barbarous temerity of your penal laws," Robespierre the abolitionist adds: "Beware of confusing the effectiveness of your penalties with an excess of severity. . . . Everything assists laws that are moderate; everything conspires against laws that are cruel." And the death penalty, for him, is the cruelest penalty. The "excess of severity" is "cruel." Cruelty comes from an excess of severity. That's what cruelty is: excessive severity.

But after a long discussion, the minutes of the Constituent Assembly record the upholding of the death penalty—a decision made "almost unanimously": "The principal question having been put to the vote, the Assembly decides almost unanimously that the death penalty will not be abrogated."

After that, the cases in which the death penalty can be applied are limited—if it is a limit—to thirty-two in the Code of 1791, all centered around two major types of crime: attacks on the nation, and attacks on persons and on the goods of private citizens; the progress consisted in condemning torture and in limiting the death penalty to the simple privation of life (without cruel suffering! and this is the whole discourse on the guillotine, that gentle and egalitarian means of punishment, more democratic than torture): "Every condemned person will have his head cut off."

Let us not forget that after the "formal" execution of the king, the very next day Condorcet dared to propose again the abolition of the death penalty, though it would be a partial and not a political abolition, to be sure. He did this immediately after the execution of the king, as if—a double hypothesis—*either* the trauma, not to say the unconscious remorse, was still vivid and intense enough for Condorcet to hope to be heard (one thinks of the sons and brothers of Freud's primitive horde after the murder of the father), *or*—but the two hypotheses are not contradictory—the death of the sovereign having accomplished the essential in an act of parri-

cide, it was possible henceforth to dispense with the death penalty. A profound logic is at work here. It gives much to be thought, for it is this Revolution, and the Terror soon to follow, that provide the occasion of the first
Declarations of the Rights of Man. And it is this revolution that Kant will
celebrate precisely in the name of right and the ideas of the rights of man
that "fill" the soul.

The day after the execution of the king, Condorcet prudently says:
"Abolish the death penalty for all private offenses, and allow us to examine
whether it is necessary to keep it for offenses against the state." A proposition that was refused, as were other, analogous ones each year—in 1793, in
1794, in 1795. The Revolutionary Tribunal of Paris and the special tribunals
outside Paris executed more than seventeen thousand people who had been
given a death sentence. There were also executions without a "formal" order, as Kant would say, without a judgment, and it is said that thirty-five
thousand to forty thousand people were executed or assassinated without a
judgment.

Revolution in the Revolution, then, and the example of Victor Hugo
attests to the necessity of distinguishing between more than one meaning
and more than one time of what is called the French Revolution.[22] When
he spoke out against the death penalty, so often and with such eloquence,
he always did so in the name of the "Thou shalt not kill," or of the "inviolability of human life," but also in the name of the *Evangiles contre l'Eglise*
[Evangels against the Church], and in the name of the Revolution, the
spirit of the Revolution, and against the Terror.[23] Not only does he propose
to raise a statue to Beccaria ("To raise a statue to Beccaria is to abolish the
scaffold"),[24] but he even divides the time of the Revolution. The Revolution is one, he says, but is not one. It is wrong to treat it as an indivisible
block. It's the Convention that, while inaugurating the Terror, will have installed the guillotine, but it is this same Convention that announced: "Beginning on the day of the general peace proclamation, the death penalty
will be abolished in the French Republic." An extraordinary formula. What
kind of time is involved here? In a certain way one could say, as I suggested
a moment ago, that all this took centuries.

Currently, a certain peace has been established in postrevolutionary
Europe, this Europe that the revolutionaries dreamed of. But this only
confirms that the death penalty was abolished not so much for reasons of
pure principle (which for Kant, we should recall, are the only reasons the
debate should be concerned with, and in this he is alone against all those

who, whether for or against the death penalty, invoke only reasons of utility or inutility, the security of dissuasive exemplarity, within a logic of means and ends, etc.), but because now it is "neither useful nor necessary."

These are the terms and the logic of Beccaria, who opposed the death penalty in a way that is in the end rather equivocal, even utilitarian. He also considered it insufficiently cruel, less cruel in any case and therefore less dissuasive than the penalty of forced labor for life. The equivocal nature of this argument has not disappeared; it has proliferated, and an abolitionist discourse based on pure principle has yet to be elaborated (this is what I am attempting to prepare in my seminar, after taking note of the highly significant fact that no philosophical discourse *as such*, and in its philosophical systematicity, has ever condemned the death penalty).

A "deconstruction" of what is most hegemonic in philosophy should therefore include a deconstruction of the death penalty, and of everything with which it is in solidarity—beginning with a certain concept of sovereignty—of its entire scaffolding (and, likewise, of the discourse on what is called "the animal"). For in a way, it was only after a certain state of security and pacification that Europe abolished the death penalty, supposedly for reasons of principle. Currently, no country can enter the European Community without suspending the death penalty. We will have to speak of the United States again, I suppose.[25] These are the durations and time spans (at once very long and very short, according to the scale one chooses—but is there a scale for death?) that must be studied in all their interrelations.

E.R.: Freud had no sympathy for the French Revolution, although he did admire Cromwell, and in *Totem and Taboo* he states that at the origin of every society there is an act of murder, a real and necessary act of murdering the father, followed by a sanction that allows for the symbolic revalorization of the place of the father. But he was also an abolitionist, and he gave Theodor Reik the task of presenting his views on this question. I noticed that he took the risk of condemning the death penalty, not as a citizen but in the name of psychoanalysis, by engaging it *as such*, which the philosophers have not done, according to you. Now, in the trial of Louis XVI, "justice was suspended." It is not a matter of judging the king, says Robespierre, but of executing him.[26] It seems to me that the regicide is necessary so that abolition can come afterward.

J.D.: Two competing discourses authorized themselves to justify this regicide. One consists in considering the king an enemy of the nation: this foreigner is therefore to be eliminated, he is "decapitated," just as in a war one kills the soldier of another belligerent country. The Revolution is a war waged to protect its nation-state. According to the other discourse, since the Revolution was under way or had already taken place, Louis Capet had to be judged like any other French citizen. As a traitor to his country, this citizen deserved death. Each of these arguments follows a very different logic. But this equivocation is everywhere; it is found, for example, on the porous border that, in the obscure concept of war, will always separate civil war, national war, and that "partisan war" of which Schmitt speaks. The modernity of this "partisan war" begins very early on. This equivocation poisons all instances of the abolition of the death penalty, which are limited, of course, to national penal law and never prohibit legally killing "in war." In the end it has to do with a concept like that of the "public enemy," which is at the center of *The Social Contract*, when Rousseau justifies, not without hesitation or remorse, the principle of the death penalty.

I do not know if it *was necessary* to execute or not to execute the king. Kant thought that nothing was worse or more ruinous for the foundations of sovereignty than the "formal" execution of the monarch. *As such*, by definition, the sovereign cannot be submitted to judgment without destroying the principle and the foundation of the state. Kant gives the example of Charles I and Louis XVI, and goes so far as to judge assassination without trial or the abdication of the king less unjustifiable. That is what is changing in this regard today: the new possibility of judging a head of state, a former head of state, or of summoning him before an international tribunal; to a certain extent, which is in any case very complicated, this calls back into question the very principle of sovereignty.

But what is certain (and I suppose this is what you are emphasizing in "the idea of the necessary regicide") is that, however unjustifiable this regicide may seem according this logic, however inadmissible the Terror may appear, these acts were *in fact* (I underscore the enigma of this *fact*) the price to pay for a large number of major gains and for some undeniable "progress": for example, the Declarations of the Rights of Man, in their historical development, with all that depends on them (the concepts of right to life, of crimes against humanity, genocide, the idea or the outline of an International Criminal Court, etc.) or the set of revolutionary principles that have been integrated into certain universal juridico-political discourses of modernity.

Yes, I am *for* the unconditional abolition of the death penalty, both for *reasons of principle* (I insist on this point: on principle, and not for reasons of utility or inutility or because of a dubious exemplarity; I spoke of this a moment ago) and for *reasons of the heart* (a notion which, like that of compassion, I try to remove from a simple pathetic sentimentality, and which I would like to ally with the "reasons of principle." I cannot explain myself here without detours that would be too lengthy).

But, *in fact*—I return to this point—did the king die? *In fact?* Did this putting to death take place? To use the Kantian distinction, was it an assassination? or else a judgment and a "formal" execution? In fact, if the execution of a sovereign as such, and a "formal" one, is an internal contradiction and is not only unjustifiable but impossible, the question remains open. A king's body was certainly put to death. One of the king's two bodies, that of Louis Capet, was put to death. But did the Restoration ever come to an end? Did the monarchic structure and the figure of the sovereign ever disappear in the history of the French Republics?

With his right to pardon and with the representation of national sovereignty that he incarnates, an elected president of the Republic is a kind of king. Without even invoking all the imagery of the Elysée Palace and of the current monarchy, it is not certain that the king died. A certain king's body[27] must have been put to death, but that does not mean that the specter of monarchy—of the sovereign father as a condition of the nation-state's unity—met its end at that moment. What must be reconsidered here is the theory of the king's two bodies and the democratic tradition of the theologico-political idea of sovereignty.

E.R.: The question, as I stressed when I brought up the idea of the necessary regicide, is whether the execution of the king was necessary so that the abolition of the death penalty could then take place.[28]

J.D.: Not until two centuries later, and under a pressure that was partly international. We are entering into a complicated debate on the death penalty. Its legal abolition (which for about ten years now has extended to the majority of states in the world, except the United States, China, and a good number of Arab-Muslim countries) does not signify the end of the decreed, organized, and in general institutionalized act of killing, putting to death. Without speaking of the unstable limit between "making-die" and "letting-die." This is why, in the abolitionist discourse— to which I subscribe in a certain way—there are inconsistencies that must be deconstructed. It is within a sovereign state—now France or Europe, the Europe of the European Community—that a certain type of legal killing has been abolished, but killing, putting to death, will continue in certain situations: in war, for example. The notion of war, I insist, is linked to a very obscure concept that is more and more dogmatic. No abolitionist state has ever decreed that the extermination of enemy soldiers was an illegal, illegitimate act punishable by law, no more than killing out of "self-defense."

E.R.: Yet it seems impossible to me that the death penalty could be reinstated in Europe.

J.D.: Oh, of course it could! In a situation of civil war or *quasi*-war. Where does civil war begin? Where does it end? If it appears that there are "public enemies" within, why not kill them, *à la guerre comme à la guerre?*[29] Today, the police kill suspects when they consider themselves to be in a situation requiring self-defense. And they are acquitted, if it is believed that they have proved this to be the case. The question is therefore indeed that of the limitation of state sovereignty and of the concept of war. What is a civil war? What is a public enemy?

E.R.: You have addressed this question in reference to Carl Schmitt.[30]

J.D.: A moment ago you spoke of regicide as the necessity of an exception, in sum. Well, yes, one can refer provisionally to Carl Schmitt (whatever one may think of him, his arguments are always useful for problematizing the "political" or the "juridical"; I examined this question in *Politics of Friendship*). He says in effect that a sovereign is defined by his capacity to decide the exception. Sovereign is he who effectively decides the exception. The revolutionaries decided that at that moment that it was necessary to suspend justice and—in order to establish the law [*droit*] and to give the Revolution its rights—to suspend the rule of law [*l'Etat de droit*]. Schmitt also gives this definition of sovereignty: to have the right to suspend the law, or the rule of law, the constitutional state. Without this category of exception, we cannot understand the concept of sovereignty. Today, the great question is indeed, everywhere, that of sovereignty. Omnipresent in our discourses and in our axioms, under its own name or another, literally or figuratively, this concept has a theological origin: the true sovereign is God. The concept of this authority or of this power was transferred to the monarch, said to have a "divine right." Sovereignty was then delegated to the people, in the form of democracy, or to the nation, with the same theological attributes as those attributed to the king and to God. Today, wherever the word "sovereignty" is spoken, this heritage remains undeniable, whatever internal differentiation one may recognize in it.

How do we deal with this? Here we return to the question of heritage with which we began. It is necessary to deconstruct the concept of sovereignty, never to forget its theological filiation and to be ready to call this filiation into question wherever we discern its effects. This supposes an inflexible critique of the logic of the state and of the nation-state. And yet—hence the enormous responsibility of the citizen and of the heir in general, in certain situations—the state, in its actual form, can resist certain forces that I consider the most threatening. What I here call "responsibility" is what dictates the decision to be sometimes *for* the sovereign state and sometimes *against* it, for its deconstruction ("theoretical and practical," as one used to say) according to the singularity of the contexts and the stakes. There is no relativism in this, no renunciation of the injunction to "think" and to deconstruct the heritage. This aporia is in truth the very condition of decision and responsibility—if there is any.

I am thinking for example of the incoherent but organized coalition of international capitalist forces that, in the name of neoliberalism or the market,[31] are taking hold of the world in conditions such as the "state" form; this is what can still resist the most. For the moment. But it is necessary to reinvent the conditions of resistance. Once again, I would say that according to the situations, I am an antisovereignist *or* a sovereignist—and I vindicate the right to be antisovereignist at certain times and a sovereignist at others. No one can make me respond to this question as though it were a matter of pressing a button on some old-fashioned machine. There are cases in which I would support a logic of the state, but I ask to examine each situation before making any statement. It is also necessary to recognize that by requiring someone to be not unconditionally sovereignist but rather sovereignist only under certain conditions, one is already calling into question the principle of sovereignty. Deconstruction begins there. It demands a difficult dissociation, almost impossible but indispensable, between *unconditionality* (justice without power) and *sovereignty* (right, power, or potency). Deconstruction is on the side of unconditionality, even when it seems impossible, and not sovereignty, even when it seems possible.

E.R.: The invention of the term *sovereignism* is recent. It designates those who are opposed to the delegitimation of the nation-state for the benefit of a European community onto which all the attributes of sovereignty would gradually devolve. Behind this apparent "desovereignization" (if I can put it this way), a process is at work in which sovereignty is transferred: one passes from theocracy to monarchy, then to the republic. One therefore always ends up delegating sovereignty to another system, which embodies it in turn.[32]

J.D.: We have become conscious of the fact that the question of sovereignty is decisive, and not only from the political point of view or from the point of view of international law and the relations between states. This is also true for the sovereignty of the subject. During the years we spoke of earlier, I was interested in the concept of sovereignty as it was set to work by Georges Bataille, where, as opposed to Hegelian mastery, it implied the experience of loss in ecstasy, laughter, or error.[33] Rereading these texts by Bataille today in another way, I wonder whether, despite the difference he indicates between mastery and sovereignty, this latter word does not still maintain an extremely equivocal theologico-political tradition, particularly in the sacrificial logic that Bataille takes up in this context. Later I would use this lexicon in a much more prudent fashion.

E.R.: Let us consider the evolution of the concept of *nation*. In the discourse of the revolutionaries, it was a new idea charged with hopes, a subversion of feudalism that led to the enthusiasm at Valmy,[34] to the idea that the entire people should defend its borders not against foreigners but against the reconstitution of feudalism. And then the ideal of the nation was partly transformed after that into a nationalism fraught with xenophobia, with hatred of the foreigner.

J.D.: How to find the right limit between the reaffirmation of the nation—I have nothing against this term—and nationalism, which is a very modern form of the struggle for survival, not to say for the expansion, of the nation-state? Nationalism, today, is always *state*-nationalism, a zealous, that is, a *jealous* and vindictive vindication of a nation constituted as a sovereign state. The difficulties begin there, but I am not certain that some kind of nationalism is not already at work, however discreetly, as soon as one has entered into even the most sympathetic national consciousness, the most innocent affirmation of belonging to a particular national, cultural, or linguistic community. Hence the difficulty of escaping from it. And besides, is it necessary to escape from it? Ought we not rather—as I would be tempted to think, and as I have attempted to say elsewhere[35]—engage it in another experience of belonging and in another political logic?

E.R.: What is so deeply moving in *Specters of Marx* is that you revive hope for revolution in an age when every desire for revolution, every fantasy of a revolutionary ideal, is placed under a compulsory repression, because of its supposed shamefulness.

J.D.: It's a rather dim hope.

E.R.: I don't see it that way. *Specters of Marx* is the anti–*Black Book of Communism*,[36] which condemns as a crime, and in advance, the very project of a revolution, by reducing the entire history of communism, including that of thousands of militants throughout the world who died for this ideal, to a question of accounting. Thus anyone who worked in the name of communism, who belonged to any communist party during an entire fifty-year period, would be subject to a purification tribunal for having collaborated in a "criminal" undertaking.

To reduce communism to the crimes committed by the regimes who claimed to represent real socialism, to reduce communism to the gulag, as we said, strikes me as horrific. One example: a friend of mine, a professor at the former University of East Berlin, whose father had been a communist hero in the fight against the Nazis and had died defending France in the Resistance, was recently accused of collaboration with the former regime because he was the son of a pro-Soviet militant. But he himself had been persecuted for his hostility to the East German regime. Such situations are not uncommon. That's what identifying communism as a crime can lead to.

I would of course add that the corruption of an ideal or a hope is the worst thing there is. It's like killing the imagination. And one day someone will have to write the history of this tragedy and of its different repressions. In this sense—and only in this sense—what happened to communism with the gulag is the worst of catastrophes. With Nazism, everything had already been said, the worst was already there in the very project itself.

J.D.: Here, too, my book goes against the current. It continually places its stakes on a contretemps, certainly, but also on heritage and memory. As for the crimes you refer to, memory and history (the historian's history) must never be separated, even if neither one can be reduced to the other. It is necessary to respond, to give an account, if possible, and therefore to attempt to *know*, to analyze, and not to forget.

E.R.: There is no question of forgetting them, but of analyzing them in a coherent fashion and without confusion. The equation of communism and Nazism, which we spoke of a moment ago, leads one to claim insidiously that fascism and antifascism are symmetrical, and that racism and antiracism (or neo-antiracism, as its opponents have dubbed it) also have a symmetrical relation, each one as fanatical as the other, and each one feeding off the other. One finds this thesis in François Furet's *The Passing of an Illusion*,[37] and especially in Paul Yonnet, who, with his battery of anticommunitarianism, aggravated anticommunism, and critiques of multiculturalism, did not hesitate, in 1993, to accuse the "neo-antiracism" of SOS-Racisme[38] of seeking to occupy the place of the "Marxist myth and of a proletarian Esperantism"[39] in order to promote a "demand for the extinction of French identity."[40] Traces of this can be seen also in Pierre-André Taguieff,[41] whose works on racism actually have a certain authority in other respects.

Today, a new vulgate is spreading: to have been an antifascist in the name of communism, or because one belonged to the Communist Party between the wars or during the war of 1939–1944, would be the same as having been a fascist. Likewise, antiracist activism, with its inevitable simplifications, would be as dangerous as racism. I think nothing of the sort, even if I remain vigilant regarding all the aberrations we have already discussed.

You propose a program that I would tend to call an awakening of consciousness. You propose the creation of a new International to fight against the ten wounds of the new world order (unemployment, exclusion of exiles, economic wars, arms trade, ethnic conflict—based on soil and blood—, the power of phantom states that take the form of mafias and drug cartels), and you put forth the idea of a "declaration on the horror of the state of the world," which echoes the title of Viviane Forrester's book, *The Economic Horror*.[42]

In short, while the world is being unified under the banner of neoliberalism, and while all those who believed in the ideal of a communist society are forced to mourn it, you are inventing a new opposition.

J.D.: But in this regard I would hesitate to use the word "program," as you just did. It implies a knowledge of norms, a preestablished authority that, using this knowledge, would dictate the decisions and the responsibilities (thus annulling them in advance and in the same gesture). There is a necessity for programs, for the secondary effects of programs, for a programmatic economy and strategy, but in the first or last instance, what is to be done is invented or inaugurated, and therefore it comes about without a program.

I speak of a new International in which solidarities seek each other, and seek unheard-of figures for themselves, throughout all humanity, today, as a way to counter these wounds. I myself could not define these original forms, but it is clear that they are not the state-oriented forms of a party, an International of parties or of the party. I am not opposed to the existence of parties in general; they are still necessary and no doubt will be for a long time to come, but the "Party" form is no longer the major form of political struggle. The International I speak of is therefore not the International of the Communist Party or of any Party whatever. But I kept this word, with a capital, as a salute to the memory of what, existing no longer, will have been a great sign.

Among all the current commotions, one can find countless symptoms of this situation, whether it has to do with the Gulf War, the war in Kosovo, or struggles like the one associated with José Bové (for example). These disturbances indicate that something is being sought, a new form of alliance, a new style of "practice." I wonder, among other reservations, whether the very idea of a political program does not still pay an essential tribute to an outdated concept of the political.

We have already addressed the question of the "program" from another perspective, with the themes of the event, alterity, and unforeseeability. What is undergoing a "deconstruction" is no doubt the very concept of the political, from its Greek origins through all its mutations. What is called the political can no longer be bound in its very concept, as it has always been, to a presupposition of place, of territory—and of what pertains to the state. Carl Schmitt emphasizes that the political cannot be reduced to the state, even if the state form still remains a privileged form, something that is fundamentally at stake in the political. Some would like to continue to think—but this is more and more difficult—that the political necessarily takes the form of a state, and that it is bound to an irreplaceable territory, to a national community. But this is exactly what is being *dislo-*

cated today, and delocalized, notably through the techno-scientific and techno-economic transformation of the global field. It has become impossible to think as one previously did of the question of place, the political place in particular, the place of *the* political and of political taking-place.

Throughout the new regime of telecommunications, one is no longer where one thought one was. There is sometimes more proximity between a Japanese and a French person than between either of them and his or her neighbor in the same building or village. It suffices, in order to realize this, to take into account the cellular telephone, the Internet, the passage through a hegemonic language, or the speed of communications at the stock exchange, etc. The state of the financial market can be modified in a fraction of a second. This general dislocation dissociates the political field from the territorial and national field. A new concept of the political is now being forged. Before speaking of a "political program," it is therefore necessary to know what is meant by "the political."

Let me return for a moment to the question of hospitality. Kant's cosmopolitan ideal, for which I have the greatest respect, still assumed that the citizen was the citizen of the world "as a citizen," that is, as the subject of a nation-state. When Kant defines the conditions of universal hospitality,[43] he refers nonetheless to a multiplicity of states that will never make up a universal state. These states, and their citizen subjects, must define the laws of hospitality. They must make sure these rules are respected, and they must therefore place limits on welcoming the foreign citizen: for a brief time, as a visitor and not as a resident (or else, on the contrary, for a longer period, etc.). This concept of cosmopolitan hospitality, as respectable and always perfectible as it is, seems to me to be still bound to a figure of citizenship in the nation-state, the very one that now finds itself in a process of dislocation, transgression, transformation.[44]

When I speak of the democracy to come—this thing that can appear a little mad or impossible—I am thinking of a democracy that would no longer be bound in any essential way to citizenship. Here again, I come back to the same apparent contradiction: I am not against citizenship; it is necessary, and one must even fight for certain human beings who have been deprived of it, so that they might finally gain it. But the rights of man must also be extended beyond citizenship. Such is the "spirit" of the Declarations of the Rights of Man (beyond the Declaration of the Rights of Man *and of the Citizen*),[45] even if this "spirit" remains, in its inspiration, hindered by the state of the letter or the letter of the State.

E.R.: What can one do?

J.D.: This cannot be done from one day to the next and through a single decision. It is necessary for this "new International" to be developed, this engagement (which is not necessarily reciprocal, in the symmetry of rights and duties) between men, I would even say, inseparably, between living beings (with "animals"!), and then, inseparably, between the living and the dead, and even between the living and those who are not yet born. It does not stop at the borders of the nation-state or with the contracts of citizenship, even if this does not efface them or disqualify them necessarily.

Something of an identity is of course necessary, *some* citizen identity, but at certain moments, the categorical imperative exceeds the responsibility of the citizen as such. You asked me a question concerning the humanitarian. I salute humanitarian logic in its "spirit." And yet I am mistrustful of it when it happens to be controlled by certain states in the service of long- or short-term calculations, and sometimes quite simply in the service of the market. Even as they rescue populations, such "great powers" thus attempt at times to protect a hegemony. Whether economic or military or both.

Let us therefore remain as vigilant as possible with regard to the humanitarian alibis and suspect policies that instrumentalize "human rights." But how can one be opposed to the very idea of the humanitarian, to the project of a nongovernmental organization coming to the aid of men and women in distress? This idea is not, is no longer, has never been (Schmitt, in another spirit, emphasized this) a "political" idea in the traditional sense of the term. It is therefore necessary to ask, each time: who is doing what in the name of humanitarianism? What are the relations between certain powerful sovereign states—it's almost always the United States—and the UN, when states impose the logic of their interests on nongovernmental or multigovernmental organizations, or else when, on the contrary, they resist the logic of international law (and this is often the case) in order to safeguard the interests of their nation-state and their sovereignty?

E.R.: In other words, you suggest that one take positions "case by case," without positing, *a priori, one* founding principle.

J.D.: There is *one* principle, but when it is put into effect, one must take account of the singularity of the context and the moment. In the name of a single principle, I will not make the same decision at different moments. I might be opposed to a particular humanitarian operation in one case, and I might support it in another. Once again, there is nothing relativistic or opportunistic in this.

E.R.: It is this approach that leads you to include the work of Freud in your analyses: the singularity of a subject, even deconstructed, exists and resists every form of *a priori* construction.[46]

J.D.: Of course, singularity resists, it remains. Sometimes it even resists being assigned to "subjectivity" (in every sense of the term: subject as substance identical to itself, subject of the unconscious, subject of the law, citizen subject or subject of right, etc.).

E.R.: Speaking of singularity, you returned to the spirit of Marx by way of South Africa and in order to pay homage to an exceptional man, Nelson Mandela, who spent nearly thirty years of his life in prison and stunned the world with his genius for reconciliation and his serenity. Of him you say: "Admirable Mandela . . . , Admiration of Nelson Mandela, as one would say Nelson Mandela's passion. Admiration of Nelson Mandela, a double genitive: that which he inspires and that which he feels. The two have the same focus, they reflect upon each other."[47] Moreover, as I said before, you reawaken the spirit of the Revolution by dedicating your book to a militant South African communist.

J.D.: Chris Hani was assassinated a few days before I presented the lecture on "the specters of Marx," which I dedicated to him. A militant of the African National Congress[48] (ANC), he was one of the leaders of the South African Communist Party (SACP).[49]

E.R.: Mandela seems to me to be one of the great figures of today's modernity. He is the heir to Western thought, which he turned against his oppressors, first by founding the first black law firm in Johannesburg, then by becoming one of the main leaders of the ANC, and finally by spending more than twenty-seven years in prison without going mad.[50]

J.D.: An immense figure indeed. He paid the highest price. I was able to visit the cell where he had lived in horrible conditions.[51] He came out with an extraordinary serenity, and he even entered into negotiations with the whites in power *against* the advice of his comrades in the struggle. Without being able to go into detail about what was called, under the presidency of the Archbishop Desmond Tutu, the Truth and Reconciliation Commission (we studied it closely in one seminar), I would say that Mandela fought for an amnesty to be proclaimed both for the exiled ANC militants and for the whites suspected of the worst. He thought that the body of the South African nation could survive only under this condition. But supposing that this condition for survival is necessary, it is not certain that it is sufficient.

Up to now, Mandela has succeeded in saving South African society from imminent disaster, but I must say with a certain sadness that this great moment, this figure who is exemplary in so many ways, already belongs to the past. Mandela has withdrawn, and South Africa is passing through great troubles. The most serious problems have not been worked out. Mandela had to make political choices that were no doubt inevitable and that consisted, essentially, in not seizing property and in leaving the country open to the world market. Poverty, insecurity, inequality, the gulf that remains between blacks and whites (and the more and more likely exodus of the latter), these are so many troubling signs.

Mandela will nonetheless have succeeded in embodying for the entire world a cause that not only mobilized irresistible forces but accelerated a coming to consciousness. Through these struggles, we have come to understand better the international nature of the stakes involved and of the struggles that were waged. This worldwide mobilization could not have taken on such magnitude if apartheid had not been defined as a "crime against humanity" by the UN. This was a real juridical lever; it made it possible for all the democratic states of the world to exert pressure on the whites in power: political pressure and economic sanctions. It became possible to abolish apartheid[52] thanks to the mobilization of Mandela's supporters. But all the countries that had invested capital in South Africa or furnished arms to the whites in power—like France for example—were frustrated by the economic sanctions. That's when they decided that democratization would be more favorable to the market.

Mandela was very adept at making the most of this conjunction of principles and interests. He is at the same time a man of principles and reflection, a strategist and a great tactician. He managed to turn the principles of the whites' power against it.

E.R.: But how was Mandela able to avoid going mad after twenty-seven years in prison? That's one of the great questions I would like to understand. How was he able to avoid being caught in the immobile temporality of the prison phenomenon?

J.D.: I, too, have thought a great deal about this question. How was he able to resist? To account for such an exceptional situation, one can follow several lines that cross at various points. Mandela himself speaks of his filial debt: the image of his father engraved within him since his earliest childhood, like a gentle and inflexible law, and the upbringing he received from his mother. In the seminar sessions devoted to him, I also considered, of course, the episode of circumcision that he describes in his memoirs.[53] In the Xhosa tradition, it is only after this ritual, at the age of sixteen, that one becomes a man. It is thus in his psycho-fantasmatic inheritance that the individual, Nelson Mandela (he also relates how he was given the name "Nelson" at school), must have found this uncommon strength. There are many ways to approach an analysis of his personal case. A certain psychic capital must have been constituted at birth or in his childhood, and must have been determined through the traits we associate with this political hero who astounded the world and without whom it is difficult to imagine the history of South Africa for the last fifty years. But once one has said this, and even attempted to explain in this way an exceptional psychic constitution, it is necessary to analyze this entire political history, the ways in which it was and remains greater than this great man, and stronger than his strength.

In fact, Mandela has expressed himself at length on this subject: both on his happy childhood, his years of apprenticeship, the pursuit of his profession as a lawyer, *and* on the way in which, engaged as he was in these stormy political transformations, he took his place in the struggles that had shaken the body of South Africa since the beginning of the century, even before the official institution of apartheid and state racism. In his youth he participated in well-organized protest movements against oppression, movements that had a mix of whites—Christians or Jews—and clergy. Throughout this entire period of his life, before the great trial in which he defended himself,[54] neither his life nor his authority were seriously threatened. It was when he was imprisoned for a long period that the situation became terrifying for him. Here, too, it is necessary to take into account the diachrony of an existence: the imprisonment was certainly harsh, at times inhuman, but it was possible to have contact with the outside, and the conditions of his detention changed over the course of the years, especially toward the end.

Not long before his liberation in 1990, when the first negotiations were taking shape, the conditions of his imprisonment were improved. His contact with the outside allowed him to survive this long period of incarceration, and the images that reached him from abroad helped him to pursue his struggle. That said, one is still stunned by the stature of this man, by what one can call, more than ever, his greatness [*grandeur*]. He is also a tall man [*un homme grand*], smiling, attractive, seductive no doubt.

I went to Mandela's house to meet with him, and he explained this to me himself. He went through some terrible moments, but at the same time he managed to found a sort of university in the prison, with a dozen political detainees who taught each other and organized real courses.

When I saw him two years ago, he was already more than eighty years old; he had just remarried and seemed as happy as a young man at the beginning of a new life. A few moments before our meeting, he had finished a three- or four-hour meeting with Yasser Arafat (helicopters, police, bodyguards, much pomp, etc.). He was still energetic, attentive, in good spirits, as if he were just beginning his day, ready to talk about anything—about prison but also about France, pretending to complain that he was no longer able to decide for himself where to travel ("No more freedom of movement, I am in prison, from now on, and that's my jailer there," he said, pointing to his principal collaborator). He also asked for news of Danielle Mitterrand. And then: "Sartre, is he still alive?"

E.R.: In bringing this chapter to a close, I would like to recall once again the memory of Louis Althusser. Like you, I loved and respected him a great deal. My book on Théroigne de Méricourt was a way for me to speak of him, as I said. He was the last great reader of Marx's work, and he awakened a sort of *reinvented* spirit of the Revolution. Overcome with madness, he sank further and further into melancholy as communism progressively collapsed. He deeply influenced my own itinerary, and his posthumous writings, particularly his autobiography and his correspondence,[55] shed new light on him: like Hugo, he intuited the anguished calm of a "twilight moment" in the history of Europe. You did not comment on his work as you did that of Lacan, Foucault, or Lévi-Strauss. And yet I had the impression that in *Specters of Marx* he is present on every page.

J.D.: *Specters of Marx* can indeed be read, if you like, as a sort of homage to Louis Althusser. A salute that is indirect but above all friendly and nostalgic, slightly melancholic. The question is open to analysis. I wrote the book in 1993, three years after Althusser's death—and of course it can be read as an address to him,[56] a means of "surviving" what I lived through with him, alongside him. He was simultaneously close and distant, allied and dissociated. But who isn't? You are asking me to speak of something, of someone who occupied such a large place in my life. To give the external measure of things, I met him when I entered the Ecole Normale Supérieure, in 1952—he was a "caïman"[57]—he wasn't teaching, and he was often ill, though at the time I didn't know what the trouble was. He was suffering, in any case, and one time he told me that it was a problem with his kidneys. He showed me a great deal of friendship and supported me in my work. I had no idea what was happening.

E.R.: You didn't notice anything?

J.D.: During those years, I knew absolutely nothing. Later, when I began teaching at the Sorbonne, between 1960 and 1964, Althusser invited me to give courses at the Ecole Normale—before I myself became a "caïman"—and that was when he spoke to me of "depression." I understood then that his absences had to do with visits to a psychiatric institution. From that moment on, we saw each other quite a lot. With his philosophical judgment, he encouraged me in a way that was very decisive. When I sent him the manuscript of *Edmund Husserl's Origin of Geometry: An Introduction*, my first publication, he wrote me an extraordinary letter. He wasn't a Husserl specialist, but like certain Marxists in his entourage, or—elsewhere and differently—like his fellow student at the Ecole Normale, Tran-Duc-Tao, he perceived (strategically) a possible alliance between Husserl's transcendental idealism, particularly its genetic and epistemological dimension, and a new Marxist problematic. I wasn't far from thinking this as well, although in another way. With Jean Hyppolite,[58] he invited me to come to the rue d'Ulm, where I taught while he was away (in 1964). After that it became a professional *compagnonnage* that lasted more than twenty years.

A great affection united us, punctuated by all sorts of difficult moments, particularly because of his periods of exile. I went to visit him regularly in various psychiatric institutions around Paris. We did not have many very deep philosophical discussions, but I attended certain classes that eventually led to *Reading "Capital."*[59] We had the same students. In 1968–69 we brought in Bernard Pautrat, a former student and a common friend, and the three of us met every Tuesday in the same room to hear the lectures of the "agrégatifs."[60] Louis was in general more accessible and affectionate when he was "depressed" than in what might be called his more "manic" periods. After the tragedy of November 1980,[61] I was for a long time the only person allowed to see him.

E.R.: I met him in 1972, and I saw him often. He gave me a lot of encouragement in my writing, even though he didn't share the criticisms I addressed to you[62] (he completely disagreed). We had numerous exchanges on psychoanalysis; he asked me to read and correct his texts because, he said, he didn't know the works of Freud and Lacan well enough. Yet his great intelligence, and his suffering, allowed him to perceive many new things in these texts.[63] I always had the feeling that he was able to mourn neither communism nor the failure of communism. There was something mystical in the way he wanted at all cost to restore the theoretical vigor of Marxism at a time when the party was oscillating between a social-democratic political line, no doubt inevitable, and sectarian withdrawal.

J.D.: In May 1968, he was doing very badly. He had to come to terms with some of his former students who wanted to push things to their limits and were trying to draw him toward the proletarian Left. I'm thinking in particular of Benny Lévy and Robert Linhart. He was quite tormented and left the Ecole Normale at the time. Before his death, I spoke about him in an interview I gave in the United States that was published in an American book entitled *The Althusserian Legacy*. That's the only time I spoke at length of my relationship with him. At length but insufficiently, of course. This book has never been published in French.[64]

E.R.: His conception of philosophy was different from yours, but one thing you had in common was psychoanalysis. Moreover, there was a certain proximity: in the passion for teaching—what you call "school fever [*le mal d'école*]"—and the place granted to language, to commentary, and to the unconscious.

J.D.: When we spoke of philosophical subjects, he did not take up a

Marxist position; he did not try to broach this subject with me. We would talk about texts that, when he asked me about them, he thought were more familiar to me than to him and that fascinated him more than is generally believed: Heidegger, Artaud, Nietzsche. Reading some of his writings after his death, I gained a better understanding; I discovered at times what he thought of me and how he perceived the path I was taking, how he read me (particularly concerning the question of the "alea," the event, a certain non-Marxist materialist tradition, in Democritus or Lucretius, etc.).

Yes, it was quite late, and often after his death, that I began to perceive what he was most attentive to in my own itinerary, and which he did not discuss with me directly. There were many avoidances; we were very close, and at the same time we always spoke of other things besides great philosophico-political issues. There was something virtual in our relationship, and few focused debates. Traces of this can be found in his writings. He multiplies references to our friendship, to everything that kept us closer, often, than I myself believed at times.

E.R.: In his correspondence, and particularly in his letters to Franca Madonia,[65] he speaks of you a great deal. You were one of "his people"; somewhat separated, since you were not a communist, but in you he sensed something fraternal.

Of the Anti-Semitism to Come

E.R.: To begin this new chapter, I would like to evoke some personal memories with you. In *La contre-allée*—and in *Circumfession*[1]—you speak of your father, a commercial traveler, a sales representative dealing in wines and spirits for the Tachet house, whose owner had come from a "good family"—meaning Catholic and traditional.[2] Your father lived as a subservient and humiliated man; he smelled of anethol because he dealt with a brand of anisette. You seem to say of him what he said of his own father: "my poor father." A Jewish father, whom you began to accompany in his travels when you were eighteen years old. Later you saw yourself as a colonized North African Jew, then as a "marrano,"[3] forced to remain "faithful to a secret you did not choose."

This figure of the humiliated father, of the Jewish father humiliated by Christians, is central to Freud. Jakob Freud was a textile merchant. One day he told his son the well-known story of a time when it was difficult to be Jewish. In this distant age, he was unable to fight back when an anti-Semite threw his fur cap into the gutter. For this scene of humiliation related by Jakob, Freud substituted another one, this time from Roman history, in which Hannibal promises his father, Hamilcar, that he will take revenge on his enemies.[4] Thus Freud identified with the figure of a conquering Semite anxious to take his revenge and to found a new empire centered around the exploration of dreams and the unconscious.[5]

Freud built his theory of the Oedipus complex on the necessity for a symbolic revalorization of the paternal function, at a time when patriarchal authority was falling apart in the West. We also know that by aspiring to a Greco-Latin culture, the sons of the Jewish Viennese commercial bourgeoisie were "surpassing" their fathers, were becoming socially and intellectually "other."[6]

As for Lacan, he found himself in a comparable situation from the point of view that concerns us here. Born into a family of the respectable Catholic commercial bourgeoisie, he was confronted very early on with the humiliation that his father (Alfred) underwent at the hands of his grandfather (Emile), a veritable domestic tyrant. Lacan took from this experience a sort of hatred for the mean and violent behavior found within the family, even while also attempting, in his encounter with Freud's work, to restore a symbolic function to paternity through the construction of a strange concept: the Name-of-the-Father.[7] In your case, rather than revalorizing the symbolic function of the father, you propose to deconstruct Western patricentrism and its corollary: phallocentrism.

J.D.: For a great many reasons, I don't know just how far I can follow you in these analogies or distinctions. Nor whether one can compare my father to these other paternal figures in Freud or in Lacan. But I love your "as for Lacan . . . " I am also not certain that my father's experience of humiliation was linked to his Jewishness, at least in terms of what I felt about it then, as an adolescent. Implicitly, yes, no doubt, but in a very indirect way.

My compassion for my father was infinite. Hardly had he begun school, when, at the age of twelve, he had to begin working for the Tachet business, where his own father had been a modest employee. After being a sort of apprentice until the age of adulthood, my father became a commercial representative: he was always behind the wheel of his car. Sometimes I would accompany him on his rounds; I drove for him when I could. At every hotel, every café, every grocery store, he stopped to take orders, and I always saw him in the persona of the petitioner or the applicant: in relation to the clients but also to the boss, whose authoritarian paternalism irritated me as much as his benevolence. What I sensed in this benevolence, more than anything, was the condescension it expressed. One of my father's many given names, Charles, was no doubt that of the Tachet grandfather (and what a peculiar family name, no? One thinks of the stain [*tache*] of some unknown original sin).

At the time, I was not thinking of any "Jewish question." There was the boss and the employee, the rich and the poor, and even within the family I saw my father as the victim of a somber ritual. Obscure, cruel, and fatal. The word "sacrifice" came up constantly: "He is sacrificing himself for us." Sometimes he said it himself. During my entire adolescence, I suffered with him, I accused the rest of the family of not recognizing how much he was doing for us. That was the experience of the "humiliated father": a man of duty above all, bending beneath his obligations. Stooped. And he was stooped; his bearing, his silhouette, the line and movement of his body, it was as though they all bore this signature. The word "stooped [*voûté*]" imposes itself on me all the more in that I have never been able to dissociate it from his destiny: my father worked in an area whose name was nothing other than "the vaults [*les voûtes*]," at the port of Algiers.

In *La contre-allée* or elsewhere, it happens that I compare myself to a commercial representative exhausted from carrying his suitcases, from "selling" his wares on some academic and cultural market. But things are more complicated, as you can imagine, and the transaction is more perverse, more contraband; but let's leave that for now. Perhaps—I also like to think this—perhaps I am avenging my father by introducing a principle of disorder into this "commerce," whose trial I would also be organizing. To do justice to my father—or, let's say with a laugh, with our friend Hamlet: "to set it right!"

When state anti-Semitism was unleashed in Algeria, in 1940–42, my father was grateful to his employers for protecting us, for keeping him in their service, whereas they could have simply fired this Jewish employee, as some people were urging them to do, and as they had the legal right to do. I felt humiliated to see him overflowing with respectful gratitude to these people for whom he had worked for forty years and who generously "consented" to "keep him on." He worked a great deal, he worked all the time, he never took any vacation. Without going so far as to say that I virtually identified with him (but how can one not do this, at bottom, even if only a little, as soon as one begins to understand and to feel compassion?), I no doubt saw in him an exemplary figure of the victim: misjudged by the "family," exploited by "society."

E.R.: So the question of the humiliated father has a central place in your critique of patricentrism. It seems to me that personal experience always plays a role in these matters, in one form or another.

J.D.: It never occurred to me to associate this experience of the humiliated father (humiliated by "paternalism"!) with any rehabilitation whatever of the paternal figure, nor, inversely, with some deconstruction of patricentrism. My indignation regarding the employers and even my mother, who (or so I thought when I was a child) did not recognize or share the sufferings of our father—this indignation was first of all, was also, a form of compassion. I was the one who could understand the sufferings of a father; and, in fact, my father often preferred to confide in me, beginning in my adolescence. Whenever we were alone together, he approached me from the bottom of his silence; he called on me as a witness to the incomprehension and indifference of the others. It is true that this experience was more or less contemporaneous with that of the intensified anti-Semitism of the time. I was expelled from the Ben Aknoun high school in 1942, and beyond any anonymous "administrative" measure, which I didn't understand at all and which no one explained to me, the wound was of another order, and it never healed: the daily insults from the children, my classmates, the kids in the street, and sometimes threats or blows aimed at the "dirty Jew," which, I might say, I came to see in myself . . .

It is very difficult for me to articulate and link together, as you have invited me to do, these personal experiences and the deconstructive gestures in the direction of Freud and patriarchy or, as you say, patricentrism. With regard to my father, there was an ambiguous mixture of compassion and hostility. My father lacked authority, while also being prone to anger, and I regretted the fact that he always came to me to complain. Sometimes, no doubt later—but these things are obscure and difficult to describe here—I must have taken the side of my mother against my father.

E.R.: To come now to the heart of what will occupy us in this chapter, the question of anti-Semitism, we must indeed remark that, in the 1970's, this question was asked less acutely than it is today. I belong to a Jewish family that is much more assimilated than yours, or in any case much more assimilationist, and I have the impression that an interrogation of Jewish identity, though it has always existed, returned with great force among assimilated French intellectuals around 1980, with the waning of those engagements connected to the grand systems of thought. In order to remain faithful to these systems without succumbing to dogmatism, it became necessary, as we have said, to deconstruct them. But in doing this, the danger of being confined within certain categories or identities emerged more clearly over the years.

J.D.: How is it possible to venture again to confront and to *face*, in an abrupt fashion, the question of anti-Semitism? The anti-Semitism that, today, is here among us, *chez nous?* Ought we to face it as if it were still not only close to us but *before us*, simultaneously present and still to come? Does anti-Semitism still have a face and a future?

It is true that the very form of my questions remains imprudent. It seems to assume that, although "before us," and however close to us it may be, even here among "us," anti-Semitism remains external or foreign to you and me, to others as well. I'm afraid that no one can claim immunity here. For my part, I always try, perhaps with mixed success, to watch myself very carefully when it comes to the authorization I sometimes risk giving myself—as a Jew or as someone identified as such, and therefore supposedly as someone who cannot be suspected of anti-Semitism—whenever I ask critical or sometimes radically "deconstructive" questions about Judaism (religion or culture), Jewishness, the notion of election, about a certain communitarian dimension, or about the foundation of the state of Israel, especially, or its politics for the last half a century.

My vigilance with regard to racism and anti-Semitism was tireless— I believe I can say this—from as early as the age of ten. I must admit, however, that it is only *just today* that, along with others, I am overcome with vertigo before something that has lately become obvious to me: French society continues to welcome back the old demons, particularly in milieus and in public spaces that, I thought, were safe from them.

Let us return to Algeria for a moment. The school system there was, at least in principle, by right, absolutely identical to that of the "metropole": the same norms, the same values, the same linguistic model. This school saw itself as republican (more "republican" than "democratic"!), and the "Republic" can be, as we know, more "colonialist," that is, more expansionist in the name of universal values, than a "democracy," if we still even hold to this fragile and misleading opposition. This republican school, of course, excluded all reference—I would almost dare to say all mention—of Algeria and the Arab language. It tended also to exclude the Algerians themselves! In primary school, certainly, there were about as many young Algerians as young students of French "stock," but in the great majority of cases, the former did not continue to pursue their education. Neither in high school nor, even less, in the university.

When I was expelled from Ben Aknoun, my parents sent me "into town" to enroll at the Maimonides high school, nicknamed "Emile Maupas," after the street behind the Algiers cathedral, at the edge of the Kasbah. This was where all the Jewish professors of the region, themselves excluded without a word of protest from their colleagues (just as in the "metropole"!), regrouped to form a place of instruction for all these pariahs. So that's where I ended up, but I have a dark and unhappy memory of the place. It was there, I believe, that I began to recognize—if not to contract—this ill, this malaise, the ill-being that, throughout my life, rendered me inapt for "communitarian" experience, incapable of enjoying any kind of membership in a group.

For it was at that moment that this tendency no doubt became fixed, in appearance, over and against a frenetic "Jewish" fusion. But I suppose that the threat I was fleeing at all cost, and with all speed (for example, I hid from my parents the fact that, for nearly a year, I "cut" classes in the Maimonides high school), came from farther away. It was, and remains, general and multiform. Similarly, one year before, I had deserted the milieu of the Scouts et Eclaireurs de France (a Boy Scout association that was very French, pro-Pétain even), into which a zealous teacher had pushed me.

E.R.: In *La contre-allée* you say that you did not want to belong to the Jewish community. You detested the word "community," as you detest today, as much as I do, ethnicism and communitarianism. You also speak, in reference to this triple identity (Jew/North African/French), of a dissociated identity.

J.D.: On the one hand, I was deeply wounded by anti-Semitism. And this wound has never completely healed. At the same time, paradoxically, I could not tolerate being "integrated" into this Jewish school, this homogeneous milieu that reproduced and in a certain way countersigned—in a reactive and vaguely specular fashion, at once forced (by the outside threat) and compulsive—the terrible violence that had been done to it. This reactive self-defense was certainly natural and legitimate, even irreproachable. But I must have sensed that it was a drive [*pulsion*], a gregarious *compulsion* that responded too symmetrically, that *corresponded* in truth to an *expulsion*.

A double suffering, then, a divided cruelty, a wound whose bleeding had a source that was perhaps more distant, and much earlier. It will have come, since always, to give a path and a form ("my" form) to everything that could be recounted, to everything that I myself could write under the rubric of a "formation novel." For this is perhaps also a reconstruction, a story, a fiction I am telling myself. So much work remains to be done.

E.R.: Although I know that conceptual productions cannot be reduced to the elements of subjective life, I almost think that when it comes to the construction of an identity, there exists a link between them, a sort of "oedipal relation."

J.D.: Of course. But it is necessary to find the most precise and subtle mediations, also the most singular. A daunting task.

E.R.: Today it seems difficult not to reflect on this question, both in order to turn away from the communitarian temptation and to preserve something—a remainder—a sort of "feeling of Jewishness."

J.D.: For me this "feeling" remains obscure, abyssal, very unstable. Contradictory. At once very powerful and fragile. As if some depth of memory authorized me to forget, perhaps to deny what is most archaic, to distract me from the essential. This active, even energetic distraction turns me away, then, from what no doubt remains most "constitutive" in me. It diverts me from it to the point where I sometimes find it to be, also, tenuous, accidental, superficial, extrinsic. Nothing for me matters as much as my Jewishness, which, however, in so many ways, matters so little in my life. I know very well that such statements seem contradictory, lacking in common sense. But they would be so only in the eyes of someone who could say "I" only in one whole piece, only by expelling from himself all alterity, all heterogeneity, all division, indeed all altercation, all "explication" or "coming to terms" with oneself. I am not *alone* with myself, no more than anyone else is—I am not *all-one*. An "I" is not an indivisible atom.

Without going very far down this well-trodden path, I will add two or three things and will limit myself to the question of Jewishness that we're addressing now. *On the one hand,* this division, this dehiscence (more than one and more than two and more than three, beyond all arithmetic and all calculability, etc.)—it is around this that I am working all the time, and always have been. This incalculable inner multiplicity is my torment, precisely, *my work* and *travail,* my *tripalium,* my passion and my labor. It is also that which, working [*travaillant*] on me body and soul, no doubt makes me work, as a number of texts attest,[8] giving me to reflect *both* on my belonging *and* on my not belonging to Judaism. *On the other hand,* I do not believe that this division or this nonidentity to oneself remains purely or exemplarily Jewish; but who would dare to claim that it is not *also* very Jewish?

Finally, and I would say *especially,* I vindicate this uprooting division; I do not consider it an absolute evil. One suffers from it, but it emancipates. As the condition for a somewhat awakened gaze, it interrupts many a dogmatic slumber. The rupture of belonging often gives me the chance, for example, for a judgment that is more just, less unjust, on the politics of communities to which I am supposed to belong and concerning which I want to remain more vigilant than ever—whether it is a question of Europe, France, Israel, or the Jewish Diaspora. It is also important for me to remain as free as possible in order to criticize them whenever this is necessary. Without giving in to any blackmail based on belonging to a particular community. I want to be as free as I am when—without giving in, either, to any form of intimidation, however virtual—I evaluate the actions or the politics of communities or states to which I am supposed *not* to belong. As you know, it is often very difficult to resist all these pressures to take sides, this "blackmail," as I'm calling it. It is sometimes almost impossible, in the general confusion created by such attempts at blackmail, to insist on complex judgments, prudent and differentiated statements, multilayered grounds for decision. This is particularly true, and sometimes in a desperate way, when it comes to questions that continue to be tragic and infernal: the Shoah, Israel, Palestine, etc.; although—I'll say this again—I do not want to recenter everything around this focal point, as if it alone were utterly unique, I mean "more unique" than another. Since every murder, every wound, all the disasters of the age (exterminations, genocides, mass expropriations and deportations, etc.) are irreducibly singular.

With regard to historical disaster, let us return for a moment to Algeria, if you don't mind. Anti-Semitism was always rampant there, this is well known; it was virulent during the occupation, then latent and diffuse after the war. Well, when I arrived in France for the first time, at the age of nineteen, I thought that I would stop suffering from it. I naively thought that in France, and especially in the intellectual and academic milieu, anti-Semitism had no chance. This illusion lasted a long time; I did not really shake it off, even if it happened that the illusion was at times brutally interrupted by certain "awakenings" (then I would say to myself: "Be careful, you're sleeping, but in reality anti-Semitism is awake, it practices the art of disguise, even in your own home!"). And then I would go back to sleep, perhaps to have other dreams, good or bad. Until the next jolt, which could sometimes be violent.

E.R.: How did you learn about the genocide of the Jews and the reality of the camps, about what, since Claude Lanzmann's film, has been called the Shoah?

J.D.: It was quite late. During the Second World War, in Algeria, anti-Semitism was unleashed in ordinary life and in legislation. The governor general was quite zealous. He anticipated or aggravated certain measures taken by Vichy, notably in relation to the national education system and state services. Despite everything that was happening to us in this regard, I did not know, at that age, we did not know (at least not in my milieu) what had happened or was still happening in Europe. Like many people, I did not take the full measure of the evil; I measured its unmeasure, if I can put it that way, only later, and gradually.

E.R.: Was it through texts, or talking with people, or through images?

J.D.: There were films (*Night and Fog*,[9] no doubt, although that was only part of it) and other sorts of texts. It was slow and gradual. I no longer recall all the paths taken by this coming to consciousness. Which in any case I always dissociated, unjustly, from what had happened in Algeria, as if there were two worlds, two histories, two communities with no connection. That's absurd, of course, from a certain point of view. But this disparity is not insignificant; I would like to be able to analyze it better some day.

In any case, I was an adult when I began to "know." I was more than twenty years old, and I lived in Paris. And then, of course, like anyone who is more or less awake, I tried, at least, to "think" the thing, not only to "think" it but to think "about it," as many others did, to think "about it" in its place, there where this thing *took place*, undeniably, over there, over there as well as here, but *before us*. It happened, irreversibly. This taking-place is precisely what resists thought, any thought that would believe it is thinking by assimilating, appropriating, habituating. Subjectivizing. By internalizing in a work of mourning that always tends to *immunize*, to deny what it idealizes—for one can also idealize, that is, sacralize the worst.

E.R.: Gradually, then, you had the illusion that anti-Semitism had disappeared. There were quite a few of us who thought this.

J.D.: When, like other people, I was horrified by a certain renewal of anti-Semitism linked to the growth of the far right in France,[10] I never believed—this was probably my illusion—that French society could become anti-Semitic in a dangerous way. I did see the grimacing gesticulations of certain groups, of this or that party, and, like other people, I was ready to denounce them. But I did not think that the society, that something like the "culture" of this country, could let itself be invaded by that vulgar anti-Semitism that gave us a few typical jolts during the Renaud Camus affair.[11]

E.R.: Today, everything happens as if anti-Semitism had once again become unremarkable and ordinary, well protected by a good conscience in denial. A sign of this is the formidable discourse of what I would call "unconscious anti-Semitism," which consists in radically condemning the Shoah even while claiming the right to "critique" the Jews "as Jews" and to "do some accounting." But this supposed "critique" is only a way to give new currency to an old form of anti-Semitism, based on the claim that there are "too many" Jews in certain professions, that they are organized into "lobbies" [English in original] for the purposes of influencing or unsettling opinion, etc. In this discourse, the famous "accounting" of the number of Jews in particular sectors is obviously an attempt to incite discrimination.

According to a survey taken two years ago, 70 percent of the French population declared themselves to be racist, even while claiming to be hostile to all forms of discrimination.[12] Here it's a matter of negation in the Freudian sense, as a way of negatively expressing a thought whose content has been repressed, a sort of "oh, I know, but still . . . ," according to the well-known formula of Octave Mannoni: "I know the Jews have suffered, but still, they're exaggerating."[13] Or else: "Sure I'm racist, but I don't want blacks to be persecuted, not that I particularly want to have anything to do with them, even though, after all, I can understand that they mustn't be too mistreated . . . ," and so on.

J.D.: When anti-Semitism spreads, even in this typed, predictable form, which is contemptible but quite easy to decipher, its "perverse effects," as one says, are numerous. The first is that one risks hesitating to criticize anything at all about the politics of Israel or of some particular Jewish community. There is always someone who will suspect you of direct or at least indirect collusion with this insidious anti-Semitism. Not to mention Holocaust denial! As I suggested a moment ago, I can no longer even say to myself, complacently: "Fortunately, I'm Jewish, which makes it possible for me not to be accused too quickly when I am disconcerted by the foundations of the state of Israel and its politics, by the opinion of a particular Jew or group of Jews, by this or that initiative of the Jewish community." This is a trap that must be avoided—at all costs! For it is a *deadly* trap, and I am choosing my words carefully. It is the programmed death of the slightest lucidity, of all responsibility (intellectual, ethical, political).

It is necessary to struggle and to fight against those who lay these traps. It is necessary to oppose them, if only by taking the time, by giving or imposing the time of a complex and multilayered discourse. For I do not want to deny to anyone the right to criticize Israel or a particular Jewish community (nor do I want to be deprived of this right myself) under the pretext that such criticism would risk resembling or being useful to some form of anti-Semitism. I recognize the difficulty, but if the word *courage* (intellectual or otherwise) still has any sense, it is precisely in this treacherous situation, when faced with attempts at intimidation from all sides. For we are surrounded; the trap is a veritable siege. The worst thing, in my eyes, from the position in which I find myself, is the appropriation and especially the instrumentalization of historical memory. It is possible and necessary, without the least bit of anti-Semitism, to denounce this instrumentalization—for example, the properly strategic calculation (political or otherwise) that would consist in *making use* of the Holocaust, of using it for particular ends. It is possible to judge these ends to be highly questionable, or to regard as detestable the strategy they dictate, without denying in the slightest the reality of this past monstrosity that is the Holocaust, which certain people would thus like to take hold of in order to make use of it.

It seems to me (this is in any case my rule or my maxim) that one must be tireless, and never let oneself be intimidated, in *simultaneously* combating every form of Holocaust denial *and* in refusing the exploitation of a bottomless tragedy, a tragedy worse than all tragedy (I mean insofar as tragedy is still too "Greek" as a figure), and which belongs to no one. Artisanal or industrial, instrumentalization begins very quickly and very early on. It imposes itself everywhere, inevitably. It does so sometimes crudely and without disguise, sometimes also under a respectable mask, in a way that is more noble and refined—for example, by showing the marked features of a face that has been frozen, so to speak, into the legitimate witness's imperturbable pain, almost as if one were reduced to professionalizing an appointed role. This strategy can also invade rhetoric, diplomacies of all sorts, the market, and even the art market. It is not always easy to perceive. But if it is necessary to be constantly on alert in order to discern this strategy, it is, for the same reasons, no less necessary and urgent to analyze anti-Semitism, and even Holocaust denial, which is also quick to use it as the pretext for a good conscience. These two evils go hand in hand; they feed off each other and comfort each other. However uncomfortable it is, I conclude therefore that it is necessary to resist both one and the other simultaneously. Without respite and without weakness.

E.R.: One must not give way on these questions. And let us not forget that anti-Semitism, even unconscious, is revealed in a particular way of speaking about Jews, in a certain way of writing. It is perfectly possible to oppose Israeli politics and support the Palestinian cause, or else to criticize a certain fundamentalist or Zionist discourse, without for all that succumbing to anti-Semitism. Besides, there is no need to be Jewish to be authorized to critique what is intolerable in certain pro-Israeli discourses. It is in fact because I know that anti-Semitic discourse is always recognizable by its language, its words, its rhetoric, by the particular logic and the arguments it uses, that I do not feel guilty for the criticisms I address to Jews or to non-Jews whose opinions I do not share. For the same reasons, it seems to me indispensable to condemn the manifestations of anti-Semitism that are developing, and even being cultivated, in the countries at war against Israel, to the point of reproducing negationist arguments.[14]

J.D.: I believe that it is indeed necessary to redouble our vigilance regarding an anti-Israeli indoctrination that rarely avoids anti-Semitism. You will grant that this is one place where, less than ever, we should not be content to "share opinions." I don't want to have a what is called an "opinion" on this matter. Look at the history of the "Jewish lobby" ["lobby" and its cognates here and below are in English in the original—Trans.]. Here, too, the expression has been imported without precaution from a place, a language, a culture, a set of political customs or habits that do not necessarily mark the expression "lobby" with suspect connotations. In the United States, "lobbying" can be an ordinary and legitimate political activity.

When it comes to the importing of certain idiomatic locutions that are potentially dangerous, perhaps we ought to apply the "principle of precaution" used today for "animals" or for toxic substances!

I do not believe that the importing of the expression "lobby" (like that of "politically correct," which we discussed before) is ever innocent or transparent. That said, why not recognize that in civil society there are something like "lobbies," pressure groups of every sort—Jewish ones among others—that is, assemblies of people who, with a mandate or not, within or without an institution, make an effort to protect what they interpret, rightly or wrongly, as the interests or the proper memory of a community? Some people, inside or outside this community, can in turn recognize themselves in it or disavow it.

One can therefore, it seems to me, criticize or regret, in certain cases, the actions of such groups—Jews, for example. Jews, too, can and sometimes should be troubled by the initiatives of such groups, without being suspected of anti-Semitism. But the importation, the *precipitous and compulsive* use of the expression "lobby," in France, and even on the part of someone who would not normally be considered anti-Semitic—I believe, to say the least, that it is impossible not to detect in this, most often, a clear token of anti-Semitism. The symptom can be more or less serious according to the case at hand, according to the context, the rhetorical or political scene. Each time, one must ask oneself "Who's saying what?" in what situation and with what status. The same expression does not signify or produce the same thing when it comes from the mouth of the president of the Republic as it does when a Jew tells a Jewish joke.

An anecdote: Some time ago, someone I didn't know called me on the telephone. From the Centre de Documentation Juive [Center for Jewish Documentation]: "My son is writing a thesis on Israel at the Sorbonne. He heard that you were in Tel Aviv two years ago and that you gave a 'speech' which the Israeli press reported on. He would like to get a copy." I didn't give a lecture in Tel Aviv, I told her; rather I spoke, in front of a large audience and as part of a discussion, about what I thought of the situation and the political stakes, and notably what I disapproved of in Israeli politics. I did so carefully, politely, I believe, but frankly and firmly. Since I had no legible trace of this improvisation, aside from a brief introduction, I told my interlocutor that if her son was interested in what I think of Israel, he could find what he's looking for in certain texts of mine. In general, I added, although the conditions of the foundation of the state of Israel remain for me a tangled knot of painful questions that I could not possibly address over the phone (and even if it is considered a given that every state, that every foundation itself is founded in violence, and is by definition unable to justify itself), I have a great many reasons to believe that it is *for the best*, all things considered, and in the interests of the greatest number of people, including the Palestinians, including the other states in the region, to consider this foundation, despite its originary violence, as henceforth irreversible—on the condition that neighborly relations be established *either* with a Palestinian state endowed with *all* its rights, in the fullest sense of the term "state" (at least insofar as anything remains of this full sense and of sovereignty in general; another very serious question I must leave aside for now while briefly relating, in an interview, a telephone interview), *or*, at the center of the same "sovereign" and binational "state," with a Palestinian people freed from all oppression or from all intolerable segregation. I have no particular hostility in principle toward the state of Israel, but I have almost always judged quite harshly the policies of the Israeli governments in relation to the Palestinians. I have often said so publicly, in particular in Jerusalem, for example, in a lecture I gave quite a long time ago, which was published in more than one language, during the period when one spoke of "occupied territories,"[15] etc. After a few more sentences along these lines, I heard on the other end of the line: "I see. Well, that's what I suspected."

I don't know what she concluded from this, but I immediately added, more or less: "You no doubt know that I am Jewish; I can feel a deep compassion, even a certain solidarity with the inhabitants of this region and with the historical victims (Jewish and Palestinian) of the atrocities of these times. But I insist on having the right to criticize all the governmental policies, including those of the great powers, dating from before and ever since the foundation of the state of Israel. I do not believe I am giving in to any anti-Semitism by saying this, and, as I have written elsewhere, I even dare to be more faithful than ever to a heritage, a demand for justice that some, rightly or wrongly, do not hesitate to consider essentially Jewish. But I have explained myself in this regard elsewhere and I cannot here address these tremendous problems, neither in depth nor very directly."

E.R.: Listening to you it occurs to me that in my childhood certain people on my mother's side of the family, descended from the haute bourgeoisie referred to as "Israelite" or (on my father's side) as "protestant," used to say of the recent immigrants from Eastern Europe: "There are Jews and there are *métèques*."[16] They saw themselves as "Israelite" (or "noble") Jews; they often belonged to the reform movement, and spoke of the eastern Jews as "*métèques*," including them in a subcategory of Jews. And I often had the feeling that my father, an eastern Ashkenazi Jew who immigrated from Rumania, suffered from this to the point of wanting to conceal his own Jewishness. He always said that "it's a misfortune to be Jewish," and that, above all, I shouldn't "marry a Jew." He himself ended up thinking, particularly after the Shoah, that Jews should absolutely assimilate and not be Jewish anymore. It's an instance of the famous "Jewish self-hatred."[17]

This assimilationism went hand in hand with the concern for telling the whole truth of the Shoah. When I was a child I was constantly being told about the gas chambers and the horrors of Nazism. I learned very early of all the details of the extermination, from which, with one exception, all the members of my family had escaped. Gaullist and anti-Pétain from the very first, they were all resisters (actively or passively) and were therefore very wary of the dangers of deportation. Seeing themselves less as Jews than as assimilated republicans, they refused to wear the yellow star, a mark of infamy, and had recourse to false certificates of baptism. But by the same token, Jewish self-hatred was exacerbated after the war. It was better not to be Jewish, *never again* to be Jewish, since the extermination could always begin again, since hatred for the Jew was eternal, interminable. So I was baptized—a *true* baptism—and was raised in the *true* Catholic religion, whereas my father was an atheist and my mother staunchly anticlerical. It was after going into psychoanalysis that she was later able to answer my numerous questions, and it's thanks to her, no doubt—and thanks to psychoanalysis—that I came to understand what a strange kind of Jewishness I had inherited. As for my father, what I owe him is not the assimilation he so desired for me, but a true taste for Italy, for painting and for art in general, which the Catholic religion was able to cultivate for centuries.

J.D.: It is said that there's nothing more Jewish than self-hatred, nothing more "exemplarily" Jewish; but most often it's a Jew who says it. As always, the logic of exemplarity leads these arguments into an abyss: if nothing is more Jewish than self-hatred, whoever hates himself begins to resemble a Jew, and this figurality undermines the entire question. If you will allow me to recall this again, I have always stubbornly pursued—and, to this end, formalized—the logic and the rhetoric of exemplarity,[18] with all the political stakes it implies.

E.R.: I fear that the anti-Semitism to come will be along these lines. We risk witnessing, against the tragic background of the Shoah, disputes *among* Jews who revert to the vocabulary of hatred for the other in order to feed their quarrels, thus giving great pleasure to the true anti-Semites. Recently, Esther Benbassa, the chair of the history of modern Judaism at the Ecole Pratique des Hautes Etudes, was accused by a journalist of supporting, *as a Sephardic Jew,* the positions of Renaud Camus and the fundamentalist rabbi Ovadia Yosef.[19] She had raised some of the questions we're discussing here.[20] Her positions were debatable—and I don't happen to share them—but they were not discussed by the journalist, who simply launched into a brutal attack.

As you know, in France, contrary to what happens in the United States, it is forbidden to distribute anti-Semitic or racist texts, even as documents framed by scholarly commentaries. One could nevertheless imagine that it might be possible to publish *La France juive,* by Edouard Drumont,[21] or the anti-Semitic pamphlets of Louis-Ferdinand Céline, in a precise context, with a critical commentary. This hasn't been done, but I am not opposed to it in principle; although I can understand that a publisher might prefer not to.

What is in any case punishable, and rightly so, under the law of 1972[22]—with which editors and authors are obliged to comply—is the publication of *current* writings that are overtly anti-Semitic or racist, or of *older* writings of an overtly anti-Semitic or racist character. If the older writings are published without comment, or with commentaries that are themselves anti-Semitic, the law is applicable to them. But it goes without saying that, if it is a matter of a critical edition, the judge will not rule against it, since in that case we are not dealing with an incitement to racial hatred.

In addition, there are all sorts of *older* writings in the French literary corpus that, without being overtly or exclusively anti-Semitic, are punctuated with passages that are anti-Semitic, racist, xenophobic, misogynist, homophobic, etc. I'm thinking in particular of Gide's *Journals,* also those of the Goncourt brothers, as well as the writings of Léon Bloy, and many others besides. Are we going to expurgate them in the name of a retroactive and "politically correct"[23] censorship, as certain defenders of Renaud

Camus actually feared? Certainly not. Brandishing such a threat amounts to masking the problem we have to face today: the *current* anti-Semitic authors, those who are publishing *here and now*, are using denial, derision, sometimes even critical introspection to get their anti-Semitic message across.

J.D.: When they call for "racial hatred," can these writings be published at the author's expense, without the mediation, and therefore without the agreement, of a publisher?

E.R.: Nothing forbids it, but the law of 1972 would still apply.

J.D.: Do you think that it should be allowed?

E.R.: No, of course not. In France, the public manifestation of racism and anti-Semitism is, if not prohibited, at least punishable under the law as an offense justifying criminal prosecution. But, I repeat, today we are confronted with something else, namely with the manifestation of an unconscious, masked, distorted anti-Semitism, which pertains neither to the law nor to conscious responsibility.

J.D.: Once again, we have to take into account (in order to work on it endlessly) this massive fact: the law in general, and penal law and criminology in particular, have not yet integrated the mere *possibility* of something like psychoanalysis. Freudian "concepts" do not have even the slightest tangential relation to them.[24] I say *possibility*, and I will leave "concepts" in quotes, for such perilous, uncertain, unforeseeable work remains to be done on the side of psychoanalysis, in the direction of the very axiomatics of European law.

When faced with explicit and violent anti-Semitic statements, one assumes that their author had the conscious intention, the explicit will to express them as such: he knew what he meant to say, he said it freely, he is therefore responsible for it, and we have the right to punish him. But there are some who will claim that he didn't quite mean that—not that exactly—that in truth he intended, in a rhetorical or literary space whose status remains uncertain, to make something else manifest, etc. And that, besides, every manifestation of anti-Semitism, racism, cruelty in general, remains a symptom. Now, what is a symptom? Can one judge a symptom?

Or summon it before the law? You know that traces of anti-Semitism can be detected in discourses in which Jews are not even mentioned. So does one have the right to judge a symptom? How can a symptom be related to a subject? How can it be attributed, as a predicate, to a subject of the law?

E.R.: In law, a subject under the sway of such a symptom cannot be judged guilty. In this case, the only weapons are critique and vigilance.

J.D.: There is a point at which the question of guilt goes beyond the juridical space. Even if one authorized oneself to judge someone guilty (from a moral or political point of view), would one have the right to prosecute before the law a person who presents only "symptoms" of racism? I doubt it. And as long as we have not rigorously delimited—and we're nowhere near doing so—this concept of symptom (and, correlatively, that of the act or the passage to the act), well, the axioms of penal law will remain crude and primitive, whatever their apparent refinement or "technical" sophistication in other respects. They may well one day resemble human artifacts that are as "prehistoric" as stone-cut axes (with which one could of course do amazing things, but they can't be compared, for example, to laser surgery, microprocessors, or cellular telephones).

For Freud, the death drive, the destruction drive, the originary "cruelty" of "sadism" or "masochism" cannot be uprooted. He himself has a few difficulties logically drawing the ethical or political consequences from this, in relation to what he calls culture or civilization.[25] He does and does not believe that progress has been made. I see him as a man of the Enlightenment who could never believe in it, in the Enlightenment. His discourse on this subject has always seemed to me unstable and equivocal. Perhaps it cannot be otherwise. We will speak of this again no doubt. But if one does not wish to abandon oneself passively to this confusion (for example, under the pretext that this aggression and this hatred of the other, even of the other in oneself, cannot be eradicated), then it is necessary both to rethink our legacies and to "start from zero"—both in terms of psychoanalysis and in terms of the law, morals, and politics. If we call this "deconstruction," we must not look to it for "theses" or ready-made answers. Here, the future-to-come cannot be reduced. And that is the sign that these tasks remain very "historical"—in a sense of this word that must undergo the same reelaboration.

Beyond or on this side of any "theses," foreign to propositions and positions, not only is the "it is necessary [*il faut*]" of these tasks and of this future announced, it comes upon us, it comes to impose itself on us *unconditionally*. That is the first event. Beginning from this unconditional, I try to *think thought*, that is, the experience of the condition, of the conditionality, the ex-posure of a limit, the exposure *to* a limit—however unstable and difficult to determine it may be—between the conditional and the unconditional, which I would like to distinguish from the sovereignty of any subject at all, whether God, the prince, the monarch, or the people, as well as from all power, performative power, for example (I have dealt with this question elsewhere).[26]

I therefore have no *thesis*, properly speaking, to propose. Only a belief, perhaps a naive one: I would like to be able to carry out, modestly, the critical or deconstructive analysis of what doesn't work and "isn't going well [*ne va pas*]," of what should *come* and remain to be thought, remain to be done—a distinction (thinking and/or doing) that I don't much believe in, either, but I would need some time to enter into this problem.

For example, in the case we have been speaking of[27] (in itself a minor case, but a very serious one in terms of what it reveals of a certain state of French, and even European, culture and public space), what "isn't going well" and never goes well is a certain relation between justice and law. It is necessary, certainly, to *fight* against whatever any such awful book is a sign of; we must do everything to oppose it *publicly* and to *justify* our opposition: by speaking, writing, analyzing, arguing, protesting, by *giving demonstrations*, and aiming well. But aiming at what? Well, for example: at all the familiar tics of vulgar anti-Semitism or of the "Old France" style xenophobia, the antiquated literary staleness, too, as well as the deep lack of culture and the social, or even "sociological," foolishness of someone who strikes pompous attitudes without ever having opened his eyes to the very tradition he vaunts or to the codes that have programmed him for so long, like a child's toy. But especially, since the book and its author seem to me to deserve less vigilant attention than the "reception" they received, we would have to ask ourselves what is happening in our public space when a publisher and a certain number of "intellectuals" close their eyes to such hideous and grotesque sentences, or even rush to the rescue of a book or an author whom they quite obviously did not *read*, did not *know how* to read, were *unable* to read, or did not *want* to read (four often inextricable possibilities, in such cases, and the analysis would have to begin from there).

That said, to face this rising tide, publicly, does not mean prohibiting a publication. I understand what, in certain situations, could have motivated the Gayssot law;[28] but to prohibit a publication seems to me unjustifiable. On principle, but also by virtue of the perverse effects that such a measure always risks producing, especially at a time when the technical transformation of public space would render it more ineffectual than ever.

In addition, beyond this struggle, which I judge to be necessary outside of all juridical recourse, I would be prepared to "condemn" Renaud Camus (whose work and person, I have to admit, interest me very little) only if I were sure that, as we say, he knew what he was doing, that he understood his own heritage, that he knew history, the history of his own country, the history of literature, of anti-Semitism, of anti-Semitism in French literature, etc., and therefore that he meant, "freely" and in all conscience, what he said and placed on the market. But the least I can say is that I'm not certain about this. I believe that he was a shrewd and calculating character but also, as is almost always the case, that he was naive, with very little experience—let us say, to abbreviate—in self-analysis. At least in any analysis of his social unconscious. We are again navigating through the same zones: penal law, criminology, and psychoanalysis—everything remains to be reinvented.

E.R.: I would tend rather to refuse to introduce the dimension of the unconscious into juridical discourse. In principle, someone is judged only for his acts, and, within the domain of criminal justice, if a criminal has no consciousness of his act, his case is referred to psychiatric discourse. As for the law of 1972, I think it is satisfactory, precisely to the extent that it resolves the problem you are posing. It makes it possible in effect not to have to prohibit a publication, and not to have to withdraw it from sale afterward, since it forces any author who is consciously or unconsciously anti-Semitic to limit the manifestation of his symptoms, whenever it is a matter of public and written expression. In other words, it is the author who must submit himself to the law in order to prevent the publisher (the author at that point being only his accomplice) from being prosecuted in court. Besides that, when an author signs a contract, he makes a de facto commitment to respect the law of 1972. And in the case we're discussing, the publisher should have insisted that the author honor his signature. But it was still necessary to be able to discern the traces of anti-Semitism and racism enunciated in this disavowed form.

This limit imposed by the law has nothing to do with the kind of censorship that exists in dictatorial or fundamentalist regimes, in which the writer risks losing his life or going to prison for refusing to bow to arbitrary edicts. The existence of the law, and obedience to the law as a limit imposed on *jouissance*, seem to me the opposite of a code of censorship.

For twenty years now I have reflected on this relation between law and writing. In my work as a historian, I myself confronted the necessity of internalizing the law, since I was dealing with the contemporary period and there could be no question of defaming or insulting anyone, nor of attacking the memory of the dead or the privacy of the living, etc. And yet it was unthinkable for me to remain silent about certain important events, for the sake of a pious history or in order to obey excessive injunctions. It was therefore necessary for me to find the proper words and to present a narration rich enough to convey the meanness, the passions, the heroism, the abjection, or the daily lives of the actors in the history: neither to destroy nor to belittle, neither to idealize nor to lie, nor to say everything and "tell all." There is a certain balance to strike, and the only way to arrive at this balance is to give a narrative status to the history one is recounting: a history that is not a fiction but that is recounted like a fiction, using the means of novelistic writing.

Following a similar line of thought, I tend to think that the more anti-Semitic a piece of writing is, the weaker it is from a literary point of view.[29] No doubt because it tends to retreat into itself and to become the expression of a simplistic, enclosed ideology, and in any case the opposite of what I see as the essence of literature: a polysemic textuality, subject to a multitude of possible interpretations and readings. You have shown this, you who are a great reader of contemporary literature, notably Artaud, Bataille, Paul Celan, Jean Genet, Francis Ponge, James Joyce, Philippe Sollers, Hélène Cixous, and Michel Deguy.[30]

Thus, contrary to what one sometimes hears, I find that in his pamphlets[31] Céline dissolves the power of his style, this style that makes *Journey to the End of the Night*[32] so powerful. Instead, he becomes merely the compulsive and delirious spokesman of an incantatory style reduced to the rhetoric of a simpleminded ideology.

J.D.: To oblige the author, as you say, to "limit the manifestation of his symptoms," in their public exposure—I don't know how far I can follow you there. For here again we encounter the question that we were unable, precisely, to delimit: What is a symptom? And what are the borders of public space? Literature, if such a thing exists in all purity, like the "fine arts"—isn't literature something that displaces the very status of these concepts, affecting them with an irreducible novelty? Wherever there is *some* literature, if there is any, the concept of public space finds itself transformed, just as it is transformed today by the "new technologies" of communication and reproduction (and remember: printing was one of these "new technologies"; literature, the literature I'm speaking of, *stricto sensu*, did not exist before printing).

How is it possible to answer for literature? For responsibility in literature? For this new institution that is called literature? Unique in its kind, this institution does not respond in principle, in spirit, or according to the letter, before any other institution. It has been granted, in principle, an absolute candor, an absolute freedom. A paradox: this liberation makes it resemble an institution that, for the essential part of its *acts* (*public writing*, if not the apparatuses and the modalities of publication), is an-institutional, almost wild and unconditional. It falls under no positive law. What this means is not irresponsibility but rather a mutation in the concept of responsibility.

This ethical and political mutation, rather than making the writer irresponsible, should increase the responsibility of literature. It is *as if* the invention of literature caused a change in the ground of responsibility, precisely by using—to the point of deliberate abuse—and by violating the modality of the *as if* (and this is a *jouissance* that demands its right, even imposes its authorization, its becoming-licit), also by inventing a new element for it, perhaps by revealing its infinity. I always associate this infinity, or rather this endless opening up to the historicity of the political, with a certain concept of *democracy to come*.

There is no doubt a synchrony, a systemic link in the history of the West, between democracy, the principled right to say everything in the public sphere, on the one hand, and the possibility of literature on the other. In principle, as soon as there is literature, one should have the right to *say everything* (or the right also *not* to say everything). Or to be more precise: one should be able to *publish* everything (there is no private literature), to manifest everything in the public space, in conformity with the very status of literature as it is defined in Europe, its unique place of origin. But this definition is the source of the extreme difficulty of the matter (concerning which I have long debated with myself and others),[33] for it determines not an *essence* (a being-literary of literature, a literarity) but a *func-*

tion subject to interpretations and conventions (historic, ethico-juridical, etc.). Hence the difficulty of treating enunciations according to whether they claim, legitimately or not, to belong—functionally and pragmatically—to something like "literature," which is not a thing but an *address*, a certain *mode of address*. This claim is the act of literature itself. It pretends to engender its own norms; it tends to legitimate itself by itself. Thus producing right, *its* right, it has no intention of answering any summons to appear before any existing law, at least not as a literary work. It recognizes in advance no statutory juridical competence or presumed competence.

Does one always make "bad literature" with "bad sentiments"? I am less certain of this than you are. It is necessary to judge according to each piece, each work. And without ever hesitating, in the experience of thought, before the abyss of good and evil, even before the beyond of good and evil (which is perhaps the only "country" of literature). Inversely, of course, it does not suffice, as certain people have tended to think, to put one's faith in "bad sentiments" and to play cheaply at transgression, anticonformism, the conformism of anticonformism (and vice versa), in evil, the diabolical, etc., in order to be interesting and to accede to "literature." By virtue of its public space, its essential *publicity*, literature is always stalked by the gesticulations of the media. What is true of the politician is also true of the writer. More than ever.

We might well be troubled, both of us, and become indignant regarding a certain publication. Protected by an "as if" covered by some ethics of literature, or even by an incontestable right of literature, such a publication is authorized to *propagate* a language with which we are familiar and whose most probable consequences and premises are in our eyes the worst. Uncultured or not, such a "literature" *inculcates* and *flatters*, it *corresponds to* an ideology that we judge to be harmful and that we fight against—racism or anti-Semitism, for example. But here, too, it is better, I believe, not to prohibit. It is better to reply (at times with the disdain it deserves, with silence, depending on the context and the real danger) or to counterattack, to analyze, to discuss, to evaluate, to critique, to be ironic.

In fact, it's true, literature has always been subjected to some kind of censorship. The modalities of this censorship are extraordinarily various: censorship by others, self-censorship, censorship by order of the Church, the state, civil society, the market, the media market, that is, again, "civil society," etc. These modalities are constantly evolving; their limits remain at bottom indeterminable. That is a *fact*. But *also*, in principle, there

thing publicly supposes an essential link between the democratic principle and the literary principle, I do not want to reduce one to the other. The subject of law, the author as citizen, is not a mere novelistic fiction. Democracy is not a literary phenomenon, nor is it merely a "Republic of Letters." But, despite being rigorously distinct, the two phenomena, each one in its place and in its way, according to original modalities, come to determine certain common *possibilities*:

1. On the one hand, an open historicity. Literature is historic through and through; it has acts, birthplaces, traditions, legacies. And democracy is the only "regime" that, welcoming *on principle* its own critique and recognizing its indefinite perfectibility, defines itself by *promising itself*—by and in its historicity, by and according to its very *future-to-come*.

2. On the other hand, still in a historical fashion, the performative legitimation of a fiction—its legitimation *as* fiction, together with the institution of a constitutional state, and, for example, of a right to say everything publicly—depends on a power of fiction, and on a credit granted to some kind of fictionality. Montaigne and Pascal knew how to think and to articulate this deep connection between right and fiction.[34]

E.R.: You touched on this problem in 1993 in "Passions": "Literature," you write, "is a modern invention, inscribed within conventions and institutions which, to hold on to just this trait, secure in principle its *right to say everything*. Literature thus ties its destiny to a certain non-censorship, to the space of democratic freedom (freedom of the press, freedom of speech, etc.). No democracy without literature; no literature without democracy."[35] I would mention in passing that this statement is also true for psychoanalysis.[36]

J.D.: If a literary work, as such, always belongs to the public sphere, then the border between literature and non-literature remains unstable by nature. The same enunciation can, in one context, be inscribed under the rubric of literature, and, in another context, under that of non-literature. No *internal* analysis can allow one to say whether a particular enunciation (an anti-Semitic one, for example) belongs to literature—thus leaving its "author" in the clear—or to ideological journalism, to political rhetoric, to an electoral campaign, etc., in which case it would then be punishable under the French laws in force.

In each case, it is necessary to analyze the context defined by the law,

and it is *in fact* up to a juridical authority, ultimately, to make a pro-
nouncement: this is a literary work, and this is not. Now, in its corpus and
in its norms, the currently existing law seems more incompetent than ever
in dealing with these questions (and I maintain that, by definition, it always has been incompetent on this subject—I'm speaking of the law, not
of the jurists). Among other reasons, this is a result of new technical and
techno-capitalist powers: all enunciations are affected by the enlargement
and the accelerated differentiation of places, but also of sites of production
and distribution. Who will decide whether some enunciation on the Web
is a literary work or a tract? Lawmakers will have more and more difficulty
in deciding what is a literary fiction, a murderous tract, or a morbid artifact. This is all the more true in that many manuscripts turned down by
publishers will in the future be published on the Internet. Only very subtle, and always debatable, analyses will allow for a reelaboration of the entire field of the public sphere of publishing and of the law.

Literature is a very recent invention, which immediately became, of
itself, by itself, threatened with death. It thinks itself, it thinks its own possibility, it repeats its birth beginning from its end, from a finitude that is
not before it but within it as its resource and also as its essential specter.
Blanchot is no doubt the one who, closest to us, has given the greatest rigor
to the thought, as well as to the chance, of this unheard-of experience.[37]

E.R.: To come back to the right to *say everything*—including publishing anti-Semitic writings today and tomorrow—I have the feeling that
the organized Far Right weighed so heavily on political life that it was impossible, particularly in certain "intellectual" circles, to give free rein to the
good old French anti-Semitism of the pre-Nazi period. The risk of being
situated within these Far Right tendencies was too great then. A party "unlike all the others" took charge, in a certain way, of an entire society's conscious or unconscious hatred of the Jews. But things have changed now,
and we must henceforth be attentive to the insidious and dangerous forms
of this "respectable" and even "refined" and "chic" anti-Semitism, if only
because we know now that it led in the end to the final solution.

J.D.: Although the return of anti-Semitism always reproduces the
same imperturbable logic, it has to invent new figures. Its resources are essentially inexhaustible. Anti-Semitism thus always maintains, like democracy, a certain future-to-come. Democracy, a certain interpretation of

democracy, often actually provides it with a paradoxical "soil," and with "pretexts" that are often difficult to discredit. I am thinking of the support that Noam Chomsky has given, if not exactly to Robert Faurisson,[38] at least to his right to public expression. Chomsky acted in the name of freedom of speech and the first amendment of the United States Constitution (the right to freedom of expression). Using the principle of the Constitution as a pretext for letting the unacceptable pass—that is what is worrisome, as a paradox or a perversity. But one must not give ground on either of the two injunctions, precisely when they seem to be contradictory. There is no decision and no responsibility worthy of the name except in the endurance of a double bind,[39] when one *does not know* in advance, when no previous knowledge can guarantee or program in a continuous fashion, without some kind of leap, the choice between two injunctions each of which is as imperative and legitimate as the other. This terrible law, which is the law itself, the law of the law, gives responsibility and decision—if there are any—whatever chance they may have, but leaves no chance for a good conscience. No one can ever *know*, no one can ever be sure, in a theoretical and determinative judgment, that a responsible decision was made and that it will have been the best.

Today it is of great urgency at least to save a certain number of principles—the right to debate, the right to discussion, non-censorship—and nevertheless the possibility of combating, limiting, denouncing what, under this guise, allows anti-Semitic temptations to pass through. This is very difficult. Don't forget, for example, that Chomsky would never have accepted anyone's saying of him that he was defending Faurisson. In his eyes, he was defending the right to speak.

E.R.: Must we, in the name of freedom, lead a campaign in favor of a Holocaust denier, whose writings are in fact so delirious that they have aroused considerable interest? One can never sufficiently stress that the more the truth is falsified, the greater the lie becomes, and that the more the imposture is obvious, the more chances it has of finding followers. Hallucination, denial, paranoia, everything, in short, that characterizes Holocaust denial as an extreme expression of anti-Semitism can become perfectly acceptable, much more easily even than rational knowledge. If this weren't the case, such discourses would not inspire such extravagant transference and would not have such a ready audience.

More generally, I find it very perverse that someone would be mobilized, in the name of freedom of expression, to support not only Faurisson, for example, but also any "ordinary" anti-Semitic author, a good Frenchman, well protected by the law in a democratic society like our own, and not oppressed by any danger, except that of being criticized by the press or by other authors. I have no compassion for this type of "nonconformist" character. They benefit from all the privileges granted them by a democracy. Why should we feel sorry for them?

Finally, I wonder what unconscious reason there could be for a Jewish intellectual like Chomsky—a leftist, a civil libertarian hostile to anti-Semitism, a specialist in cognitive rationality, an enemy of what he calls the irrational, and a staunch opponent of Freudian theories—to adopt such a position.

J.D.: One hypothesis: the difference between us, as European intellectuals, and Chomsky (whose personal history and experience should also be taken into account) is in part the difference between Europe and the United States. There is of course the weight of the customs of his country and of its Constitution, but there is also the fact that for Chomsky, the Shoah—an event that is first of all and in many respects European—does not represent what it represents to us. Far from the real situation of French or European public space (but distance is not always a bad thing, in this case), he invoked a principle that, in itself, is unassailable. All this seems respectable to me.

I believe that, regarding the way in which this principle is then invoked, put to work, and regarding the connotations, the alliances or the objective complicities to which they give rise, it is a question of the context, as one says, of places and customs. That is where the most difficult discussions begin, even if it is within the same "camp" and among people of good faith who share the same convictions. In the combats he wages, in particular against the perversions or the hypocrisies of American democracy, Chomsky is a "radical" in the American sense. Any limitation of the right to speak worries him, and first of all in the "context" he has to confront as his own.

Why should we prohibit Faurisson? It's a difficult question for me, too, I won't hide this from you. I know that it is necessary not to risk publicly legitimating the propagation of a negationist discourse or one "calling for racial hatred." But it is imperative that we allow anyone whatever to speak. And to write, in the public sphere, and to seek to reach an addressee. I confess my embarrassment. It is necessary simultaneously to respect freedom and not to provoke martyrological groupings of people who feel censored and who therefore might with good reason denounce the democratic society in which they live. I confess that the principle and the workings of the Gayssot law[40] leave me ill at ease.

It's true that in the United States, because of this supposed freedom of speech and expression, Nazi groups have the right to manifest themselves as such, and to demonstrate. But there are also other ways of fighting. I recently saw an extraordinary American film called *Mr. Death.*[41] A man, often shown in hideous close-up, testifies. He was the industrial promoter of lethal injection. In the name of "humanitarian" principles, he claims to have spoken out against the electric chair, against hanging, against the gas chamber. He promoted lethal injection, which he presents as a more humane method of ending a life, somewhat as Dr. Guillotin did for his machine. Behind all this there is the history of the death penalty in the United States since 1972.[42]

This odd character raises the question of the gas chamber, at first, as a mode of capital execution used by certain American states, and he goes on from there, quite naturally, to speak of gas chambers elsewhere in the world, and therefore at Auschwitz. He asks: "Were there really gas chambers? Is it true?" So he goes to Auschwitz to "conduct a personal investigation." Calling himself an "engineer," he takes some rock samples, goes to a laboratory, and concludes that none of it happened, that the examination of the rocks proves it. So he becomes a Holocaust denier after being a champion of lethal injection. Lauded as a hero by all the negationist groups of the United States, Canada, and the United Kingdom, he gives all sorts of lectures to explain that he went through scientific verifications and is therefore in a position to affirm: the gas chambers did not exist.

However, this man ended up being condemned in certain northeastern states for what he was saying. He was deprived of work; his engineering degree was questioned; and in any case it was obvious that he wasn't really an engineer. He defended himself by claiming that in the United States "only ten out of a hundred so-called engineers have a degree." That's how the negationist discourse is penalized in the United States. I am also thinking of another character whose group I came into contact with, since over there I am sometimes the target of extreme right-wing groups.

The representatives of Lyndon Larouche, a sort of American neo-Nazi, wrote a pamphlet against me that was widely distributed, notably in the universities where I teach. During a conference being held on my work, in New York, a militant from his group violently intervened and was about to attack me; he was on the verge of physical violence.

E.R.: Of what did they accuse you?

J.D.: Of being a Marxist, a destroyer, a nihilist, an enemy of the people, I don't know what all. And I am one of their *bêtes noires*. Well, this Larouche was prosecuted not for his political discourse (discourses are not actionable in court) but rather, like Al Capone, I think, for tax fraud. So he was prosecuted for something other than his writings, and I believe he is still in prison. As for Mr. Death, he says that he lost his job. He had agreed to appear before the camera to calmly recount his story in all good conscience. But he fell into the filmmaker's "trap." The question is therefore whether Mr. Death is out of work because he didn't have an engineering degree or because he became, publicly, a Holocaust denier. In any case, nothing is more damning for him than his own filmed testimony. That is still the best weapon.

E.R.: Faurisson is also a fraud in his own way. A fraud who thinks that *others* are frauds. Before becoming a Holocaust denier, he published "literary" studies showing that the works of Rimbaud, Nerval, and Lautréamont were not written by their authors.[43] At that time he said that he was a specialist in the search for "meaning and misinterpretation, the true and the false," and in the "critique of texts and documents."

In the case of Mr. Death, there is a link—which Lanzmann clearly identified in his film—between "killing with clean solutions" (lethal injection) and the methods of mass extermination used by the Nazis. They, too, put into place a "clean solution," if I can put it that way. With the gas chambers and the crematoria, all trace of the living was effaced, in an industrial process and with no apparent massacre. To kill, in such conditions, is to wipe out the trace both of the murder and of the living. With lethal injection, the ritual of capital execution disappears. Not only is there no torture, but there is no longer even a killing machine: no guillotine, no gallows or noose, no firing squad. It's the degree zero of execution, and the most horrible symbolically because it makes it possible to reduce legal murder to an almost natural act, to something resembling the ordinary end of a life, a palliative treatment.

It's a matter, then, of a death penalty administered as a negation of it-self, as an attempt to efface the shame of wanting to accept its continued use. Without comparing lethal injection to the extermination of the Jews, nevertheless it is necessary to remember how certain Nazis, and especially certain of those directly responsible for the extermination (Eichmann, for example), were afraid of blood, violence, and murderous acts: no blood, no torture, no visibility of death, etc.

J.D.: It is indeed a negation, a disavowal of death, a way of denying death while imposing it, or of whitewashing the act of killing, with the help of an anonymous machine: here, too, lethal injection, purification, if I may say, the purifying neutralization of the death penalty, consists in making sure that there is nothing visible: no blood, no suffering (suppos-edly!). However, if you look closely, lethal injection is something truly ter-rifying. What is called for here is a history of blood, and of the economy of blood, of the sacrificial theatricality channeled through it; we are working on this in the seminar I am conducting on the death penalty.[44] Everything was accelerated with the guillotine: "A slightly cold feeling in the neck," said Guillotin.[45] One abandons the ax-wielding executioner for a machine that works by itself.

I want to return to the difficulty of thinking the question of Holo-caust denial in the United States—where, as you know, the debates devel-oped for the most part over the last ten years, for better or worse. One of the worst things (I say one of the worst, but it's not the worst), I think, is the properly terrorist or perverse attitude of those who are quick to throw around the accusation of denial. They use it like a projectile, launching it against anyone who poses a critical, methodological, epistemological ques-tion—and especially one in the style of "deconstruction"!—concerning the establishment and interpretation of historical facts, the archive, or, more generally, history and the value of truth, etc. I expressed some worry over this already in *Specters of Marx*,[46] where I gave a few examples, but the dan-ger remains more threatening than ever. Here, too, this strictly obscuran-tist attack must be vigorously resisted.

That said, as for the "legal" barriers to be raised against "negationist" discourses or propaganda, I confess that I do not "know." I do not know if there is a "measure" to be taken, or what the "good measure" is. Here, too, it depends on the situation, and this can be said without any relativism. In a period of security and peace, when the danger is not massive and immi-nent, but perhaps also somewhere beyond, I believe it is necessary to allow people to express themselves, to discuss, to contradict, to present proof. Similarly with the death penalty. If it was abolished in Europe, it was not only for reasons of principle; it was also because the state of European society is such that people don't believe they need it any more. Its dissuasive effect is not indispensable. But if some serious social upheavals were to return, that would be enough for certain people to consider reinstating it. This touches on the immense question of the principles on which abolitionism is founded. As long as an abolitionist discourse has not been elaborated and effectively accredited (and this has not yet been done) at the level of unconditional principles, beyond the problems of purpose, exemplarity, utility, and even the "right to life," we will not be shielded from a return of the death penalty.

E.R.: I am among those who think that this is not possible. The abolition is inscribed into European law. It has become, in a way, *outside the law*, out of the reach of the law, since it falls under a higher order, that of international treaties.

J.D.: Certainly, unless a situation verging on civil war were to arise. In France, the Parliament voted for abolition in 1981 with a majority that included parliamentarians on the Right. But even today, if the question were submitted to a referendum, the death penalty would perhaps be reinstated. In terms of public opinion, a majority wanted and perhaps still wants the death penalty; it was in a sort of divorce between the Parliament and public opinion that it managed to be abolished. If a situation of great civic and political turbulence were created, the principle of abolition could be called back into question. There are enough people for this, and the majority would make itself heard. The history of this problem is immense and complex: how to abolish the death penalty in a way that is based on principle, that is universal and unconditional, and not because it has become not only cruel but useless, insufficiently exemplary?

E.R.: Before addressing this question directly, I would like to come back to anti-Semitism and the Shoah; I would like to know what you think of the famous injunction laid down by Adorno and taken up in various ways, according to which one can "no longer write poetry after Auschwitz"?[47] It always seemed to me very debatable, very much open to question.

J.D.: It seems to me impossible and unacceptable. Not only can one write, which is a fact, but perhaps one must write. Not in order to "integrate" the Shoah, not in order to undertake or to finish "mourning" it, to watch over it, or to cultivate its memory, but to give a *just* thought to what happened there, which remains without a name and without a concept, unique like other unique tragedies (and for which, as I suggested before, the Greek name *tragedy* still risks being inadequate—it is still too Greek, and it also names an art of the theater).

What I call a *just* thought is a thought that attempts, beginning from there, from this singularity without a norm and without a concept, to approach something like justice. A justice to be invented. How to watch over something that one can, however, neither watch over, nor assimilate, nor internalize, nor categorize? This is the paradox of fidelity to the other: to take into oneself, to watch over, to welcome the wholly other without this wholly other dissolving or being identified with the same in the same. To begin again to think, after Auschwitz, *to begin* to write otherwise rather than no longer to write, which would be absurd and would risk the worst betrayal. At any rate, in both cases it is impossible—the Impossible. Affected by what happened there, affected without even having decided to *let* ourselves be affected, we *testify* to what we can neither forget nor recall. Why should literature, fiction, poetry, philosophy disappear? It is even more difficult to see why this *testimony* would have the force of a verdict or a death sentence: end of history, end of art, end of literature or of philosophy, silence. A "voice of sheer silence,"[48] if I hear correctly, seems to enjoin us, on the contrary, to begin again wholly otherwise.

should not be any censorship of writings that come forth under the name of literary fiction. It is at the "moment" when an enunciation is presented with a status different from that of literature that one can envision judging it, forbidding it, or sanctioning it. This moment is always difficult to "grasp."

E.R.: In the case that interests us here, the author and those who defended him invoked this right to say everything because it was a question of a particular literary genre: the diary. But the diary is not exactly literary fiction, since the persons one speaks of and makes speak are not characters but real people, and therefore subjects of the law who can themselves invoke a right—to the protection of their privacy, for example—or who can file suit against these racist, anti-Semitic, defamatory (etc.) statements.

J.D.: Yes, but what is a diary when it has been published? At what moment, under what conditions, can a diary be part of a literary corpus? Is it enough for it to be signed by someone who is recognized by certain people as having the status of a writer? The ambiguity is deepened when this diary purports to exceed the boundaries of fiction and proceeds to designate real people, to evaluate social or political events, even to propose authoritarian measures (for example, a different "ethnic" mixture in the makeup of a team of journalists working for a national public radio station).

So the great question remains that of responsibility. In principle, of course, an author of fiction or a poet is *responsible* before the law since he signs a contract with a publisher and commits himself to a certain number of rules. He is responsible, as is the publisher, for the *fact* of publishing, but he is not responsible, at least not in the same way, for *what* he publishes, for the literary content—fictional, novelistic, or poetic (at least if we can *decide* on this literary fictionality or leave undecidable the relation between literature and its other). In a fictional world, a narrator, the character in a novel or a theatrical work, can say anything at all. The civil responsibility of the author-citizen is therefore exonerated.

As soon as there is "literature" (if there is any, or any that is pure), the "I" who speaks remains, with respect to the law, in the position of a fictive "I." He does not commit the real author or signatory, as a subject of law. The author can have him say or let him say anything at all, without being, in principle, punishable by law. When I suggest that this right to say every-

8

Death Penalties

E.R.: We passed from a reflection on Jewishness and anti-Semitism to the question of the death penalty; we have already alluded to the seminar you have been conducting on this subject since 1999. The man who abolished the death penalty in France is a Jew. Perhaps this is not by chance. Robert Badinter lost his father in the death camps. He has also said that he became a committed death-penalty abolitionist out of the guilt he felt for having been unable to save the life of Roger Bontemps,[1] and that the pain of this failure grew from old anxieties experienced during the occupation.

J.D.: Yes, but I don't know whether, or why, or to what extent someone's Jewish origin would predispose him to abolitionism, at least in this century. Such a question would require a slow and careful approach, along several lines at once. But you are right to point this out. I have noticed, I think, that many Jewish American lawyers were also committed abolitionists, in a country that remains today the last Western "democracy," with a largely Christian, or even Judeo-Christian culture, to maintain and to apply the death penalty on a massive scale, even more intensely than before, despite certain more recent signs of disquiet or worry, even in what are called the most "death-prone" states in the U.S.

To stay with your remark and with what we said in the previous chapter on anti-Semitism, you recall that, immediately after the election of François Mitterrand,[2] certain people authorized themselves to count the number of Jews in his government. And a few years earlier, at the time of the vote authorizing abortion in certain situations, there were the incidents around Simone Veil.[3] In *L'abolition*,[4] Badinter recalls the sinister debates in Parliament that preceded the adoption of the law. Through the torrent of hatred and confusion that was unleashed, in particular against Simone Veil, one could discern a specious argument that is widely used, and not only in France: How can you, without contradiction, both advocate the abolition of the death penalty and accept the voluntary termination of pregnancy?

Aside from everything one might object to in this alleged "comparison" (and we often do just that in the seminar you alluded to), one "fact" seems no less troubling, and highly significant: almost everywhere, as statistics show, those who are the most violently opposed to the voluntary termination of pregnancy, those who sometimes try to kill doctors in the name of the "right" to life, those very people are often the most ardent supporters of the death penalty.

E.R.: Yes, that's right, and Simone Veil, who had been deported during the war, was insulted by the opponents of abortion. They almost accused her of having authorized a new genocide. As for Robert Badinter, he was called a "dirty Jew" as well as a friend of the "baby killers." In both cases, the anti-Semitic theme from Edouard Drumont's *La France juive* has returned: the Jew is the one who introduces the virus of death into the entrails of the French people.

J.D.: It's especially in the United States that the, so to speak, "armed" opposition to abortion is easily reconciled with a rabid opposition to the abolition of the death penalty, or even to the moratorium that would suspend executions, on account of the large number of judicial errors recently discovered. These so-called unconditional defenders of life are just as often militants for death. It is sometimes a matter of Christian fundamentalists who associate the struggle against abortion with the struggle against the abolition or suspension of the death penalty.[5]

E.R.: How can the two positions be reconciled? I have on the contrary often heard devout Catholics declare themselves opponents both of abortion and of the death penalty, in the name of the right to life.

J.D.: An immense question. I would like to take the time here to explain myself at greater length than in the other chapters, and to recall some of the schemas of the seminar I am giving, which I have not yet published.

Here it seems we have been dealt a *contradictory* hand; at play is an internal tension that works through *almost* all the history of the death penalty in the West. Up to the twenty-first century, almost without exception, the Catholic Church has been in favor of the death penalty. Sometimes in an active, fervent, militant way. It has always supported state legislation on the death penalty—like the principle of sovereignty, without which the death penalty has no chance. Saint Thomas was not the only eloquent partisan of capital punishment. This has also been the case with "systematic" theoreticians of traditional Catholicism. I am thinking in particular, to illustrate this truth with an exemplary hyperbole, of Donoso Cortès,[6] often cited and praised by Schmitt. Cortès articulated Catholic dogma and the doctrine of capital punishment with a fierce consistency, at once a bit delirious and hyperrational, "rationalizing," as has been known to happen. And in an equally remarkable way, he welded this system (Catholicism + capital punishment) to a general interpretation of blood sacrifice, from Cain and Abel to Christ and beyond.[7] What strikes me as interesting, revealing, in fact typical, in this ultra-reactionary, excessive, and somewhat mad theorizing is the extreme rigor of the approach.

On the one hand, even if, *stricto sensu*, the penalty of death did not appear as a sacrifice and if all sacrificial cultures (which is to say *all* cultures) had not produced, in the strict sense here again, a system of criminal law[8] in which a penalty of death might have this value of calculating rationality, Cortès would not be wrong to inscribe the death penalty within a history of sacrifice. And even of blood sacrifice, even if the blood tends to disappear, at least *shed* blood, blood in the immediately visible form of its effusion, while the death penalty survives, and undoubtedly will survive for a long time yet, despite its general retreat in the world. This is one set of questions that we are dealing with in the seminar I just mentioned; and when I use the name *sacrifice*, I am aware that I designate less a clear and distinct concept than an immense problem to be reelaborated from top to bottom in one of the most obscure, most fundamental, least circumscribable zones of the experience of the living, *all* the living, human or not.

On the other hand (and a bit like what Walter Benjamin will do in "The Critique of Violence"[9] regarding the "great criminals" who horrify but also fascinate inasmuch as they contest the state's monopolization of legitimate violence—*Gewalt*), Cortès thinks, not without profundity, that the distinction between common-law crime and political crime is always fragile and that the abolition of the death penalty for the latter (in France in 1848, for example, and this is his example, as it is Marx's) would have as its ineluctable consequence a universal abolition of the death penalty—in which he sees, like Kant in fact (and this is the real site of the philosophical discussion), the very elimination of all criminal law. There would be no more law, and above all no criminal law, without the mechanism of the death penalty, which is thus its condition of possibility, its *transcendental*, if you like (at once *internal*, included: the death penalty is an element of criminal law, one punishment among others, a bit more severe to be sure; and *external*, excluded: a foundation, a condition of possibility, an origin, a non-serial exemplarity, hyperbolic, more and other than a penalty).

It is this, the death penalty's paradoxical effect of transcendentalization, that a consistent abolitionism must take on. To contribute to this, one would have to attempt a kind of history of blood within a history of the concept of the *exception* (no sovereignty without the right of exception, without the right, Schmitt will say, to suspend the law [*droit*], for example where there is a right to grant mercy), and a history of *cruelty*, of the scrupulous use or abuses of the word, of the concept, sometimes of the word without the concept of "cruelty," whether it is visible, theatrical, or not.

Not all cruelty is bloody or bloodthirsty, visible and external, to be sure; it can be and no doubt is essentially psychical (pleasure taken in suffering or in making suffer in order to make suffer, to see suffering; *grausam*, in German, does not name blood). But *cruor* certainly designates shed blood, its effusion, and thus a certain exteriority, a visibility of red, its outward *expression*—this color that inundates all of Victor Hugo's texts against the death penalty, from the red made to flow by the guillotine, "the bloodswigging old crone,"[10] "the infernal scarlet machine,"[11] up to the posts of red wood that supported the blade ("two long joists painted red, a shelf painted red, a basket painted red, a heavy crossbeam painted red in which a thick, enormous blade of triangular shape seemed to be fit together by one of its sides . . . this was civilization arriving in Algiers in the form of a guillotine").[12]

Let us return to the "Catholic question." Despite all the motions of repentance and forgiveness he has never stopped calling for, despite his discourses on the subject of the Inquisition and the past errors of the Church, despite certain statements he made on the cruelty of capital punishment during a recent trip to the United States, and even though the Vatican state abolished the death penalty some twenty years ago, John Paul II, to my knowledge, has never, any more than any of his predecessors, formally engaged the Church and the Vatican in the abolitionist struggle. Only a few bishops, notably in France, have publicly taken a stand against the death penalty, at least against its maintenance in France.[13]

How can this be justified? It would be necessary for us to take the time for a close rereading of all this. Because this undeniable *fact* (that there has never been any political opposition to the death penalty by the Church) appears to contradict *another* Christianity, another spirit of Christianity. Take the example of Victor Hugo. He devoted so many struggles and magnificent texts to the abolitionist cause, to the "abolition pure and simple"—which is to say the unconditional abolition—of the death penalty, and always in the name of what he called, rightly or wrongly, the inviolability of human life.

Now, for reasons that were not only strategic, opportunistic, or rhetorical, Hugo also claimed to be inspired by the evangelical message and the passion of Christ. He did so at the very moment when he sometimes denounced the priests and the "politics" of the Church (as he condemned the Terror and castigated the guillotine in the name of the French Revolution, of its "truth," its memory, and its spirit—of what it *should have been*, the death penalty always remaining "the only tree that revolutions do not uproot":[14] "I am not one of those capped in a [revolutionary Phrygian] *red* hat and heady with the guillotine." I again underscore *red*).

At the very moment when he takes on "the social edifice of the past," which rested on "three pillars: the priest, the king, and the executioner," Hugo appeals to the "merciful law of Christ" and to the day when it "will at last suffuse the Code, which will glow with its radiance."[15] He thus wishes to "aim his axe into the widening notch marked sixty-six years ago by Beccaria on the old gibbet that has towered for so many centuries over Christendom."[16] This is why Albert Camus, though he was not entirely wrong, simplifies things somewhat on this point as on others, when, in his beautiful and courageous "Reflections on the Guillotine,"[17] he claims that the death penalty will not be able to survive in a secularized world, or that its abolition will occur through a humanist and atheist immanentism.[18] Christianity has other resources of internal "division," self-contestation, and self-deconstruction.[19]

One cannot treat the question of the death penalty in the West (perhaps this concept of criminal law, *in the strict sense*, is actually only European, and perhaps the death penalty is not a "penalty" among others, neither a law among others nor even an element of criminal law), one cannot recognize its deep bases, without taking into account the theologico-political discourse that underlies it and that in fact has always founded it. For the death penalty has always been the effect of an alliance between a religious message and the sovereignty of a state (if one can even assume, speaking of an *alliance*, that the concept of the state is not in its essence deeply religious).

Whether or not it has to do with the paradigmatic cases of Socrates, Christ, Joan of Arc, or Al-Hallaj, everything is decided, in an exemplary fashion, on the basis of a religious accusation (profanation or violation of a sacred law), launched or inspired by a religious authority, which is then taken up by that of the state, which decides on the death sentence—and which carries it out. In the figure of the monarch, the people, the president, the governor, etc., state sovereignty thus defines itself by the power of life and death over subjects. And therefore by the right of exception, by the right to raise itself, if one may say, above the law. This is how Schmitt defines the sovereign: the ability to decide the exception, the right to suspend the law. In the figure of the president, this right remains; but as it is conferred by an electoral mandate for a limited period, this right to grant mercy may be affected by electoral considerations or public opinion, which is not the case for the absolute monarch of hereditary and divine right.

In any case, one cannot again place the death penalty in question in a radical, principled, unconditional way without contesting or limiting the sovereignty of the sovereign. The great Beccaria tried to do so,[20] and there he was caught in one of his numerous contradictions.

E.R.: That's why Louis XVI was executed. It was indeed necessary to put an end to monarchic sovereignty in order to institute that of the nation. That is how a new principle of sovereignty was substituted for another.

J.D.: But a sovereignty was reinstated whose principle had never fundamentally been abandoned, to say the least, when it was passed on to the "people" made up of "citizens." This took the form (among others) of the Terror, even though (as we have already mentioned), after the conversion of the abolitionist Robespierre to the death penalty, after a series of dilatory rejections of abolition, and despite the eloquent pleas of Condorcet, the Convention was adjourned at the end of 1795 with a promise to end capital punishment on the day peace was reestablished ("general peace"!) and publicly declared. "Effective on the day of the general peace proclamation, the death penalty will be abolished in France."

It would take more than two centuries. This is a very long or a very short time in view of the immensity of such an event and the emergence of such a symptom, depending on the scale chosen—here, to put it briefly, the historical scale of European peace, of a postrevolutionary and relatively pacified, secure, reassured Europe, a Europe in which democracy is being laboriously built. For everywhere that the death penalty has been abolished in this European community, which now makes this a condition of membership, some pressure of an international origin was necessary. It was necessary to limit sovereignty—even where, according to proper parliamentary conventions and by all appearances, abolition was a national, internal, spontaneous, sovereign decision, as it was in the case of France. I am convinced that the French parliamentarians (including those of the Right, like Jacques Chirac, for example) who abolished it in 1981 against public opinion—which favored and perhaps still favors the death penalty—did not simply listen to their hearts and obey a principled conviction. They knew that this European and international trend would be irresistible. China and the United States still resist it, with a certain number of Arab-Muslim countries.

In any case, it is impossible to treat the question of the death penalty without speaking of religion, and of what, through the mediation of the concept of sovereignty, secures the right to religion. When I speak of a theologico-political or a theologico-juridico-political alliance as the basis or the principle of the death penalty, and of what makes it effective, when I thereby invoke a concept of sovereignty (over the life and death of creatures and subjects, including the right to grant mercy), I do not rely on an *already available* theologico-political concept that it would suffice to *apply* to the death penalty as one of its "cases" or examples. No, on the contrary, I would be tempted to say that one cannot begin to think the theologico-political, and even the onto-theologico-political, except from this phenomenon of criminal law that is called the death penalty.

In fact, what is involved here is less a phenomenon or an article of criminal law than, in this tradition, the quasi-transcendental condition of criminal law and of law in general. To put it in a brief and economical way, I will proceed from what has long been for me the most significant and the most stupefying—also the most stupefied—fact about the history of Western philosophy: never, *to my knowledge*, has any philosopher *as a philosopher, in his or her own strictly and systematically philosophical discourse*, never has any philosophy *as such* contested the legitimacy of the death penalty. From Plato to Hegel, from Rousseau to Kant (who was undoubtedly the most rigorous of them all), they expressly, each in his own way, and sometimes not without much hand-wringing (Rousseau), took a stand *for* the death penalty.

This continues in post-Hegelian modernity, *either* in the form of explicit discourses (like Baudelaire, Marx suspected the interest of abolitionists who wanted to save their own heads, whether it was during the brief episode of the 1848 Revolution that abolished the death penalty for political crimes—and Hugo himself expressed this suspicion—or else during the age of the great abolitionist demonstrations, in which the latter took an active and spectacular part),[21] *or* in the troubling form of silence or omission, as if it were not a philosophical problem worthy of the name. Here there are innumerable silences, no doubt different in their implicit axiomatics, from Heidegger (the thinker of being-toward-death who, *to my knowledge*, never took up the problem of the death penalty, to which he certainly did not think he had a duty to be opposed), to Sartre, Foucault, and many others.

To my knowledge, Levinas devoted only a single sentence to it in 1987, after its abolition in France: "I don't know if you accept this rather complex system which consists in judging *according to the truth* and in treating the one who has been judged *with love* [*dans l'amour*]. The abolition of the death penalty seems to me an essential thing for the coexistence of charity with justice."[22] But, like Kant and Hegel, he tries to extricate the biblical and Roman *lex talionis* from its common interpretation—vengeance, revenge, etc., which is precisely what the Gospel of Matthew protested against (5:38–44)—and to see in it, just as Kant did, the origin and rational foundation of criminal justice.[23]

Some of them were no doubt, in their hearts, horrified by capital punishment without thinking that they had any duty to devote a philosophical argument to it; this, it seems to me, is the case with Levinas. Others believed, rightly or wrongly, that they saw in it a particular phenomenon or a mere exacerbation of the penal system, even of imprisonment in general, or again a superstructure of juridical forms that had to be traced back to its infrastructural basis and to the *interests* of the (socio-economico-political) "ultimate authority." Those who maintained a public discourse against the death penalty never did so, to my knowledge—and this is my provisional hypothesis—in a strictly *philosophical* way. They did so either as writers (Voltaire, Hugo, and Camus in France) or as jurists and men of the law (Beccaria, in the first place, whose influence was considerable and decisive in the nineteenth century, and of whom I would like to speak again in a moment, in order to complicate things a bit more; Robert Badinter, of course; etc.).

If this massive and highly significant "fact" can be proven, we then have to ask ourselves what *welds*, so to speak, philosophy and, more precisely, ontology, in their essence or, what amounts to the same thing, in their hegemonic tradition—what *welds* them, then, to the political theology of the death penalty and to the principle of sovereignty, which, through different figures, reigns there supremely and in a sovereign manner.

At once powerful and fragile, historical and nonnatural (this is why the image of a technical *alloy* occurs to me here), this *welding* of ontology to the political theology of the death penalty is also what has always held together, adjoining or held fast in a single piece,[24] the *philosophical* (metaphysics or onto-theology), the *political* (at least where it is dominated by a thought of the *polis* or the sovereign state), and a certain concept of what is "proper to man," of what is man's own: the proper to man would consist in his ability to "risk his life" in sacrifice, to elevate himself above life, to be worth, in his dignity, something more and other than his life, to pass through death toward a "life" that is worth more than life. This is Plato's *epimeleia tou thanatou*, the philosophy that enjoins us to exert ourselves unto death; it is the incomparable *dignity* (*Würde*) of the human person, who, as an end in himself and not a means, according to Kant, transcends his condition as a living being and whose *honor* it is to inscribe the death penalty within his law; it is the struggle for recognition between one consciousness and another, which for Hegel passes through the risk of one's own life; it is the being-toward-death of *Dasein*, which alone can *properly* die and die its own death, so that according to Heidegger the animal merely comes to an end and ceases; etc.

The death penalty would thus be, like death itself, what is "proper to man" in the strict sense. At the risk of once again shocking those who do not want to hear it, I will dare to say that the death penalty has always answered deeply "humanist" pleas. That is how it is in European law (and I do not know whether, in the strict sense—despite all the phenomena of mass killing and even ritualized mass killing that commonsense thinking tends to place outside Europe—there is a "death penalty," dare I say worthy of the name, outside of European law). And that is how it has been, therefore, at the unique crossroads—which is Europe itself—between, *on the one hand*, the biblical tradition (immediately after the "Thou shalt not kill," in the "Judgments," which are a true, instituted penal code, God commands putting to death those who transgress this or that commandment—and we will have to speak again of the *lex talionis*, whose interpretation is so controversial), and, *on the other hand*, the onto-theological tradition that I recalled a moment ago.

For a long time I have thus been persuaded that the deconstruction of the speculative scaffolding (not to mention the scaffold) that upholds the philosophical discourse on the death penalty is not one necessity among others, a particular point of application. If one could speak here of an architectonic and of edification, the death penalty would be the keystone or, if you prefer, the cement, the weld, as I just said, of the onto-theologico-political, the prosthetic artifact that keeps it upright, along with the nature-technique distinction and everything that follows from it (*physis/tekhnè, physis/nomos, physis/thesis*), a nonnatural thing, a historical law, a properly and strictly human and supposedly rational law.

Kant believes that he recognizes a "categorical imperative" and an *a priori* idea of pure reason in a criminal law that would not be possible if the death penalty were not inscribed within it, and if it were not commanded by a *jus talionis* to be reinterpreted. When I say "philosophical discourse on the death penalty," and thus a discourse "to be deconstructed," I am thinking not only of the death-prone discourse prevailing in the majority of nation-states that maintained the death penalty until around 1990 (in the last ten years a majority of nation-states have, in one way or another, put an end to the death penalty; the process of "deconstruction" is thus picking up speed in a critical and highly significant way, and this in effect goes for sovereignty, the nation-state, religion, etc.).

I am also thinking, without in any way trying to make things symmetrical, of the abolitionist discourse (to which, as you know, I give my most convinced sympathy). This abolitionist discourse, in its present state, seems to me greatly perfectible, philosophically and politically fragile, also deconstructible, if you prefer. For at least *three reasons*:

A. First of all, when it is inspired by the logic of Beccaria, which is almost always the case, abolitionist argumentation becomes more fragile. This can be said even while giving to Beccaria, as has often been done since the end of the eighteenth century, the homage that is owed to this great man and to his historic initiative. If one were to apply to the letter the list of exceptions Beccaria places on the suspension of capital punishment, it would be administered almost every day. As soon as the order of a society is threatened, or every time it is not yet assured, it is admissible to put a citizen to death, according to Beccaria, even if for him the death penalty is not a "right." In other words—and here we touch on one of the more obscure stakes of the problem, insofar as one has not clearly defined the concept of war, the strict difference between civil war, national war, and partisan war, "terrorism" whether domestic or not, etc. (so many concepts that have always been and are still more problematic, obscure, dogmatic, manipulable than ever)—the abolition of the death penalty within the secure borders of a prosperous and peaceful nation will remain something seriously limited, convenient, provisional, conditional—which is to say not principled. Abolition will be conditioned, as Beccaria himself saw quite clearly, in fact—and this gives us much to think about today—by the proper functioning of the liberal market.[25]

Beccaria, then, concerned with dissuasive exemplarity, judges the death penalty less necessary, more *ineffective* than *unjust*, and hardly cruel enough to dissuade.[26] Perpetual forced labor would be more fearsome, crueler, he thinks, and therefore more effective in the art of dissuasion. It is this utilitarianism or this "exemplarism" that Kant will criticize very strongly and on both flanks, so to speak, as much among those who believe that the death penalty is a good means in view of an end—security, peace, the well-being of the community or the nation, etc.—as among the abolitionists, who for the most part, and like Beccaria, think the opposite. To this means/end pair that dominates the debate on both sides (for and against the death penalty), Kant opposes an idea of justice and a "categorical imperative" of criminal law that appeals to the human person, in his "dignity" (*Würde*), as an end in himself.

This dignity requires that the guilty party be punished because he is punishable, without any concern for utility, without sociopolitical interest of any kind. As long as the flaws of such a line of argument are not made to appear from the inside, in the rigor of the concept; as long as a discourse of the Kantian or Hegelian type, which claims to justify the death penalty in a principled way, without concern for interest, without reference to the least utility, is not "deconstructed," we will be confined to a precarious, limited abolitionist discourse, conditioned by empirical facts and, in its essence, provisional in relation to a particular context, situated within a logic of means and ends, falling short of strict juridical rationality. It is this difficult "deconstruction" that I am trying to carry out in my seminar on the death penalty. I cannot reconstruct its process here. In a few words, it would make the following appear untenable from within:

1. The founding distinction of the concept of "punishment" in Kant, i.e., the difference between (a) *poena naturalis*, a punishment, entirely interior and private, which the guilty party can inflict on himself, before all laws and institutions, and (b) *poena forensis*, punishment strictly speaking, administered from the outside by society, through its judicial apparatus and its historical institutions.

2. The distinction between self-punishment and hetero-punishment: the guilty party, as a person and a rational subject, should, according to Kant, understand, approve, even call for the punishment—including the supreme penalty; this transforms all institutional and rational punishment coming from outside (*forensis*) into automatic and autonomous punishment or into the indiscernible confines of interior punishment (*poena naturalis*); the guilty party should acknowledge the reason of the sentence, he would have to acknowledge the juridical reason that gets the better of him [*a raison de lui*][27] and leads him to condemn himself to death. To follow this consequence to the end, the guilty party would symbolically execute the verdict himself. The execution would be like a *sui-cide*.[28] There would be, for the autonomy of juridical reason, nothing but self-execution. It is "as if the guilty party committed suicide."

But here one can no longer distinguish, in all rigor, the sphere of pure, immune[29] law, intact, not contaminable by everything we would want to purify it of: interest, passion, vengeance, revenge, the sacrificial drive (moral and juridical reason are moreover, in their essence, expressly sacrificial for Kant), the logic of conscious and unconscious drives, everything that Freud and Reik wrote under the heading "*lex talionis*" in its most archaic and indestructible form.

I did not say that for Kant the execution *is* a suicide. That would be as stupid as saying that capital punishment is murder, pure and simple. All these outlines, hypotheses, aporias, all these paradoxes, do not have as their aim or function to confound obviously different things, to reverse oppositions or replace them with others, but to suspend, to mark or recall the necessity of suspending our naive confidence, that of common sense or conscious belief, in distinctions or oppositions such as inside/outside, natural and interior/nonnatural and exterior (*poena naturalis*/*poena forensis*), self and other, self-punishment and hetero-punishment, execution and murder or suicide.

It is the quaking of these borders, as well as their permeability, their undecidability, that matter to me here, and not reinstating other reassuring oppositional distinctions that would allow one to say: yes, *there* is suicide, *there* is execution and/or murder. Or: that was an execution or murder and not a suicide, and this was a suicide and not the opposite.

3. Kant's reinterpretation of the *lex talionis*, whose biblical and Roman traditions he powerfully reactivates by displacing them. An enormous question, an enormous thorny tangle of texts that we cannot reopen here. Kant would be closer to a literally Jewish or Roman tradition than to a certain evangelical spirit (Matthew, I just said, denounced the principle of the *lex talionis*). Kant fails, in my view, on questions that are moreover often sexual, on sex crimes—pederasty, rape, bestiality—to produce a principle of equivalence, and therefore of calculability. This concern with equivalence (not simply literal or quantitative, but spiritual and symbolic: the figure of the unfigurable) in fact intersects, in Kant as in Hegel, what we just said about the becoming-self-punishment of hetero-punishment: regulating the talionic categorical imperative, equality (*Gleichheit*) insists first of all that whatever the harm done to the other, I inflict it equally, *a priori*, on myself. Kant literally says: "Whatever undeserved evil you inflict on another within the people, that you inflict upon yourself; . . . if you kill him, you kill yourself."[30] Or again, and here I cite from memory: in stealing from the other, you destroy the principle of property and you steal from yourself.

The question of the death penalty is not only that of the political onto-theology of sovereignty; it is also, around this calculation of an impossible equivalence between crime and punishment, their incommensurability, an impossible evaluation of the debt (Nietzsche says some very strong things on this subject), the question of the principle of reason, of the interpretation of reason as the "principle of reason," and of this latter as the principle of calculability. This question of "accounting" and of the account to be given, of "giving reasons" (*reddere rationem*), must be debated among others, but first of all, in my view, among the Heideggerian and Kantian interpretations of reason, both of which, although differently, attempt at once to *remove* rationality from and to *submit* it to its calculating vocation. Pardon me for not entering into this here, it would be too long and too difficult; but I would like to situate its principled necessity.

4. The exception that, in all logic, would have to allow the sovereign or the legislator (the horrified Kant names above all Charles I and Louis XVI) to escape all trials and all formal executions; here is what, along with the Terror, would have corrupted the French Revolution, which Kant hailed, as you know, as one of the *signs* demonstrating, recalling, announcing the possibility of progress in human history. This sovereign exception, this absolute immunity, is something that many national laws and a certain international law are tending, very laboriously and at the price of many contradictions, to call into question again. There is doubtless nothing fortuitous in the fact that at the very moment when the immunity of heads of states or armies is being, let us say to remain prudent, called again into question by international criminal authorities, we know that, whatever the worst crimes they are accused of, the accused will never again be condemned to death.

5. The de facto inapplicability of any death penalty at the very moment when Kant judges it necessary to inscribe its rational principle into a system of criminal law worthy of its name and worthy of man, worthy of the human person as an end in himself. Kant insists with so much rigor on the imperative that commands, out of respect for the person of the condemned, that no "mistreatment" be inflicted on him, no violence that would tend to demean the "person" in his essential, inalienable "innate personality" (which one can never lose, even if one loses one's "civil personality"); but one could never demonstrate that an execution does not entail any "mistreatment" of this order. No more than one can demonstrate, in all Kantian logic, that the crime was committed freely, in a responsible and not a "pathological" way, in both the Kantian and the common senses of this word.

B. If, as I suggested a moment ago, abolitionist discourse in its present state remains perfectible, fragile, or, if you prefer, deconstructible, it is because it limits the respect for life, or the prohibition on killing, to national law and to a national territory during peacetime. But today nothing seems more uncertain and porous than a border in general or a border between the concepts of war and peace, civil war and international war, war and the so-called "humanitarian" operations supposedly conducted by nongovernmental authorities. Wars of independence that are not legitimated as such by colonial powers, "terrorisms," everything Schmitt calls "partisan war"—these are some of the phenomena that confound the concept of the "public enemy" (Rousseau).

Authorizing supposedly "legitimate self-defense" and cursory killing without a "death penalty" (without judgment, without verdict, without public execution, etc.), these phenomena recall that this penal question is played out not between life and death but somewhere else altogether. The question of the death penalty is not a simple question of life or death.

C. This is why a good number of international declarations since the Second World War have remained, at least in their letter, highly precarious. In a way that was moreover deliberate. We cannot study them here, but in a word we can say that they relied on a "right to life" (one of the human rights) whose concept and axiom are more than problematic; they advised avoiding torture and cruel treatment (a notion whose obscure equivocation I have already mentioned); and, avoiding above all any binding resolution, they were always formulated as recommendations that would not have the "force of law," and that, with the best intentions in the world, had to stop at the threshold of the principle of sovereignty and right of exception of states—whom they only *advised* not to practice the death penalty except in an exceptional way and according to legal procedures protecting the rights of the accused. The pressure of the United States (often represented by Mrs. Roosevelt) was not insignificant with regard to this respect for sovereignty. But it would be impossible to reconstruct here the rich history of debates that followed the Second World War, the Nuremberg trials, the institution of the concepts of crimes against humanity, genocide, etc.

E.R.: Is it not also necessary, from this point of view, to reexamine the Shoah?

J.D.: The Shoah does not fall, *stricto sensu*, under the concept of the death penalty. Here there was never any pretense of the least legality, not even of a simulacrum of legality. Here there was neither judgment, nor guilty parties, nor accusation, nor defense. Mass killing (extermination or genocide) requires categories other than that of the death penalty. This explains, without justifying it, why some people feel authorized (incorrectly, in my view) to consider debates about the death penalty (always individual and applied to a nameable citizen) as relatively or statistically minor in the light of great crimes against humanity, genocides, war crimes, the denied phenomena of nonassistance to hundreds of millions of people in danger (malnutrition, AIDS, etc.), not to mention the immensity of the phenomenon of imprisonment (where the United States also holds records).

But here it would be necessary to take into account all the "impure" phenomena of executions following cursory, even secret, judgments. In principle, according to European law, the death penalty must be accessible to the public in its procedures of judgment, verdict, and execution. It must be the subject of an official announcement (prior to the execution). Where this is not the case (in China and Japan, it seems, and no doubt in numerous other places in the world and moments in history), it is not certain that we can, in all rigor, speak of the "death penalty."

E.R.: Hence the "cleanness" we spoke of before, and especially the elimination of traces. When I speak of reexamining the Shoah, I am thinking of the evolution in the application of the death penalty that tends to erase the traces of legal death. The way in which prisoners are executed in the United States, with the attempt to make every form of suffering disappear, has something pathological about it that makes the death penalty all the more intolerable in that one seeks to deny, not the execution, but the suffering or rather the trace connected with the passage, necessarily painful from life to death.

In the past the condemned prisoner was heroized in a certain way. Executions with an ax evoked the theory of the king's two bodies, and, for a moment, the victim could identify with a monarch whose head was violently detached from his body. In the history of the death penalty, we have shifted from the excessive *jouissance* procured by the spectacle of a violent execution to the elimination of pain (the guillotine), then from this to the elimination of the very traces of the passage from life to death. The direct scene of the execution has been banished, although its reestablishment by way of television is being seriously considered, which shows in any case that voyeurism and exhibitionism know no bounds. But above all, the act of putting to death tends today to be erased, in favor of a palliative care and therefore of a disappearance of the horror that *necessarily* accompanies being put to death. We are somehow ashamed of the violence of the execution.

J.D.: "Elimination of the traces," as you said. This is the great question of burial and laying to rest. For example, in Greece, in an age when the death penalty was found to be fully justified—with Socrates or Plato— something worse than death was inflicted on the citizen worthy of respect. For certain particularly serious crimes, the corpse of the condemned was thrown over the city walls. He lost his right to a burial. Today, in the United States, the situation is in a sense the opposite. The pretense is to re- spect the subject who is put to death, notably in states, like Texas, where the sanction is applied massively. The condemned prisoner is allowed to speak before his execution; his last words are recorded and then circulated on the Internet. Indeed, there exists a veritable corpus of "last statements" [English in original]. And they are posted "on line" [English in original]. The speech of the condemned is respected; the corpse is given to the fam- ily; and the traces are not hidden. There would be much to say on the question of the visual and audio archive of executions in the United States.

E.R.: It seems to me that the death penalty is still desired, that it fas- cinates, but that henceforth it is connected to a sort of social pathology. And in fact, in countries where it is applied, more and more "falsely ac- cused" people are being executed, people against whom there is no evi- dence that they committed a crime. All the judicial errors, which are legion in the United States and which lead to executions, make the "abnormal" character of the death penalty evident. I think that if it is abolished in the United States, it will be, as you say, not on principle but for contingent rea- sons. It will be a pragmatic abolition and not a principled one, a hypocrit- ical abolition, linked to the fear of executing either innocent people or the mentally ill or people guilty of murder but belonging to minorities who are victims of discrimination (blacks, transsexuals, homosexuals, etc.). In his arguments for abolition in 1981, Robert Badinter remarked that the last people to be executed in the Fifth Republic never should have been: one was doubtlessly innocent, another was mentally handicapped, a third was infirm . . .

J.D.: It is true that the manifestations of disquiet proliferating in the United States point less often to the principle of the death penalty than to the large number of "judicial errors" that, under suspect and monstrously unequal conditions, lead to executions. Perhaps it is necessary to recall a few figures. As of today, 73 countries have completely abolished the death penalty; 13 have abolished it for common-law crimes, for so-called nonpolitical crimes (which raises our old question again: are all crimes not essentially political, like the "great crimes" and "great criminals" that, as Walter Benjamin said, threaten the very foundation of a state law as it aims to monopolize violence?—and I think on the other hand of the example of Mumia Abu-Jamal,[31] who has always claimed the status of a political prisoner); 22 states have abolished it *in practice*, not in law (the criterion of this distinction: no executions for ten years). In total, a majority of states—108— have abolished the death penalty, in law or in fact; 87 have kept it.

Every year since 1979 two or three countries have abolished it, thus expanding this majority. In 1999 East Timor, Ukraine, and Turkmenistan abolished it for all crimes, Latvia for common-law crimes. In 1999 more than 1,813 people were executed in 31 countries, and almost 4,000 were condemned to death in 63 countries. Amnesty International reports these facts with a kind of precision that is more important to us than any other, from a geopolitical perspective (here the quantitative is more than mathematical; it is quantitative in a dynamic way—if I may thus transpose the distinction proposed by Kant concerning the "sublime"—and the question of the death penalty has some relation with that of the "sublime," not to say of sublimation).

Eighty-five percent of executions are concentrated in four countries: China comes far ahead of all the others in absolute figures (at least 1,076). And the figures of the last two years are frightening. Next comes Iran (at least 165), then Saudi Arabia (103), and finally the United States (98). We should also not forget the Democratic Republic of Congo (about 100) and Iraq (hundreds, but sometimes without judgments). At present, aside from a large number of Arab countries, only two "very great" powers maintain the death penalty: China, where it is applied in a massive way, and the United States, where there has nonetheless been a strong abolitionist current since the nineteenth century.

In 1972, as is well known, the U.S. Supreme Court decided that the application of the death penalty was incompatible with two constitutional amendments: one concerns discrimination; the other concerns anything that can be considered "cruel and unusual punishment" [English in original]. From this moment, the Supreme Court found the application of the death penalty to be a "cruel and unusual punishment." It was therefore suspended, in fact.

Its principle was not thereby abolished, but executions were suspended. It was thus that between 1972 and 1977 no one was executed in the

United States. No state was able to transgress this prohibition by the federal Supreme Court (whose democratic character was in fact contested in this case by certain people, since the judges are appointed and not elected. This was argued by a Chicago law professor who claimed that a democratic government could not contradict "public opinion" when a majority favors the death penalty. After objecting that parliamentary democracy does not obey public opinion but the elected majority, and that in France the Parliament had abolished the death penalty against majority public opinion or the probable result of a referendum, I thought it was fitting to ask: how then do you explain that the Supreme Court suspended the death penalty in 1972? Is it not a democratic institution? The answer was "no," and it gave me much to think about. In fact, my feeling is that if one day the death penalty is abolished in the United States, it will be by a progressive movement, state by state, moratorium by moratorium, de facto, and not by a single federal decision).

After 1977, certain states judged that death administered by lethal injection was neither cruel nor unusual, in contrast to the electric chair, hanging, or the gas chamber. Executions thus resumed, and the Supreme Court was obliged to submit. In certain states like Texas, executions were massive, notably during George W. Bush's term as governor.[32]

To return to the question of pathology that you raised, the symptoms of a veritable crisis have begun to multiply in the American consciousness and conscience, notably because of international pressures.

Let us take an example. It was discovered in the state of Illinois that thirteen prisoners on death row, some of whom had been there for decades, were innocent. This was discovered only accidentally when, in a journalism school in Evanston—at Northwestern University, I believe, near Chicago—some professors and students had come across serious irregularities in these cases. So the cases were reexamined, and the thirteen condemned men were cleared! The governor of Illinois, a very respectable Republican but a supporter of the death penalty, immediately declared a moratorium: "If there are so many innocents, so many who are sentenced to death but are found to be victims of judicial error, then I am suspending the executions."

Recently, during one of my last visits to the United States, I saw a television program in which thirteen innocent men who had been condemned to death participated—twelve black, one white. They told the story of their many years in prison, and then of their liberation. Without compensation! Only one of them had managed, after legal proceedings, to obtain reparations. None of them could find a job; they remained suspect even though their innocence had been established. DNA tests are now making it possible to proliferate the evidence of grave judicial errors leading to the death penalty. And it is the American judicial system as a whole that is "under examination" at the moment.

Bush is famous for, among other things, never having granted so much as a single pardon. During the same television program, he was asked: "Do you think that in Texas all the people you are refusing to pardon were guilty?" And he answered imperturbably: "Yes, in Texas they are all guilty."

Every day, during my seminars, in New York, in Chicago, in Irvine, California, we spent the first part of our sessions analyzing items from the written and televised press on the subject. Among other things, I recall the remarkable case of a nurse who had killed her two children by mimicking the legal method of putting to death (through lethal injection). She refused any pardon, so that she could "join [her] two children," and requested a lethal injection. This woman was executed. She was probably judged to be of sound mind.

E.R.: And yet in the United States there is an equivalent to article 122.1 of our penal code (formerly article 64), which allows the mentally ill to be spared the death penalty. The execution you're talking about attests to an extraordinary regression. For in the countries where the death penalty has been abolished, the allowances made for crimes committed in a state of insanity were modified. The objective of the former article 64 was to rescue insane criminals from the guillotine by effacing the trace of the crime.[33] Today, this is no longer necessary, and article 64 has disappeared. Consequently, there is an attempt to restore responsibility to the insane person who has committed murder, through various treatments (including psychoanalysis) so that he or she might become conscious of the gravity of his or her act. If, therefore, the insane criminal is not legally responsible, his or her act is no longer expelled from consciousness as it was before abolition. Hence the possibility of treatment, of a return to reason.

J.D.: Whether it is a question of a "mental handicap" or of age (but what is an age? a mental age?—an individual can have many ages according to the perspective chosen by the experts), the practice is becoming in-

creasingly harsh in the United States, sometimes in violation of the recommendations of international law. Alleged mental handicaps and the
young age of the accused are being taken into account less and less.

On the question of whether "to see or not to see killing or cruelty,"
Foucault speaks of a progressive disappearance of spectacular visibility. This
is true, but at the same time, thanks to television and cinema, one sees
more and more films that, under the perfectly good pretext of abolitionism,
exhibit not only the condemnation to death but the process of execution,
up to the last moment. Visibility is thus deferred. The transformation of
the media makes it so that one should speak not simply of invisibility but
of a transformation of the field of the visible. Never have things been as
"visible" in global space as they are today; this is itself an essential element
of the problem—and of the struggle. Spectral logic invades everything, especially at the intersections of the work of mourning and the *technè* of the
image—which is to say everywhere. (It was this intersection that interested
me in *Specters of Marx*, and, however far back one goes, the thematic of the
phantom or rather of the revenant[34] runs explicitly through most of my
texts, almost to the point of merging with that of the trace itself.)

E.R.: The world of our thinking has indeed been invaded by a large
number of productions in which phantoms, specters, or revenants are
staged.[35] As if the specter were the symptom of our globalized world. This
strikes me as energizing to the extent that the work of mourning consists
in not forgetting what one owes to a heritage and to the dead, but also terrifying when we seem to be possessed—if it's a question of possession—by
the dead acting on us in the manner of a "real" in the Lacanian sense: a
mortiferous real, a perpetual lamentation.

J.D.: It's true; attention to a certain spectral logic, almost everywhere,
seems to be taking a remarkably insistent form these days. It is thus, of
course, essentially connected to the question of the technical prosthesis, of
technics in general, of the inevitability of the work of mourning—which is
not one work among others but the overdetermining mark of all work. It
also concerns the impossibility of mourning. Mourning *must* be impossible. Successful mourning is failed mourning. In successful mourning, I incorporate the one who has died, I assimilate him to myself, I reconcile myself with death, and consequently I deny death and the alterity of the dead
other and of death as other. I am therefore unfaithful. Where the introjec-

tion of mourning succeeds, mourning annuls the other. I take him upon me, and consequently I negate or delimit his infinite alterity.[36]

This also happens with the integration of the immigrant, or the assimilation of the foreigner. This "mourning effect" thus does not wait for death. One does not wait for the death of the other to deaden and absorb his alterity. Faithfulness prescribes to me at once the necessity and the impossibility of mourning. It enjoins me to take the other within me, to make him live in me, to idealize him, to internalize him, but it also enjoins me not to succeed in the work of mourning: the other must remain the other. He is effectively, presently, undeniably dead, but, if I take him into me as a part of me, and if, consequently, I "narcissize" this death of the other by a successful work of mourning, I annihilate the other, I reduce or mitigate his death. Infidelity begins here, unless it continues thus and is aggravated further.

E.R.: It seems to me, on the contrary, that a successful work of mourning is not an act of infidelity. It makes it possible to invest in a new object that perpetuates the memory of the old one. It is less difficult to mourn the people one has loved than the people one has detested. In one case, one is faithful to the love that was given to the one who has died by loving another object; in the other case, one is faithful to the detestation by introjecting it in order then to direct it toward another object.

J.D.: Yes, but the loved object is perpetuated in being betrayed, in being forgotten. The one who has died must of course be forgotten, must be forgotten well [*Il faut bien, il faut* bien *oublier le mort*]. As I once said— and it is basically the same transubstantiation—"of course one must eat/ one must eat well [*il faut bien manger*]."[37] Faithfulness is unfaithful.

E.R.: The formula "faithful infidelity" or "successful mourning as impossible mourning" recalls the double character of melancholy: it is the source both of creativity and of destruction. But I am also thinking of what you say about forgiveness. Why must one "forgive the unforgivable" for someone who does not ask for forgiveness?[38]

J.D.: I didn't say that *one must* forgive the unforgivable; I proposed analyzing the concept of forgiveness that we have inherited. It is again a question of heritage. This heritage is simultaneously Jewish, Christian, and

Islamic, with a very strong Christian imprint. Two contradictory logics are in dispute in this heritage. The one that is prevalent imposes a condition: forgiveness has no sense except when the criminal asks for forgiveness. The guilty party recognizes his fault; he is already on the path to repentance and self-transformation. This is a pardon *on condition.*

The second logic, also present but less represented, not to say "exceptional" (and it grants the essential exceptionality of forgiveness), is that of a gracious and unconditional forgiveness: I forgive regardless of the attitude of the guilty party, even if he does not ask for forgiveness, even if he does not repent. I forgive him *as* someone who is guilty, presently, actually guilty; I forgive him *insofar as* he (or she) is guilty, or even insofar as he (or she) remains guilty. These two logics compete with and contradict each other, but both of them are active in the discourse of our heritage. One is prevalent, as I said; the second is more discreet, only slightly or scarcely visible.

But, in the analysis of pure forgiveness, as in that of pure hospitality, I maintain that pure forgiveness must forgive the one who or which remains unforgivable. If I forgive something or someone that remains forgivable, I don't forgive; it's too easy. If I forgive the fault (the "what") of the one who has repented, or the one who has repented himself (the "who"), I forgive something or someone other than the crime or the criminal. The true "meaning" of forgiveness, therefore, is to forgive even the unforgivable and even someone who does not ask for forgiveness. This is a logical analysis of the concept of forgiveness, of the aporia to which this logic is and *must remain* devoted, if it is to be faithful to its vocation, its call, and to the measure of its extraordinary unmeasure.

E.R.: Concerning unconditional forgiveness, you are right, and in fact the abolition of the death penalty somehow obliges such forgiveness, not only for the criminal in a state of insanity but for all others. I think it will be necessary one day to consider abolishing what abolition has produced: the condemnation to "life in prison," with no parole and no possible release. Perhaps we must not concretely abolish it, but pose the *principled* possibility of its abolition. It applies particularly to certain repeat offenders and murderers or to those susceptible to uncontrollable, unconscious murderous drives, and who are necessarily presumed to be dangerous. It seems to me that from the moment when the death penalty no longer exists, this type of punishment for life should be abolished, if not in fact, at least in principle. It should in any case be rethought. Which is not the case today. Abolition has rather reinforced the principle of the life sentence. I wonder if, one day, our society will be able to face the idea—almost inadmissible, not to say intolerable—that zero risk does not exist, that there is always a risk of recidivism, necessarily, even if only a minimal one. There is always a risk, even if the criminal has become *another man*, after a very long detention for example, even if he has *consciously* recognized the horror of his crime, and even if he is certain that he will not commit another. It seems to me that for a punishment to have any sense, it must take on this idea of unconditional forgiveness you speak of.

I'm reminded of Eichmann's trial.[39] Can one forgive Adolf Eichmann?

J.D.: The notion of forgiveness remains foreign to the order of the juridical and the political. In the course of a trial, one can very well condemn someone to death, inflexibly and without amnesty, and on the other hand, outside the trial, forgive, forgive him his crime. These are different orders. Eichmann was condemned to death, which is an exception in the history of Israel, a country where the death penalty was abolished at the time of the trial. There would be much to say concerning the history of law in this country, the only one, to my knowledge, where, despite euphemisms that fool no one, torture was officially authorized, in certain conditions, by the highest authorities of the country.

E.R.: You no doubt know that what was unforgivable for Eichmann was not killing people but inflicting useless suffering on them. We find here again the theme of the "clean death." Thus he was indignant when, in the course of the trial in Jerusalem, witnesses recalled the atrocities committed by the SS. When I saw the film by Rony Brauman and Eyal Sival (*The Specialist*), I was struck to see that Eichmann's hypernormality, which Hannah Arendt thought in terms of the expression "the banality of evil"— this normality, then, encloses one in madness. Indeed, one is seized with horror upon hearing Eichmann claim that he condemns the Nazi system, even as he vindicates his oath of fidelity to this very same system, which made of him the submissive servant of an abominable crime.

Contrary to a certain post-Arendtian vulgate, I do not think that Eichmann was a peaceful little functionary, nor that anyone at all can become an Eichmann or a Nazi. His "madness," that is to say, his extreme normality, was in perfect conformity with Nazi discourse, which claimed to be using the most rational, the most "normal," science in order to carry out the most horrifying crime, "beyond all norms," in its quest for the absolute (the final solution). No doubt only Freudian, and Lacanian, categories allow us to grasp the workings of this normality that encloses one in madness, this reversal of the norm into a pathology. Consequently, I believe that the central problem of this trial was the attitude of the prosecutor, Gideon Hausner. Far from understanding who this criminal was, far from grasping the significance of his aberrant but logical and normal discourse, he in a sense expelled Eichmann from the order of the human by turning him into a monster, a subhuman, who could not be judged according to human law. In these conditions, no forgiveness was possible for this man who in fact did not ask for forgiveness and who knew he was condemned. It seems to me that in this case, involving someone who was directly responsible for carrying out the genocide, we must maintain the idea that every person, whatever his acts, belongs to the order of the human and does not have to be expelled as *nonhuman*. Cruelty, the destructive drive, the madness of the norm, are inscribed in the heart of humankind. And that is where the problem lies.

J.D.: In principle, law is a human institution. It is assumed to be such even if it is always authorized, founded, and in sum legitimated by some divine sacredness, whether this is explicitly recognized or not. According to the logic of Christian doctrine, it is not man who forgives man; God alone can forgive. Man asks God for forgiveness, or asks God to forgive another. Think of the declaration made by the Christian Church of France to the Jews. It asked God for forgiveness, while calling on the Jewish community as witness, but it did not itself ask the Jews for forgiveness, not immediately. It is God who forgives and whom one asks for forgiveness. The power to forgive, conditionally or unconditionally, is always an essentially divine power, even when it seems to be practiced by man. One could believe the contrary, namely that only a finite being can be harmed, wounded, or even killed, and therefore only a finite being can have to forgive or can make one forgive.

That is why the question of the human dimension of forgiveness is difficult to treat. It would be difficult for me to enter into this while improvising, for example to discuss, as I have done elsewhere, the statements of Vladimir Jankélévitch[40] or Hannah Arendt on this subject. For the latter, forgiveness remains a purely human experience, even in the case of Christ, whom she always refers to as Jesus of Nazareth, in order to recall his terrestrial roots, the *human* place of his birth and of his speech—of the *action of his speech*. She does this precisely in "Action," the chapter of *The Human Condition* in which she analyzes these two conditions of the social bond, forgiveness and the promise.[41] We must be able to forgive, she says, so that social life will not be interrupted. She therefore proposes in principle—and I find this highly debatable—that forgiveness has meaning only there where the right to punish can be exercised.[42]

E.R.: You don't agree with that?

J.D.: It seems to me that it simplifies things somewhat. I would be tempted to think that forgiveness responds to its pure vocation—if it ever happens that forgiveness is able to do this—only when it forgives the unforgivable and thus rises above law, beyond all calculable sanction. Forgiveness is and must remain heterogeneous to juridical space. Like pardon itself: the right to pardon is not a right among others. Forgiveness has no symmetry, no relation of complementarity with punishment. It has nothing in "common," precisely, with punishment. I will not do so here, but one can read the texts she cites completely differently; all of them leave to God, literally and explicitly, the ultimate power to forgive. The problem, by definition, cannot be purely anthropocentric. There is something transhuman in the idea of forgiveness. And one does not need God in order to speak of the transhuman or the ahuman. The impossible is at work in the idea of unconditional forgiveness, since this forgiveness that forgives the unforgivable is an impossible forgiveness. It *does the impossible*, it makes one do and give the impossible, it forgives the one who or which is not forgivable.

Consequently, to forgive the unforgivable is to cause human reason to shatter, or at least the principle of reason interpreted as calculability. It makes a sign in the direction of something from which the human is announced without immanence. In the idea of forgiveness, there is that of transcendence. Perhaps one does not need forgiveness, nor to believe in the *possible existence* of such a thing; but precisely, it is a question here of the possibility of the impossible, and, if we want to speak of this, if we want to use this word in a consistent way, it is necessary to admit that to forgive the unforgivable is to accomplish a gesture that is no longer to be measured by human immanence. Hence the origin of religion. Beginning from this idea of the impossible, this "desire" or this "thought" of forgiveness, this thought of the unknowable and the transphenomenal, one can indeed also attempt a genesis of the religious.

E.R.: Don't you think that what we are invoking without naming it is the Judeo-Christian legacy, so as to provide a counterweight, on one side, to scientism, to a certain atheism and to globalization—all of which limit the human to a sort of militant positivity—and on the other side to the danger of irrational sects and discourses (sects of fundamentalism, for example and once again), which claim to bring a new spirituality to the human?

J.D.: I don't know how to respond here in any simple way. I am pursuing as far as possible the necessity of a hyper-atheological discourse, but at the same time, I do not cease to meditate on Abrahamic culture (Jewish, Christian, Muslim)[43] without the least desire to destroy it or to disqualify it. To explain this double gesture, if not to justify it, and to explain that despite appearances it remains the same, at once divided and indivisible, it would be necessary for me to read, to write or rewrite everything I have already written. To limit myself to a single sentence, I will say this: for a few years now, in numerous texts (for example, but not only, in *Le toucher: Jean-Luc Nancy*), I recall that there are literally Lutheran origins in this Heideggerian deconstruction (*Destruktion*) that I have spent my life questioning—precisely as one of the legacies we are speaking of, legacies to receive, to mine, to discuss, to filter, to transform, faithfully unfaithfully.[44]

Well, what is important to me, since always, would be a deconstruction of *this* deconstruction, of this "Christian" landscape of deconstruction. It is necessary therefore *to pass* through this place. Can one pass through it? Can one limit oneself to passing through? What does it mean "to pass"? To surpass or overstep? To measure and mark one's step [*pas*]? Is it possible for this step not to be forever marked by what it has passed through? One *will* never *be able*—this is the destiny of the heritage—one *should* never want to avoid getting caught in a tight spot. Or even of stepping right into it. No one would go anywhere, nothing would ever happen otherwise.

In Praise of Psychoanalysis

E.R.: We will now speak of something that has been our common reference throughout this dialogue, and well beyond: psychoanalysis. As soon as I say this, I think of Sandor Ferenczi's beautiful idea, which was to found a Society for the Friends of Psychoanalysis. Such a society would bring together writers, artists, philosophers, and jurists interested in the discipline.[1] It was Freud who inspired him with the project—for Freud had surrounded himself with the intellectuals in the Psychological Society that met every Wednesday, which he founded in Vienna at the beginning of the century. He believed that psychoanalysis should in no case remain the property of a corporation of practitioners.

In 1964, Lacan took up this idea when he founded the Ecole Freudienne de Paris (EFP, 1964–1980), which was to welcome members who were not psychoanalysts. When I entered it, in 1969, I had not yet been analyzed.[2] Thanks to my mother, Jenny Aubry, a founding member of this school and a close friend of Lacan's, I benefited from a particular status in this community: I had been immersed in the culture of this movement since my childhood.

Your life and your work have been marked by psychoanalysis. Your wife, Marguerite Derrida, is a psychoanalyst and has translated some of Melanie Klein's texts; one of your longtime friends, Nicolas Abraham,[3] was a psychoanalyst, and he introduced you to René Major,[4] more than thirty years ago. With him, you have played an important role in the history of psychoanalysis in France. I myself crossed paths with you again, if I may say, thanks to him, beginning in 1977. During that period, having been inspired by your work, he was "deconstructing" the dogmas and rigidities of the psychoanalytic thought that was dominant at the time; he did this in part by bringing together under the name "Confrontation" all the younger people in the psychoanalytic community in France, a young group with institution *fever* [*en* mal *d'institution*], so to speak, and of which I was a part; this was a young group confronted, on one side, with the bureaucracies of the International Psychoanalytic Association (IPA) and, on the other, with the final throes of the last great living master of psychoanalysis: Jacques Lacan.

I owe a great deal to René Major, who encouraged me to write the history of psychoanalysis in France and who always embodied a spirit of resistance and tolerance at the heart of psychoanalysis: notably in his struggle against every form of collaboration or complicity, past or present, between psychoanalysts and Nazism, torture and dictatorship.[5]

A highly moral figure of the international Freudian community, Major has always recognized a theoretical debt to you,[6] and you have always supported him in this struggle, which was how I met him, and which gave rise to the States General of Psychoanalysis, held in July 2000.[7]

J.D.: I like the expression "friends of psychoanalysis." It evokes the freedom of an alliance, an engagement with no institutional status. The friend maintains the reserve, withdrawal, or distance necessary for critique, for discussion, for reciprocal questioning, sometimes the most radical of all. But like friendship, this engagement of existence itself, the engagement at the heart of experience, the experience of thought and experience *tout court*, assumes an irreversible approbation, the "yes" given to existence or to the event, not only of something (psychoanalysis) but of those whose origin and history will have been marked by their thinking desire—which will also have paid the price.

In a word, this "yes" of friendship assumes the certainty that psychoanalysis remains an ineffaceable historical event, the certainty that it is a *good thing*, and that it ought to be loved, supported, even when, as in my case, one has not practiced it within an institution, neither as an analysand nor as an analyst, and even when one cultivates the most serious questions concerning a great number of phenomena referred to as "psychoanalytic," whether it's a question of theory, of institution, of right, of ethics or of politics. "The friend" salutes a sort of Freudian revolution; he assumes that it has already marked and should continue to mark, always otherwise, the space in which we live, think, work, write, teach, etc. Of course, it will not surprise you if I say that I implicitly load this word "friendship" with all the worries, questions, affirmations, even mutations that are at work in my book *Politics of Friendship*, which itself assumes a certain psychoanalytic "legacy" without which it would not have been possible (notably in its deconstruction of the fraternalist privilege), but which also doesn't spare Freud and certain of his disciples (here Jung and Ferenczi)—in one chapter in particular—nor especially the psychoanalytic interpretation of inheritance and of the generations "*up until now.*"[8] A certain "up until now" marks both the threshold and the limit of the friendship we are speaking of, that of the "friend of psychoanalysis." However difficult and contradictory this may appear, the friend can consider, in the name of psychoanalysis itself, that psychoanalysis has taken place without yet having taken place: "up until now." What does this mean, "up until now"? That is the question.

The friend is therefore the one who holds to his vigilance and who exercises it from a distance that is always being negotiated and displaced. The friend of psychoanalysis does not belong to the corporation, but he claims the right, if not the duty, to speak the truth to those who work or who suffer within the body of the corporation. The right, if not the duty, I said. One must be more attentive than ever to this porous, permeable, unstable border, which simultaneously assures and forbids the passage between psychoanalysis and right, all the questions of right. Today, as you know, this border is undergoing great turbulence. "The friend" is the one who approves, acquiesces, affirms the ineffaceable necessity of psychoanalysis, that is, above all, of its future-to-come, but who is also interested in the problematic, sometimes artificial, artifactual, and therefore deconstructible and perfectible character of the relations between psychoanalysis and its right, as between its theory and its practice, between the necessity of knowledge and its institutional inscription, between the public space of psychoanalysis and the absolute originality of its "secret" space, irreducible to all "publicity," beyond even what we commonly recognize and legitimize under the concept of the "professional secret" (medical, judicial, etc.). Far from authorizing everything, this other "secret" calls, with at least equal rigor, for another ethics, another right, another politics. In short, another law (a law of the other, of course, another heteronomy).

E.R.: You have maintained a very personal relationship with Freud's texts. I am thinking in particular of your lecture of 1966, "Freud and the Scene of Writing," and your radio interview with Jean Birnbaum, in which you speak of the legitimacy of your reading of Freud: "I am willing to accept the hypothesis that if one has not been analyzed, nothing is possible." You were responding to certain practitioners of psychoanalysis, whom I would qualify as "religious," and who consider that only psychoanalysts or those who have been analyzed are qualified to read the works of the psychoanalytic corpus. A transferential reading, in a way, reserved for initiates. I do not at all share this opinion, and you responded to it by saying: "I, too, deal with people who are suffering, and I think sometimes that I am more of an analyst than those who are paid to be one."[9]

As for Lacan, you knew him and you read his work, unlike other intellectuals from a period previous to yours, who knew him but did not have the same proximity with his work. I'm thinking of Georges Bataille, Maurice Merleau-Ponty, Claude Lévi-Strauss, Roman Jakobson. They were friends of Lacan's, but they considered his teaching too hermetic. It must be said that before the publication of the *Ecrits* in 1966, this teaching was known only in a fragmentary way through typewritten transcripts or articles, published in specialized journals that were hard to find. For my part, although through my mother I knew Lacan very well from the age of nine, it wasn't until the publication of the *Ecrits*, when I was a student in linguistics at the Sorbonne, that I understood the importance of his thought.

Lacan suffered from the incomprehension of his friends who didn't read him.[10] At the same time, he did not recognize the importance of the philosophers of your generation, who began to read his work later, between 1964 and 1970. I remember that at that time he had become quite intolerant, as you yourself recall in your lecture for the conference "Lacan avec les philosophes," and as you confided to me in 1986.[11]

J.D.: I had read Freud in a very fragmentary, insufficient, conventional way, and Lacan in a way that was even more incomplete, barely preliminary, at the time—between 1964 and 1965—when the "matrix," so to speak, of *Of Grammatology* took shape, which conditioned all my later work.

But first I would like to say a word about Lacan, since you have invited me to. At the time when I wrote *Of Grammatology*, I didn't know Lacan. I had looked superficially at "The Instance of the Letter in the Unconscious," and partially, I think, at "Function and Field of Speech and Language in Psychoanalysis."[12] From 1963 to 1965, I elaborated the problematics of the trace, which governed a deconstruction of logocentrism and phallocentrism. That's when I began to perceive and to analyze Freud's debt to metaphysics. If psychoanalysis is unthinkable outside of this philosophical tradition, this latter makes psychoanalysis possible but also limits it. In short, as it often happens, and no doubt always, X makes Y impossible at the very moment of making it possible.

Up until 1965, I had not yet realized the necessity of psychoanalysis in my philosophical work. Beginning with *Of Grammatology*, I sensed the properly *deconstructive* necessity of again calling into question the primacy of the present, of full presence, as well as self-presence and consciousness, and therefore of putting the resources of psychoanalysis to work. Of course, up to then I was not totally blank or ignorant, but my knowledge of psychoanalysis was not, by right or in theory, integrated into my "own" problematic, nor even really articulated with it.

And yet, what had not yet clearly appeared was beginning to emerge "point by point." Concerning the problematic of the trace, as an important principle of contestation and a strategic lever of deconstruction, situating it within and along the edges of psychoanalysis was indispensable. In *Of Grammatology* and especially in "Différance," I tried to situate, at least, the necessity of reinterpreting a certain path opened and left behind by Nietzsche and Freud. The question of differance, or of the trace, is not thinkable on the basis of self-consciousness or self-presence, nor in general on the basis of the full presence of the present. I felt indeed that there was in Freud, in reserve, a powerful reflection on the trace and writing. Also on time. There were others, I think, who were also sensitive to this proximity between what I was saying and psychoanalysis. Invited by André Green to give a lecture at the Société Psychanalytique de Paris, I wrote the essay on the "mystic writing-pad," which was first accepted, and very well received, if my memory is correct, in *Tel Quel.*[13] You see, in this one sentence, I just named and left suspended I don't know how many historical threads, a whole spider's web of misunderstandings that were then beginning to be woven, or even fabricated. Without end. (I will here leave in peace, or in reserve, an entire work of the archive, of history and sociology—of ideas and of people. This has all been published and is accessible to whoever wants to read and has the means to do so.)[14]

It was then—roughly from 1968 to 1971—that I began to read certain texts by Lacan and to discover many exciting things in them, as well as many sites of resistance and residues of metaphysics. Since then I have confronted these issues often and at length, whether it is in terms of a certain conception of "true speech" or "full speech," a "logic of the signifier," or the reference to Heidegger. After that, without wanting to reduce Lacan's work to the famous "Seminar on 'The Purloined Letter,'" I proposed what one could call an analysis of it, in 1975, in the text entitled "The Purveyor of Truth"[15]—which gave rise, as you know, to a number of debates, and a number of publications, notably in the United States. There was never, to my knowledge, any public response from Lacan or from anyone close to him.

To return to Freud: my concern was to find, in a "logic of the unconscious" (but I never made this expression my own), something with which to support a discourse that, from another place, according to another approach, I felt to be necessary. It was a question of the motifs of deferred action, delay, or "originary" differ*a*nce, everything that ruined or threatened the absolute phenomenological authority of the "living present" in the movement of temporalization and the constitution of the ego or the alter ego, the presentation of sense, of life, and of the present in phenomenology—which was for me, at the time, like the very element of thought and discourse, even if my relation to Husserlian phenomenology was also the privileged site for deconstructive questions.

But the "friend of psychoanalysis," faced with so many metaphysical schemas at work in the Freudian and Lacanian projects, remained on his guard. Always, therefore, a double gesture: to mark or remark in Freud a resource that had not yet been read, it seems to me, as I thought it should be, but at the same time to submit Freud the "text" (theory and institution) to a deconstructive reading. Since no text is homogeneous (this has become for me a sort of categorical axiom, the charter of all my interpretations), it can be legitimate, and is even necessary, to do a reading of it that is divided, differentiated, even contradictory in appearance. This reading—active, interpretive, performative, signed—must be and cannot not be the invention of a rewriting.

E.R.: You didn't directly take on the great metapsychological texts of Freud. You approached him either through works considered "speculative" (*Beyond the Pleasure Principle*, for example), or through marginal texts: those on the "uncanny" or on telepathy, for example.[16]

J.D.: That's what I have always done, not only with Freud.

E.R.: Freud saw in what he called metapsychology a way to take psychoanalysis out of psychology and to prevent it from being subservient to philosophy. Unable to bring psychoanalysis into the natural sciences, he invented metapsychology,[17] that is, a speculative model, in order to inscribe it at the intersection of the natural sciences and speculative reflection. Hence the idea of translating metaphysics into a metapsychology, that is, of renouncing the knowledge of being for that of unconscious processes.

It is striking to see that his approach is similar to a movement of return—often found at the end of the nineteenth century, and notably in Nietzsche—to the pre-Socratics, to these old Greek philosophers for whom nature was traversed by great myths. You yourself have worked on this question a number of times. Freud often pays homage to Empedocles, and if at times he places philosophical discourse in the category of paranoia, he also makes it the paradigm of a high degree of civilization. In *Moses and Monotheism*,[18] he compares philosophy to monotheism. Why did you not take the notion of metapsychology as an object of reflection?

J.D.: I acknowledge that the grand conceptual framework was no doubt necessary. It was necessary for breaking with psychology within a given context of the history of science. But I wonder whether this conceptual apparatus will continue to survive for long. I may be mistaken, but the id, the ego, the superego, the ideal ego, the ego ideal, the secondary process and the primary process of repression, etc.—in a word, the large Freudian machines (including the concept and the word "unconscious"!)—are in my opinion only provisional weapons, or even rhetorical tools cobbled together to be used against a philosophy of consciousness, of transparent and fully responsible intentionality. I have little faith in their future. I do not think that a metapsychology can hold up for long under scrutiny. Already, it is hardly being talked about anymore.

I prefer in Freud the partial, regional, and minor analyses, the most venturesome soundings. These breaches and openings sometimes reorganize, at least virtually, the entire field of knowledge. It is necessary, as always, to be ready to give oneself over to them, and to be able to give them back their revolutionary force [*puissance*]. An invincible force. Finally, whatever the inequalities of development, the "scientific" incompleteness, the philosophical presuppositions, this force always involves the reaffirmation of a reason "without alibi," whether theological or metaphysical. This reaffirmation of reason can go against a certain state or a certain historical concept of reason,[19] and this force can provoke thought beyond even "power [*pouvoir*]" and the "drive for power" identified by Freud, and therefore the drive for sovereignty.[20]

But the very aim, and I do say the *aim*, of the psychoanalytic revolution is the only one not to rest, not to seek refuge, in principle, in what I call a theological or humanist alibi. That is why it can appear terrifying, terribly cruel, pitiless. Even to psychoanalysts, even to those who, on both sides of the couch, more or less pretend to put their trust in psychoanalysis.[21] All the philosophies, the metaphysics, the theologies, the human sciences end up having recourse, in the deployment of their thought or their knowledge, to such an alibi.[22]

Among the gestures that convinced me, seduced me in fact, is its indispensable audacity of thought, what I do not hesitate to call its courage: which here consists in writing, inscribing, signing theoretical "fictions" in the name of a knowledge without alibi (therefore the most "positive" knowledge). One thus recognizes two things at once: *on the one hand*, the irreducible necessity of the stratagem, of the transaction, the negotiation in knowledge, in the theorem, in the *positing* of truth, in its demonstration, in its "making known" or its "giving to understand," and, *on the other hand*, the debt of all theoretical (but also all juridical, ethical, and political) *positing*, to a performative power structured by *fiction*, by a figural invention. For the convention that guarantees every performative inscribes within itself the credit that is conferred upon a fiction. For example, in the most "speculative" moments of *Beyond the Pleasure Principle*, a text I have often returned to (and recently, at the States General of Psychoanalysis, to a beyond of its beyond, to a beyond of the death drive, the drive to destruction and cruelty),[23] one can show—and Freud says this himself—that the opposition between the reality principle and the pleasure principle, with its unlimited consequences, is a theoretical fiction. There are many others in Freud's discourse.

The "friend of psychoanalysis" in me is mistrustful not of positive knowledge but of positivism and of the substantialization of metaphysical or metapsychological agencies. The grand entities (ego, id, superego, etc.), but also the grand conceptual "oppositions"—which are too solid, and therefore very precarious—that followed those of Freud, such as the real, the imaginary, and the symbolic, etc., or "introjection" and "incorporation"—these seem to me to be carried away (and I tried to demonstrate this more than once) by the ineluctable necessity of some "differ*a*nce" that erases or displaces their borders. Which in any case deprives them of all rigor. I am therefore never ready to follow Freud and his followers in the functioning of the grand theoretical machines, in their functionalization.

E.R.: In my opinion, on the contrary, it is necessary to take account of the break introduced by Freud and to continue to work *with* the metapsychology. For if one gives way on what you call the grand theoretical machines, one runs the risk of liquidating the very principle of the Freudian "subversion," the principle of its innovation, and of going back to old notions of the unconscious (cerebral, neuronal, cognitive, subliminal, etc.),[24] historically very interesting, but extremely poor compared to the inventive force of the Freudian system, which gave birth to an interpretive richness found nowhere else. I have the impression that in philosophy, one is faced much less with such a risk of regression. There is a specific fragility to psychoanalysis that has to do with its very object: the unconscious, in the Freudian sense, can always be avoided, refuted, judged "dangerous," and therefore banished from consciousness and reason, etc. Hence the necessity, in order to maintain a certain creativity, to return incessantly to Freud's original gesture, to counter the dogmas arising within psychoanalysis itself when it claims to "go beyond" Freud, that is, to "bury" him.

J.D.: No doubt. But the specificity of the struggle waged by Freud still needs to be sharpened. From a historical point of view, I can understand perfectly well how one can justify the "construction" of a Freudian discourse, but on the condition of knowing that the field in which it did its work is no longer our own. Certain elements endure, but I would not make the "unconscious" and the agencies of the second topography into scientific and scientifically assured concepts.[25] I do want to cite them and use them in certain strategically defined situations, but I do not believe in their value or their pertinence beyond this battle field. Other "theoretical fictions" are henceforth necessary. This is not a relativist or opportunistic response on my part. On the contrary, it is a concern for scientific truth and a lesson drawn from the history of science, from the life or the progress of scientific communities, which are also "productive," "performative," and interpretive communities.

One day, the best part of the psychoanalytic legacy will be able to survive without the metapsychology, and perhaps even without any of the concepts I just mentioned. Hence a sometimes troubling and anguishing strategic difficulty. Indeed, in saying such things, one always risks giving help to those who would like to "liquidate" psychoanalysis. I do not mean to say that we have "gone beyond" Freud's work, but I would like to be able to say what I am now saying without concluding that the battle is over.

E.R.: You did not write a "Specters of Freud," but I am convinced that *Specters of Marx* is a profoundly Freudian book, more Freudian, without any doubt, than any of the texts you have written explicitly on psychoanalysis. Just as I am sure that it is necessary to make the spirit and the desire of the Revolution live, beyond the failure of communism, likewise I want to ask questions about how to make the spirit of the Freudian subversion live, precisely because psychoanalysis, as a treatment and a therapeutic practice, has not failed in the way that communism did, whatever people may say. However, despite its clinical force, psychoanalysis has enclosed itself, through the ossification of its institutions—whose usefulness I do not dispute—within a certain academicism, and I am convinced that creativity will return to it from the outside, from work like yours or like that of people working in literature, historians, writers, and perhaps scientists, if they give up wanting to enclose this discipline within the ghetto of an ideology of experimental proof, of counting or measurement, which is in no way appropriate to it.

Personally, I find myself in the very strange situation of being both outside and inside. I am a "daughter of psychoanalysis," as I have said, through my origins and my formation, but I feel more and more in the position of a "friend," because of the dichotomy that has been established between clinical practice, internal to the milieu, and intellectual production, in which I participate and which is rather external. It will one day be necessary to form a conjunction between the real clinical force represented by the anonymous practitioners and the patients, and the creative power of theoretical reflection expressed more and more outside the Freudian community.

J.D.: One point of disagreement, perhaps: philosophy is familiar with scenarios and stakes that are at least analogous. One does not deconstruct simply by progressing, without risks. One must always reaffirm something of the past in order to avoid a relapse into something worse. Strategic problems are therefore also essential, and always inevitable in philosophy. Philosophical concepts, sentences, discourses, or arguments are always *also* stratagems.

You are right to compare these two premature "death notices," these two alleged deaths, that of Marx and that of Freud. They attest to the same compulsion to bury the malcontents alive and to initiate an impossible mourning. But the survival of each of these two "dead men" is not symmetrical to the other. One affects the totality of the geopolitical field of world history; the other casts the shadow of its half-mourning only on what are called "constitutional" states, on the European, Judeo-Christian democracies, as one says too quickly—but one cannot say "Abrahamic" in this case, since Islam has remained, on the whole, inaccessible to psychoanalysis (an enormous problem, which I bring up in "Psychoanalysis Searches the States of Its Soul").

You asked me how to maintain the subversive virtue of Freud. I try to do so, as you have said, in texts devoted to psychoanalysis, as in others. Isn't the urgent task today that of bringing psychoanalysis into fields where up until now it has not been present? Or active?

Once again, it is not the Freudian theses that count the most in my view, but rather the way in which Freud has helped us to call into question a large number of things concerning law, right, religion, patriarchal authority, etc. Thanks to the impulse of the initial Freudian send-off [*coup d'envoi*], one can, for example, renew the question of responsibility: in place of a subject conscious of himself, answering for himself in a sovereign manner before the law, one can introduce the idea of a divided, differentiated "subject" who cannot be reduced to a conscious, egological intentionality. And the idea of a "subject" installing, progressively, laboriously, always imperfectly, the *stabilized*—that is, nonnatural, essentially and always *unstable*—conditions of his or her autonomy: against the inexhaustible and invincible background of a heteronomy. Freud helps us to place in question the tranquil assurances of responsibility. In the seminar entitled "Questions of Responsibility," which I have been giving for twelve years, I have treated questions such as testimony, the secret, hospitality, forgiveness, and now the death penalty. I am trying to see what terms such as "answer before," "answer to," "answer for," "answer for oneself" can mean when one looks at them from the point of view of what is still called "the unconscious."[26]

E.R.: For my part, I try to analyze what in 1981 you called "geopsychoanalysis." You used the expression during a French and Latin American gathering organized in Paris by René Major, the aim of which was to denounce both the Latin American dictatorships and the collaboration of certain psychoanalysts with this type of regime.[27]

You noted at the time that, during the thirtieth congress of the International Psychoanalytic Association, held in Jerusalem in 1977, the direction of the IPA had divided psychoanalysis into three zones: (1) everything located north of the Mexican border; (2) everything located south of this border; and (3) *the rest of the world.* This classification was unheard of, when you think about it, since this "rest of the world" included Europe, the birthplace of psychoanalysis—a continent without which it would never have existed elsewhere—together with other parts of the world that are non-Judeo-Christian, where it exists only as an enclave (India and Japan), but where it is bound to develop eventually. This is already visible in the interest shown in these countries in reading and translating texts; I'm thinking particularly of China, Korea, etc.

I was very sensitive to what you said in your intervention, and on my side I tried to show that psychoanalysis could only have taken root in constitutional states and therefore almost always in what are customarily called "Western societies." Today, with the fall of communism, psychoanalysis is taking root again in places where it had been banned for political reasons: Russia, Poland, Rumania, etc. But, with globalization, we are witnessing a process of "ready-for-occupancy" exportation. The IPA exports its standards the way one exports a factory with its technicians, without taking into account the local situations, or what happens after everything is set up, or the attitudes of the indigenous labor force, or that of the consumers.

For example, it obliges the practitioners in Eastern Europe who want to be given the label of "study group"[28] to set up treatment facilities that for the moment do not correspond to any local reality. It's not because of the universality of the unconscious, madness, or desire that, to grasp their functioning, one would have to impose on newly emergent locations things like couches, training sessions, lengths of treatment, or session times, which do not correspond to the demands made by those awaiting a psychoanalysis to come.

Moreover, in the countries where it has met with considerable success, psychoanalysis is always attacked, mocked, threatened, and derided. We never stop hearing the announcement of its end, or of how we have gone beyond it, or of its alleged incapacity to "care for" the maladies of the soul, and we continually hear prophecies of the death of Freud (like that of Marx). Moreover—this is the case in France—it is not considered an integral and independent discipline apart from the schools in which clinical training is transmitted. Despite all the struggles that have been fought, and in which you recently participated, psychoanalysis remains "forbidden" in the high spheres of republican teaching: no chair at the Ecole des hautes études en sciences sociales or at the Collège de France.

J.D.: What is exported by way of imperialism, by way of colonialism, by way of every other mode of diffusion of Western thought, is not, generally speaking, only norms, advancements, and positions. It is also crises and destabilizing interrogations, in the course of which the "subject" finds himself only by finding himself put to the test. Today, we are witnessing *simultaneously, on the one hand,* the consolidation of everything that binds right, law, and the politics of citizenship to the sovereignty of the subject, and, *on the other hand,* a possibility for the "subject" to deconstruct himself, to be deconstructed. The two movements are indissociable. Hence the paradox: globalization is Europeanization. And yet, Europe is withdrawing; it is being fissured and transformed. What is exported, in a European language, immediately sees itself called into question again in the name of what was potentially at work in this European legacy itself, in the name of a possible auto-hetero-deconstruction. Or even, I would say, of autoimmunity. Europe is in my opinion the most beautiful example, and also the allegory, of autoimmunity. I say "beautiful example" because if Europe is beautiful, it is because of this strange beauty: autoimmunity as survival; invincibility as autoimmunity. The immense tragedy of a beautiful suicide, you see . . .

Consequently, the European legacy is not a set of values or of spiritual goods; it is not a legacy of movable or real property. It would be rather an inexhaustible potential for crisis and deconstruction. It is difficult today, for this very reason, for this double reason of a reason that is getting the better of itself [*a raison d'elle-même*], to think the relations between Europe and its others, the non-European "cultural zones." These latter, while developing a powerful and indisputable contestation of Eurocentrism, are in the process of letting themselves be Europeanized far beyond the imperialist or colonialist forms we know. We are therefore witnessing, we are participating in—whether we like it or not—this double movement: globalization of Europeanness and contestation of Eurocentrism. Whether we are Europeans or not, we have to think this double solicitation.

As for psychoanalysis, we must take note of the fact that, as you were saying, it has taken root, certainly in a limited fashion, in a world of European traditions, in a world that includes the two Americas. And this is so even as it continues, in that very world, to encounter numerous resistances, which oblige it to penetrate certain institutions in a clandestine or marginal fashion. It has at bottom very little influence in the university. When it does, it is not through direct teaching; it is rather smuggled in, through literature or otherwise. Even within its place of birth, its cultural territory, the place occupied by psychoanalysis remains so narrow!

E.R.: That can be explained by the fear aroused by the idea of the unconscious.

J.D.: A "subject," of whatever kind (individual, citizen, state), is instituted only out of this "fear," and it always has the force or the protective form of a barrier or a dam. A dam interrupts energy, which it then accumulates and channels. For throughout all the differences that must not be forgotten, our European societies are always dominated by something like *one* ethical, juridical, and political "system," *one* idea of the Good, of Right, and of the City (of citizenship or the state). What I am calling, too quickly, a "system" and an "Idea" must still be protected against that which risks emerging from psychoanalysis—which, however, grew in Europe and, more often than not, through the person of Freud, continues to cultivate a European model of culture, civilization, and progress.

This "system" and this "Idea" are above all constructions produced to resist what is felt to be a threat. For the "logic of the unconscious" remains incompatible with what defines the identity of the ethical, the political, and the juridical in its concepts, but also in its institutions, and therefore in its human experiences. If one took psychoanalysis [la *psychanalyse*] into account, seriously, effectively, practically, this would be a nearly unimaginable earthquake. Indescribable. Even for psychoanalysts.

There are times when this seismic threat passes through ourselves, through the interior of each individual. In our life, as we well know—we know it all too well—we present equivocal, hypocritical discourses, in the best cases ironic, structurally ironic. We proceed as if psychoanalysis had never existed. Even those who are convinced, as we are, of the ineluctable necessity of the psychoanalytic *revolution*, and at least of the psychoanalytic *question*, well, in their lives, in their current language, in their social experience, they act *as if* nothing had happened, if I may say, in the last century. In an entire zone of our life, we proceed as if, at bottom, we believed in the sovereign authority of the ego, of consciousness, etc., and we speak the language of this "autonomy." We know, certainly, that we speak several languages at once. But that changes almost nothing, neither in the soul nor in the body, in the body of each one and in the body of society, in the body of the nation, in the body of the discursive and juridico-political apparatuses.

What had already struck me in 1981, when I wrote "Géopsychanalyse," was that the large national and international institutions of psychoanalysis are constructed according to political models that are themselves in crisis, or even in ruins—the state, a certain international law—according to models that are not in themselves psychoanalytic. Certainly, the reference to Freud is there, but as a whole, the charters that govern the psychoanalytic institutions are not in themselves psychoanalytic. In Freud's time the models were already outdated, inadequate in any case to what was required by the psychoanalytic revolution. No doubt this was strategically inevitable. But today? I do not see most analysts taking account of all the problematic new configurations in national and international law ("crimes against humanity," "genocide," limitation of sovereignty, the project of an international criminal court, the problems or progress of abolitionism with regard to capital punishment, etc.). From this point of view, and despite exceptions, the institutional discourse of psychoanalysis appears archaic. At times to the point of becoming comical.

There are many different forms of institutions, and, seen from a distance, the IPA seems to me the most archaic. But neither do I see, in the other associations, any greater degree of organized and fundamental (or even re-founding) reflection that measures up to these new juridical, ethical, and political configurations linked to "globalization."

E.R.: There are two major models. The first was the one inaugurated by Freud with the Wednesday Psychological Society in Vienna: this is the Platonic model corresponding to an aristocratic organization of the movement and referring back to Greek culture—a master surrounded by his disciples. The second, which came after the first one historically and was adopted by the IPA, is a corporatist, associative model. It is consciously based on each member's renunciation of the place of the master. Intent on reserving for Freud the historical place of a "unique" founder—that is, the founder of a discipline—his successors created the IPA so that the associative model would prevent any particular member from setting himself up as a charismatic leader.

For the first Freudians,[29] psychoanalysis was the property of a founding father, who designated those close to him as a "savage horde." The ones who left him saw themselves as dissidents no longer belonging to the circle of the elect. Beginning in 1910, the sovereign function of power was delegated by Freud to the IPA. For almost twenty years, this latter was the sole legitimate, not to say legal, authority of psychoanalysis, directed not by the founder who continued to embody its creative force, as a *master without commandment*,[30] but by his first-generation disciples. With successive schisms, beginning in 1927, the IPA gradually ceased to be the site of sovereignty of psychoanalysis, even while remaining, for some time yet, its only legitimate authority. In effect, those who split off did not leave the community, of which Freud, while still alive, was still the principle agent, but they sought to create other currents within this community. The secessionism that took place between the wars was in this respect a symptom of the impossibility for psychoanalysis to be represented in its totality by a single government. This secessionism reflected something that was the very essence of the Freudian invention: the decentering of the subject, the abolition of mastery, the defeat of monarchical authority.

This is why, after the Second World War, the IPA was no longer regarded as the sole institution capable of uniting all the various currents of psychoanalysis into an indivisible community. Not only did other associations emerge then, seeking to remain at the heart of a single empire, but *multiple* groups emerged who refused the very principle of a unique membership. Some of them made claims to the disappeared father and his doctrine; others called for a surpassing or an abandonment of his system of thought. This type of secessionism in particular was a sign that psychoanalysis was being transformed into a mass movement.

With the passing of time, the IPA became such a bureaucratic and corporatist association that it was abandoned or contested from within by all those who sought to revive a creative spirit through theoretical renewal. It must be said in all fairness that it was subjected to the constraints imposed by the "market" (and today by globalization), particularly in the United States, where the practitioners were obliged to submit to the arbitrary demands of financial groups, responsible for their own insurance and that of the patients, and more concerned with making profits than with contributing to any intellectual reflection. In a word, the "commodification" of psychoanalysis, and the sterile battles it had to wage for status— or for a rejection of all status (which amounts to the same thing)—against the background of a newly developing spirit of competition that placed it on a path of rivalry, whether with the psychopharmacological laboratories or with all sorts of other psychotherapies—all this ended by making nearly everyone forget the original splendor of the grand Platonic symposium orchestrated by Freud at the beginning of the century.

In 1964, forced to leave the IPA, Lacan attempted a return to the Platonic model, to the grand symposium of the Viennese origins. Hence the appellation "Ecole" in the sense of the philosophical schools of ancient Greece. Lacan is the only heir to Freud who really attempted to think the question of a school of psychoanalysis that would be neither a professional corporation, nor a party, nor a sect, nor a bureaucracy. He pushed the reflection on this subject very far, and I can testify to this, having participated in this adventure as a member of the EFP [Ecole Freudienne de Paris] beginning in 1969.

However, I have always thought that this type of experience could last only for a short time. In relation to the original Platonic model, which assumes the real presence of a real master, the producer of an innovative body of work, the associative model has all of eternity before it. On one side, the force of a subversive event, bound up with the singularity of one destiny, and necessarily limited in time; on the other, the long duration of institutional conservation (the model of the "hedgehog" we spoke of before).

The current situation is a reflection of this history that we have inherited. We know henceforth that no International can claim to embody the legitimacy of psychoanalysis. Consequently, all of its institutions are marked by a certain mourning for a sovereignty lost forever, or they are engendered by the interminable mourning for this figure of a master to whom each one wants to be faithful, at the risk of reconstructing it in the form of a simulacrum.

J.D.: I am convinced, as you are, that Lacan was without doubt one of the rare people who have tried to change the institution. And like you, I believe that *something of an institution* [*de l'institution*] is necessary. That said, I have no ideal "solution" either, if by that we mean a discourse or arrangement that would leap fully armed, like Athena, from the paternal head. One cannot wait passively for something to happen, in the form of a new constitution, a new charter, or a new institution. It would be unwise to believe that the day after the States General, for example, a new international or national psychoanalytic institution will be able to emerge. Institutions change, even the oldest ones, and I hope in any case that the IPA will see that something important took place.

Globalization not only creates more permeable borders but also transforms the modes of communication, the transmission of knowledge and of norms. I think it's important that the States General of Psychoanalysis were prepared on the Internet. This implies a speed, a multiplicity of messages, but also a dehierarchization, that is, a new way of addressing the psychoanalytic community that short-circuits the bureaucracy. As soon as one disturbs the hierarchization, one disturbs the entire institution. What is hierarchy from the psychoanalytic point of view? You spoke of master and disciple. Yes, this is certainly important, but there are other forms of hierarchization.

I have always been struck by the extraordinary concern for hierarchical status within psychoanalytic institutions. The ones I am familiar with are at least as concerned with status and hierarchy as the most traditional university. They resemble the medical corporations, in which one sees those in charge ruling as masters over assistants in submission. I'm not saying that all this must be reduced to a blank slate—I am for a certain hierarchy—but these models ought to change by being inspired, in their very change, by psychoanalytic teaching. That has never yet taken place, as far as I know.

When one speaks of Lacan, of the Lacanian space or the Lacanian legacy, it is necessary to keep from overly identifying things. Everything about it is conflictual and heterogeneous. The only place where I see any life is in sites of dissidence—more interesting at times than centrality. Control over this Lacanian enclave, quite large in France and in Latin America, is being disputed by more or less aleatory forces and movements. Keeping the proper proportions in mind, one could push quite far the analogy—in terms of an enclave to be controlled and a sovereignty to exercise—with Balkanization and with the recent or current tragedies in the former Yugoslavia.

E.R.: At the heart of the Lacanian field, not only has the rigid model of treatment, clocked at five times a week, been spontaneously called into question, but so have the intolerance of homosexuality, racism, and all the most conventional forms of submission in the medical hierarchy, of which Freud, it must be remembered, was the victim in turn-of-the-century Vienna. Lacan gave the initial send-off to a phase of Freudianism that I have described as "orthodox," since it aimed not to go beyond Freud but to return to the famous "original splendor" of a discovery. However, he was much more open than other Freudians to all the various movements of emancipation, in France at least.

J.D.: That's not by chance. Lacan was interested in the symbolic spaces of culture to a degree matched by very few psychoanalysts of his time: an enlightened interest in law, politics, literature. Hence the fact that in these neo-Lacanian, para-Lacanian, or post-Lacanian spaces, there is, more than elsewhere, a certain openness to these transformations.

I do not know where all this will lead. I would not even know how to trace the outline of what is going to happen. A complex process is evidently under way, both within what is given the name of psychoanalytic community, corporation, or institution, and along the outer borders of psychoanalysis: psychiatry, the domains of "therapy," and, at least if there are any, the foreign domains with therapeutic concerns, the general culture, the media, the law. *On* these mobile, unstable, and porous borders, affecting precisely the form and the existence *of* these very borders, change will continue to accelerate. Leading where? I don't know. It is necessary to know, to know this, but it is necessary also to know that without some kind of non-knowledge nothing happens that deserves the name of "event."

E.R.: I do see, in fact, a true change among young psychoanalysts, a greater desire for transverse movements and connections, and for democracy.

J.D.: What psychoanalytic institutions have to rethink, in their very charter, in their mode of sociopolitical functioning, is first of all the relation to the state. In every country, institutions are defined in relation to the state—in France in particular. But the crisis of state sovereignty will oblige psychoanalytic institutions to work out their relation to something other than the state—not necessarily to a governmental type of international institution (to a superstate, in sum) or to a nongovernmental one—to something other than citizen sovereignty. In other words, to something other than a "subject," but to something that remains nevertheless in the order of law. A law, however, that would have taken into account, in an effective way, the psychoanalytic revolution. This won't happen tomorrow. But if something still remains to come, if there is something of a future-to-come, if there is any event to come, beyond all performative sovereignty and all foreseeability, beyond every horizon from which one believes one sees it coming, it will be, it would be on this condition.

E.R.: To come back to Lacan and to the subject we are concerned with, I would like to talk about the conference "Lacan avec les philosophes," organized ten years ago by René Major.[31] At the time there was a controversy between the different interpretations of Lacan's work. Now that some time has passed, this controversy seems rich and alive. I wonder if we could organize a similar event again today, as the hundredth anniversary of Lacan's birth is celebrated.

In 1993, I published a book on Lacan[32] that shocked both my Lacanian friends and the anti-Lacanians. The former reproached me with the crime of lese majesty; the latter, who were even worse, declared that they were furious that I had taken from them the object of their scorn by relating the excesses committed by Lacan, notably when he reduced the time of his sessions to a duration close to zero. But I did it without ever belittling the man. As an epigraph, I quoted a sentence from Marc Bloch: "All of you who are for Robespierre and who are against him, we beg your mercy: have pity and tell us, simply, who was this Robespierre." I remember that at the time—just after the book had come out and when you were about to take a flight to the United States—you told me to "retreat to the Aventine," because the projectiles would come flying from all sides. Since then, I have often thought of these words you abruptly offered me at the corner of the rue des Saints-Pères and the rue de Grenelle.[33] For years after that, I took part in dozens and dozens of discussions, confrontations, critical debates. But when I read certain books on Lacan by the psychoanalysts of my generation, I have to acknowledge at times that very few of these books measure up to the debates that took place during that conference in 1990. Fortunately, there are some notable exceptions, which testify in their way to significant changes. But despite these exceptions, the contemporary writings on Lacan have a difficult time escaping from two dominant categories: catechism and anticatechism, discourses that are either pious or destructive.

I also notice a fear of approaching, of thinking about the psychic cruelty that marked Lacan's childhood, and that, without any doubt, explains his capacity to grasp in such a modern fashion not only the essence of human madness but some of the major forms of abjection in this century. I say this without animosity and with all the more hope in that, from another perspective, I think that my Lacanian friends are in the process of actually carrying out the mourning I mentioned earlier.

J.D.: At the time of that conference on Lacan, nine years after his death, it seemed that the moment had come to recount something directly, the apparently anecdotal history, at least, of my personal relations with him. This text did not really have any new "contents"; in it I recounted a personal story while recapitulating the elements of the theoretical discussion. What was new, perhaps, was the necessity of saluting Lacan in a context that had been transformed. Psychoanalysis already appeared to be receding. At that period, I sensed, as many others did, a regression in relation to the Lacanian exigencies. From this point of view, and at that transitional juncture, the alliance with Lacan seemed to me a just one.

Besides that, whatever their points of divergence, all the speakers showed that they took Lacan's thought very seriously. Even in the debates and conflicts one may have had with Lacan, there was a great philosophical and theoretical exigency. Elsewhere this was, and still remains, on the verge of being lost. And even of being denounced. At the time when the conformist philosophical discourse that we discussed at the beginning of this dialogue was being reconstituted, I thought it necessary to remember and to remind others that we would do well to read or to reread the texts of that period.

E.R.: Another "event" or encounter took place that means a great deal to me, namely your failed and yet successful dialogue with Yosef Hayim Yerushalmi. In June 1994, with René Major, we organized a conference at the Freud Museum in London entitled "Memory: The Question of Archives."[34] Yerushalmi was ill and was unable to come, so he did not speak with you then. His paper, which was read by someone else, dealt with the Sigmund Freud Archives,[35] and yours was an "explication" dealing with his book *Freud's Moses*.[36] Later you actually met Yerushalmi in New York, but he never responded to your commentary, at least not to my knowledge.

For quite a long time I had wanted to bring a great historian of Judaism into dialogue with a great philosopher, both of them with an excellent knowledge of Freud's work and deeply concerned with the problems of memory, the archaic, and the interpretation of Jewishness in a world after Auschwitz. This encounter interested me all the more in that I have always found myself in a situation "divided" between several disciplines, particularly between philosophy, science, and the texts of history. Philosophers accuse historians of historicism; the latter reproach philosophers for not taking the archive into account and for an excessive propensity for abstract interpretation; and literary people don't want to hear anything about the history of ideas.

However, in my opinion, one cannot do "good" history without a certain philosophical theorization of history, nor can one do "good" philosophy without a solid historical and historiographic approach. As for the literary analysis of texts, it is indispensable to anyone who wants to escape ideological, teleological, or quantitative history. I wanted to shake things up a little on this terrain. I will add that the question of the archive was a concern of mine since, in writing my book on Lacan, I had almost no concrete sources: neither on his childhood nor on his manuscripts, etc.[37] There are a lot of oral testimonies available on Lacan, but very few written documents, and even fewer letters. Very few images, only two black and white films, and a few photographs, only some of which are in color.[38]

In *Archive Fever*, you pose the problem of the archive's *archontic*[39] power in history, and you address the question of Freud's Jewishness, which has been the subject of many studies. I would like to come back to it here. Three orientations emerge in this regard: the first (David Bakan) aimed to inscribe the Freudian theory into the tradition that secularizes Jewish mysticism; the second, the most common, presented a Freud who was decentered from his Jewishness and at the mercy of the double problematic of Spinozian dissidence and integration into German and Greco-Latin culture;[40] the third, that of Yerushalmi, reintegrates Freud into the history of Judaism without denying his atheism or his integration into German culture. In this perspective, psychoanalysis becomes the continuation of a godless Judaism and therefore of an interminable Jewishness.

Although I do not agree with all of Yerushalmi's choices, I find it exciting that he reopened this question concerning the Jewishness of psychoanalysis, the archive, and the interpretation of Freud's texts.

You reproach Yerushalmi for wanting to assert, in reference to a lecture by Anna Freud from 1977,[41] that Freud would have accepted the idea of psychoanalysis as a "Jewish science," not in the pejorative sense in which the Nazis meant it, but in the sense that Freud would have conceived it as a new Covenant. You also criticize the way in which Yerushalmi makes use of the Archive. He does provide archival proof for his argument by reproducing and commenting on the dedication written in Hebrew by Jakob Freud—whom you call "the archpatriarch of psychoanalysis"—in a Bible he gave to his son Sigmund Freud for his thirty-fifth birthday. According to Yerushalmi, this dedication would signify that Freud knew the sacred language better than he claimed and that *Moses and Monotheism* would be a delayed response to the paternal injunction of fidelity to the faith of his ancestors.

According to you, everything happens as if Yerushalmi had placed himself in the position of archon of the archive in order to "circumcise" Freud a second time[42] and to bring him back into Judaism. You also stress that you are all the more sensitive to the approach taken by the historian here in that your own father was named Hayim and you yourself had been marked by the problematic of circumcision.

J.D.: If we follow Yerushalmi, one would not need psychoanalysis to understand the question of the murder of the father in the story of Moses. Everything happens as if this attempt at murder could not be taken into account since the murder was not effectively or *actually* [English in original] carried out in reality.[43] At the center of a discussion that I cannot reconstruct here, we find again the Freudian distinction between "historical truth" and "material truth." Freud's argument relies on a conceptual difference between two types of history: one based on the real archive, that is, on facts that took place and are publicly recorded, the other invoking a psychical truth discernible in symptoms and making it possible to say that a *temptation* to murder *can* be equivalent *to* a murder. This would be true *a fortiori* for an *attempt* to murder, a real attempt in which an acting out is initiated. Now, Yerushalmi ought to recognize, as a historian who cites his archive, that there was at least such an *attempt* to murder. It is attested and taken into account by what he calls the "rabbis in the Midrash."[44]

Yerushalmi does not take sufficiently seriously, it seems to me, the Freudian propositions on repression, the formation of the symptom, the distinction between "historical truth" and "material truth"—which he nonetheless evokes.[45]

I also interrogate the distinction between "Jewishness" and "Judaism" [both words in English in original].[46] At bottom, Yerushalmi seems ready to abandon Judaism. Not out of infidelity to Judaism, but out of fidelity to Jewishness, which, from his point of view, is marked by two fundamental vocations: the experience of the promise (the future) and the injunction of memory (the past). This was troubling to me—and I discreetly said so.[47] Every culture, every non-Jewish community would claim these two fundamental traits.

After asking Yerushalmi a few questions, I began to see, I think, that despite everything, when it came to Moses, he wanted to erase the originality or the necessity of the psychoanalytic explanation. There is (according to him), in a certain tradition of Jewish interpretation, a wealth of resources prior to psychoanalysis, which for its part, seen from this perspective, essentially brings little more to bear on these questions. In sum, at the heart of a certain Jewish tradition, the interpreters had *already* been, according to him, very subtle psychoanalysts.

This celebration of a "Jewish specificity" (having to do with memory, the future, the anticipation of psychoanalysis, etc.) seemed very debatable to me in its content (but as always over the course of our conversation, I will refrain from reproducing arguments that have already been published; it would be difficult and too lengthy; I prefer to refer the interested reader to these publications). I also wondered whether Yerushalmi did not risk giving sustenance, willingly or not, to a *political* use of the very serious theme of election (so difficult to interpret), and more precisely of the "chosen people."

E.R.: I agree with you in mistrusting any glorification of some specificity or of a chosen people. And yet there is something like an almost inexpressible specificity, it seems to me. You know that the Nazis attempted to eradicate psychoanalysis as a "Jewish science." Not only did they persecute the Jewish representatives of the discipline, but they also sought to "exterminate" the doctrine itself: by burning books, abolishing the vocabulary, suppressing the concepts, etc. But they did not act in the same way with the school of individual psychology founded by Alfred Adler, although he was just as Jewish as Freud. Among all the other theories of psychic life, only psychoanalysis was declared a "Jewish science" by the Nazis and condemned *as such*.[48]

From this I conclude that there is something specific about it that strikes directly at Nazism. I wonder if the unconscious in Freud's sense—this thing that is not seen, this *invisible* thing, this thing of a universal nature—was not for Nazism an equivalent of the Jewishness it considered all the more dangerous for being invisible, recognized only as an identity or an abstract entity, detached from all real membership in a group, all ethnicity.

We have already stressed, in an earlier chapter, the extent to which the anti-Semitism to come is discernible only through a style, through words, rhetoric, and turns of phrase marked by denial. I wonder if Jewishness would not be considered all the more dangerous for being invisible. To the point, in any case, that its identification by anti-Semites could take place only indirectly and by way of a denial.

Michel Foucault pointed out, in 1976, that after Freud's rupture with the theories of heredity and degenerescence, and in reaction to the rise of racism that was contemporary with him, he grounded sexuality in "the law—the law of alliance, tabooed consanguinity, of the Sovereign-Father." In short, he had endeavored to "surround the question of desire with all the trappings of the old order of power." And Foucault added: "It was owing to this that psychoanalysis was—in the main, with a few exceptions— in theoretical and practical opposition to fascism."[49]

This judgment by Foucault, with which I agree, points to the discipline itself. It is indeed *as a discipline* that psychoanalysis is in essence incompatible with the dictatorial forms of fascism and with every type of discrimination associated with it (racism, anti-Semitism, xenophobia, etc.), and this is true independently of the practitioners who saw fit to collaborate with such regimes. In its rejection, on principle, of the death penalty and in the fact of engaging psychoanalysis *as such* in this rejection, Freud had grasped this reality, I think, although without theorizing it. He had understood, no doubt unconsciously, that psychoanalysis *as such* opposed everything that one might call "the crime industry." I am thinking of the excellent formula from Thomas Mann, with regard to the *Anschluss*: "How such a man [Hitler] must hate analysis! I secretly suspect that the fury with which he marched against a certain capital city was directed at bottom at the old analyst living down there, his true and actual enemy, the philosopher and revealer of neurosis, the great disillusioner, the very one who knows, and shows, the ways of 'genius.'"[50]

J.D.: It seems to me that the Nazis also wanted, in a certain way, to eradicate science itself, the "universalistic" and "abstract" principle of science.

E.R.: But why this science, and not other theories of the mind invented by other Jews? Is there not something in this Freudian conception of the unconscious that touches on an invisible universal, of which Jewishness would be a sort of mirrored expression? We would find there again

Freud's idea according to which Jewishness would be transmitted by "our blood and nerves,"[51] that is, by the path of a hereditary unconscious and therefore through a phylogenetic inheritance.

In sum, with Freud, Jewishness becomes the emblem of a sort of perpetual memory of the human, a memory that Freud thinks in Darwinian or Lamarckian terms, but that today we can translate otherwise, with other concepts. It is not limited to Jewish identity but extends to man in general. Between the (Freudian) unconscious and Jewishness, there would thus be a specific equation that would forbid one to reduce the human to a race or an archetype, at the price of convoking the symbolic Law (that of the defeated and humiliated father) so that it will occupy the place of the old authoritarian sovereignty (that of the tyrant). This is only a hypothesis, of course, but it relates to what you have said about the archive in the Freudian sense. Just as, with regard to the law, you propose to introduce a Freudian dimension into the understanding of history.

For you, the archive is not only the document but an "imprint," the "weight of something radically unthought" that governs the relation of memory to knowledge: a "Freudian impression," as you say. This Archive (with a capital A) would ceaselessly subvert the authority of the patriarchal state (the sovereign patriarchal state) since it thinks itself as the holder of an archontic power over the archive.

J.D.: I believe that this science characterized as "Jewish" carries within it a formidable question concerning the leader and the political organization. Freud's major political texts are a threat to the Nazi organization. It seems to me, however, that psychoanalysis did not survive the communist regime, either.

E.R.: Here, too, there is no symmetry between Nazism and communism. Psychoanalysis was condemned as a bourgeois science in the Soviet Union only starting in 1947–49, at a time when there were no more psychoanalysts in the country. In addition, it was condemned for its supposed complicity with American imperialism.

J.D.: Is it less grave to condemn a science as "bourgeois science"?

E.R.: No, of course not, but all the other theories of psychic life underwent the same fate at a time when the only reference point in this domain was Pavlov's work on conditioning. Besides that, in the case of Zhdanovism,[52] the adjective "bourgeois" was used everywhere: bourgeois literature, bourgeois philosophy, etc.

J.D.: Under Nazism, there was talk of degenerate science, degenerate Jewish art, degenerate literature, etc. When it comes to psychoanalysis as a Jewish science, I find myself incapable of reconstructing the logic of the argument. But as you know, Freud himself did not exclude the existence of something Jewish in psychoanalysis.[53]

E.R.: Freud oscillated between two positions; like you, and contrary to what Yerushalmi says, I don't believe that he ever considered psychoanalysis really as a Jewish science. Early on, he wanted to avoid such an equation for strategic reasons. Freud, the Jewish man of science, the heir of the Haskalah,[54] wanted to de-Judaize psychoanalysis in order to make it the universal theory of a universal unconscious. Thus he designated Carl Gustav Jung, a non-Jew, as the head of his movement (the IPA).

Beginning in 1913, after the split with Jung, which he experienced as a betrayal, Freud reversed his course and withdrew, in a way, into the ghetto of his Jewish and Viennese disciples. This was the time of the so-called "Secret Committee," during which Ernest Jones, the only non-Jew in this restricted group, felt he was the victim of a certain anti-goy ostracism. It is certain that at that time, Freud dreamed that psychoanalysis might be "Jewish," but he did not believe in this dream. Later on, he never gave way to any return to a religious or ethnic type of Jewish identity. He remained a man of the Enlightenment, in the manner of a thinker drawn to the dark side of the *Aufklärung.* Thus he did not reclaim his Jewishness until he was confronted with anti-Semitism. We find here again your model of unfaithful fidelity. In *Moses and Monotheism,* he "deconstructs" the notion of the chosen people, which he rejects.

J.D.: Independence and contradiction: there is nothing I understand better. Uprooted despite myself, I have, rightly or wrongly, made no sufficient effort to reroot myself; in fact I have cultivated withdrawal; I am even on my guard before any Jewish community. But when confronted with the least sign of anti-Semitism, I do not deny and will never disown my Jewishness, the one I search for in myself—which can be read in so many signs—or the one that others believe they can attribute to me.

Sartre said, quite a long time ago, that the Jew is produced by anti-Semitism.⁵⁵ If this were simply true, if it were really a question of being produced by others, if the Jew were really projected by anti-Semitism, one would not need first to be Jewish to be thus engendered by the other, anti-Semitic or not. (At the end of his life Sartre seems to have acknowledged the ignorance, not to speak of the misrecognition, of the Jewish tradition, or traditions, shown in this book, which was written immediately after the war.) But to be born Jewish and, for a man, to be circumcised, this can never be reduced to a projection of the other, anti-Semitic or not. This heritage can be neither disowned nor denied. Asymmetrical, heteronomic, it precedes speech, the oath, the contract.

You yourself are unlike any ordinary Catholic citizen, even though you were baptized. You feel that you were marked, passively, even before anti-Semitism instituted this mark in you. You are *affected* by Judaism *even before* anti-Semitism produces or transforms your identity for you. And this identity is not the same for you as for someone who is born a Breton, for example.

I have a great deal of trouble with the "doctrine" of election. I would be capable of expressing the worst suspicions against it, but, whether I wanted it or not, I was designated, assigned, signed, even before my birth, even before I had any choice to make. There is a universal "structure" of heteronomic election: I am the only one to be called to do this or that; I am irreplaceable in the place of this decision, in being obliged to respond: "It is me," "I am here," etc. This *election of each* seems to me to give to all responsibility worthy of the name, if there is any, its chance and its condition.

As for Jewishness "by birth," there it is a question of another form of election (which one may or may not see as a blessing; that's secondary), which a good number of Jewish thinkers would like to *bind together* [*relier*] with the universal one I just evoked. That is for me the site of this problem, this *bond*, but, in any case, something, some One marked my destiny even before I had a word to say. That is what I call circumcision, in the literal or figural sense. I am marked even before being able to speak. And this is true for women too. You were not circumcised, but you know that a mark preceded and traversed your Catholicism.

E.R.: You were circumcised, and therefore the mark was inscribed on the body?

J.D.: I will not dare to say that it's a metaphor. But whenever I have spoken of this (and I have done so abundantly, from *Glas* to *The Post Card*, from *Shibboleth* to *Circumfession*, and again recently in the film by Safaa Fathy),[56] I have also treated the rhetoric that has always worked the literality or the tropic value of circumcision into the body: the circumcision of the sex, that said to be "of the heart," of the lips, and of the tongue, etc.

E.R.: But if you hadn't been circumcised, you would still feel Jewish in the same way!

J.D.: If someone had told me in one way or another that I had been born into a Jewish family, indeed, that would have been equivalent. For girls too. I'm not saying this in order to erase a mark that really, concretely, exists. I am interested—and I insist on this—in all the *figures* of circumcision, in what makes it such that one need not be literally circumcised, nor even a man, for this to exist, this marking prior to speech.

We know very well, however, that literal, "physical," "traumatic" circumcision has original effects. There is too much to say on this subject. And this remains, like female excision (which is massively practiced in the world, and which I consider an even more violent aggression, with murderous and in any case irreversible effects that are much more grave than circumcision, with which it has no common measure), it remains a question that will not fail to be submitted, more and more, like the death penalty, to "globalized" debates. I therefore try to have an interest, for myself and elsewhere, both in the general and universal figure of circumcision, of excision and in all the ethno-religious markings of the body.[57] These inscriptions do not take place just anywhere.

E.R.: Circumcision is not specific to Jews, but it became the mark one ought to renounce if one was a Freudian. Freud refused to circumcise his sons because he was hostile to bodily marks. He accepted the intellectual heritage of Judaism and never hesitated to underscore his Jewishness, but he also saw himself as an "unfaithful Jew."

J.D.: Many Jews, faithful and unfaithful, have spoken of circumcision—notably Spinoza. He stressed that circumcision assured the continuity and the survival of the Jewish people. I recall this in *Circumfession*.[58]

E.R.: But can one maintain such a position today?

J.D.: Orthodox Jews, and hardly the least refined among them, will tell you that if circumcision is abandoned, Judaism risks losing something essential. More generally, if circumcision is abandoned (literal or figural circumcision, but everything is played out around the letter, in Judaism as well as in Islam), one is on the road to an abandonment of phallocentrism. This would apply *a fortiori* to excision. This abandonment applies also to Christianity, since these three religions are powerfully, although differently, phallocentric. In any case, phallocentrism and circumcision link Islam and Judaism. I have often stressed the profound irreducibility of the Judeo-Islamic couple, or even its often denied privilege, in comparison to the confusedly accredited couple Judeo-Christian.[59]

E.R.: I would tend to think that one can abandon circumcision but not phallocentrism, in the sense in which Freud made it the Law of the father, a law coming from a defeated sovereignty that is no longer the sovereignty of tyranny but of its transfer to the symbolic, and to the universality of sexual difference. In other words, to be much more modern than the "postmodernism" that would want to abolish every form of symbolic function by a sort of unbounded deconstruction, I think that militant antiphallocentrism is always condemned, despite its good intentions, to valorize a matricentric power—or a nihilistic one—which is as formidable as the phallocentrism it claims to abolish. It is therefore necessary to break out of this symmetry and not to oppose antiphallocentrism to phallocentrism.

Better a defeated father who is rid of his tyrannical authority, a deconstructed father, humiliated and conscious of the necessity for humbling his former sovereignty, which has become impossible, than an absolute—and necessarily sovereign—power attributed to mothers: a power that is all the more "phallic" for being exercised as revenge and especially as the simulacrum of a conquest of femininity, or of the unlimited *jouissance* of which women themselves would risk, in the end, being the primary victims.

In this respect, and to take up your comparison between the couple Judeo-Islamic (which has been denied) and the couple Judeo-Christian (which has been affirmed), I notice that psychoanalysis is for the moment *forbidden*, as it were, in the Arab-Muslim world, that is, in Islam, even though a few people are practicing it and attempting to institutionalize it (particularly in Morocco and in Lebanon). In this world, and contrary to the Judeo-Christian world, the law of the father is still oppressive, and not "oedipal," "deconstructed," "defeated." Even if, as you say, we must not confuse Islam and Islamism,[60] in Islam today, this tyranny is exercised on women's bodies, in particular in the form of the "veil," which, as I see it, symbolically forbids them to speak in their name. And it is for this reason that many women do not wear it anymore or fight in order not to wear it anymore. The fact that this alienation may be *unconscious* makes it all the more formidable. But, as we know, the freedom to speak in one's name, and therefore to interrogate the essence of one's own alienation, is indispensable to the exercise of free association that characterizes the Freudian treatment, which was "invented" by a woman.[61]

J.D.: You are more Lacanian than I am. But indeed, if one reverses the hierarchy in order to attribute to mothers the old power of the fathers, that changes nothing.

E.R.: We are struggling for equality and emancipation. But psychoanalytic experience shows that the power exercised by the mother over the child and the infant can also show itself to be as destructive, from the point of view of psychic life, as that of tyrannical fathers, and even more formidable. I would like it if women, on their way to becoming all-powerful in democratic societies, attributed a new place to these fathers who have accepted the narcissistic wound of sharing their former privileges. If not, what will happen to them, and what will happen to the men?

J.D.: What if we suspended the dialogue on this question, which is yours? It would be in the end rather humorous, and would no doubt give more to be thought than a response from me.

Notes

Notes written by Jacques Derrida are marked "J.D."; those by Jeff Fort are marked "Trans." Unattributed notes are by Elisabeth Roudinesco.

In citations, the date of original publication is given in parentheses after the title of the translation unless the work was published first in translation.

FOREWORD

1. "Spectre toujours masqué qui nous suis côte à côte./Et qu'on nomme demain!/Oh! Demain, c'est la grande chose!/De quoi demain sera-t-il fait?" ("The specter, always masked, that follows by our side./We call it tomorrow!/Oh! Tomorrow is the great thing!/For what tomorrow will be, no one knows.") Victor Hugo, "Napoléon II," in *Les chants du crépuscule* (1835), vol. 1 (Paris: Gallimard, Bibliothèque de la Pléiade, 1964), pp. 838 and 811.

[Hugo's verse "De quoi demain sera-t-il fait?" (literally: "Of what will tomorrow be made?") has become a common saying in French, often occurring in another form: "Personne ne sait de quoi demain sera fait" ("No one knows what tomorrow will be").—Trans.]

2. I would like to thank Colette Ledannois who transcribed the tape for the speed and quality of her work.

3. This formula is found in Robert Louis Stevenson and is repeated by a character in Fritz Lang's *Moonfleet* (1954).

CHAPTER I

1. *Héritage*, translated here and in this chapter's title as "heritage," can also be rendered as "inheritance" and "legacy." The term occurs frequently throughout the present work. In each case I have chosen one of these three translations based on context, connotation, and consistency, but it is worth keeping in mind that they render a single French word.—Trans.

2. Jacques Derrida first used the term "deconstruction" in 1967 in *De la grammatologie* (Paris: Editions de Minuit, 1967) (published in English as *Of Grammatology*, trans. Gayatri Chakravorty Spivak [Baltimore: Johns Hopkins University Press, corrected ed. 1998]). It was initially borrowed from architecture, where it

signifies the laying out or decomposition of a structure. In its Derridian definition, it refers to a work of unconscious thought ("it deconstructs itself [*ça se décon-struit*]") and consists of undoing, without ever destroying, a hegemonic or dominant system of thought.

To deconstruct is in some way to resist the tyranny of the One, of the logos, of (Western) metaphysics, and to do so in the very language in which it is articulated, by using the same material that one displaces and moves for the purposes of reconstructions that remain in motion. Deconstruction is "what happens [*ce qui arrive*]," without our knowing whether it will arrive at a destination, etc. Derrida also attributes a grammatical meaning to the term, according to which it designates a disarranging of the construction of words in a sentence. See Jacques Derrida, "Letter to a Japanese Friend" (1985), in *Derrida and Differance*, eds. David Wood and Robert Bernasconi (Warwick: Parousia, 1985), pp. 1–5. In the Littré dictionary we read: "Modern scholarship has shown us that in a region of the timeless East, a language reaching its own state of perfection deconstructed itself [*s'est déconstruite*] and was altered from within itself, according to the single law of change natural to the human mind."

3. Claude Lévi-Strauss, *Tristes Tropiques* (1955), trans. John and Doreen Weightman (New York: Penguin Books, 1992); Michel Foucault, *Madness and Civilization* (1961), trans. Richard Howard (New York: Random House, 1965); Michel Foucault, *The Order of Things* (1966) (New York: Random House, 1970); Louis Althusser, *For Marx* (1965), trans. Ben Brewster (London: New Left Review Editions, 1977); Jacques Lacan, *Ecrits* (Paris: Seuil, 1966), a portion of which was translated as *Jacques Lacan, Ecrits: A Selection*, trans. Bruce Fink (New York: Norton, 2002).

4. Jacques Derrida, *Writing and Difference* (1967), trans. Alan Bass (Chicago: University of Chicago Press, 1978).

5. See Elisabeth Roudinesco, *Généalogies* (Paris: Fayard, 1994), and François Dosse, *History of Structuralism* (1992), trans. Deborah Glassman, 2 vols. (Minneapolis: University of Minnesota Press, 1997).

6. This conference was attended by intellectuals with widely varying tendencies, and, more specifically, by writers involved with three journals: *Tel Quel, Change*, and *Action Poétique*. On this occasion, I presented a paper in which I showed that Derrida's theses were inspired by a Heideggerian vision of the archaic similar to those of Carl Gustav Jung. I recounted this episode in Elisabeth Roudinesco, *Jacques Lacan & Co.: A History of Psychoanalysis in France, 1925–1985* (1986), trans. Jeffrey Mehlman (Chicago: University of Chicago Press, 1990), pp. 540–42. [This is a translation of volume 2 of Roudinesco's *Histoire de la psychanalyse en France*. Volume 1 has not been translated and will therefore be cited by the French title in what follows.—Trans]. See also Elisabeth Roudinesco, *L'inconscient et ses lettres* (Paris: Mame, 1975). Jacques Derrida had responded to me in *Positions* (1972), trans. Alan Bass (Chicago: University of Chicago Press, 1981).

7. Jacques Derrida, "Unsealing ('The Old New Language')," in *Points … : In-*

terviews, 1974–1994 (1994), ed. Elisabeth Weber (Stanford, Calif.: Stanford University Press, 1995), p. 130. See also "Rencontres de Rabat avec Jacques Derrida: Idiomes, nationalités, déconstructions," ed. Jean-Jacques Forté, *Cahiers Intersignes*, 13 (1998).

8. Jacques Derrida, "Violence and Metaphysics: An Essay on the Thought of Emmanuel Levinas" (1964), in *Writing and Difference*.

9. Luc Ferry and Alain Renaut, *La pensée 68* (Paris: Gallimard, 1986); published in English as *French Philosophy of the Sixties: An Essay on Antihumanism*, trans. Mary S. Cattani (Amherst: University of Massachusetts Press, 1990).

10. Jacques Derrida is the author of more than fifty books, as well as numerous prefaces and contributions to various collections. He has participated in approximately one hundred interviews.

11. Derrida writes *à-venir*, thus dividing the word *avenir*, "future," into its parts: "to-come." It will therefore be translated as "future-to-come."—Trans.

12. *S'en prendre*: This idiomatic French expression can mean "to attack," "to take it out" on someone or something, in the sense of "to blame," also "to challenge" and thus "to take on" in a contest.—Trans.

13. The last part of this sentence reads: " . . . une déconstruction qui se prend, qui se fait prendre et se laisse prendre dans ce qu'elle comprend et prend en considération tout en s'en éprenant."—Trans.

14. This double meaning involves a play on the verb *devoir*, "to owe, to be obligated," whose present participle, *devant* ("owing"), is identical to the preposition meaning "before" (in a spatial sense).—Trans.

15. *Devancer* ("to come or arrive before or ahead of") extends the set of associations of the previous sentence, giving it a temporal sense as well—and suggesting another word (analogous in its formation to *la différance*): *la devance*, which would be a situation of "owingness" in which what one has made one's own would be traversed by all the temporal and spatial relations of debt and obligation implied in this passage.—Trans.

16. The idiom, as a particular language, refers by extension to the manner of expression proper to an age, a social group, or a person. According to Derrida, the idiomatic is "a property that one cannot appropriate. It signs you without belonging to you; it appears only to the other and never comes back to you except in flashes of madness that bring together life and death" ("Unsealing 'The Old New Language')," in *Points . . .* , p. 119.

17. Jacques Derrida, "Force and Signification," in *Writing and Difference*, p. 3 [translation slightly modified].

18. Jacques Derrida, *Specters of Marx* (1993), trans. Peggy Kamuf (New York: Routledge, 1994). See below, Chapter 6, "The Spirit of the Revolution."

19. Jacques Derrida, *Politics of Friendship* (1994), trans. George Collins (London: Verso, 1997), chap. 4, pp. 75–111. Carl Schmitt, *The Concept of the Political*, trans. George Schwab (Chicago: University of Chicago Press, 1996).

Carl Schmitt (1888–1985) was a German jurist. A student of Max Weber, he took part in the political life of his country at the end of the Weimar Republic and at the beginning of Hitler's regime. Threatened by the SS, he abandoned his activities in 1936. After his arrest by the Allies in 1945, he was put on trial because of his ties with Nazism, but later his case was dismissed.

20. Derrida, *Politics of Friendship*, p. 135 n. 17 [translation slightly modified]. See also Sigmund Freud, "Thoughts for the Times on War and Death" (1915), in *The Standard Edition of the Complete Psychological Works of Sigmund Freud*, 24 volumes, trans. and ed. James Strachey, in collaboration with Anna Freud (London: Hogarth, 1953–74) [hereafter *SE*, followed by vol. number], vol. 14, pp. 273–302; and *Group Psychology and the Analysis of the Ego* (1921), *SE* 18, pp. 67–143.

21. Jacques Lacan, "Intervention sur l'exposé de Michel Foucault" (1969), *Littoral*, 9 (June 1983). The title of Foucault's presentation to the Société française de philosophie was "What Is an Author?"; the paper was published in *The Foucault Reader*, ed. Paul Rabinow (New York: Pantheon, 1984), pp. 51–75.

22. See Jacques Derrida, "The Violence of the Letter: From Lévi-Strauss to Rousseau," in *Of Grammatology*. See also Claude Lévi-Strauss, *The Elementary Structures of Kinship* (1949), trans. James Harle Bell, John Richard von Sturmer, and Rodney Needham (Boston: Beacon, 1969); and Claude Lévi-Strauss, *La vie familiale et sociale des Indiens Nambikwara* (Paris: Société des Américanistes, 1949).

23. Jacques Derrida, "Cogito and the History of Madness" (1963), in *Writing and Difference*.

24. "But on what grounds," writes Descartes, "could one deny that these hands and this entire body are mine? Unless perhaps I were to liken myself to the insane, whose brains are impaired by such an unrelenting vapor of black bile that they steadfastly insist that they are kings when they are utter paupers, or that they are arrayed in purple robes when they are naked, or that they have heads made of clay, or that they are gourds, or that they are made of glass. But such people are mad, and I would appear no less mad, were I to take their behavior as an example for myself." René Descartes, *Meditations on First Philosophy*, trans. Donald A. Cress, 3rd ed. (Indianapolis: Hackett, 1993), p. 14. In "Propos sur la causalité psychique" (1946, in *Ecrits* [1966], pp. 151–93), Lacan had already pointed out, as Derrida would do later, that the foundation of modern thought by Descartes does not exclude the phenomenon of madness. See Elisabeth Roudinesco, "Lectures de *Histoire de la folie* (1961–1986)," in *Penser la folie: Essais sur Michel Foucault*, ed. Elisabeth Roudinesco (Paris: Galilée, 1992).

25. In Derrida, *Writing and Difference*.

26. Claude Lévi-Strauss, *Introduction to the Work of Marcel Mauss* (1950), trans Felicity Baker (London: Routledge and Kegan Paul, 1987).

27. Michel Foucault, *Discipline and Punish* (1975), trans. Alan Sheridan (New York: Random House, 1979).

28. In Derrida, *Writing and Difference*.

29. Jacques Derrida, *Of Spirit: Heidegger and the Question* (1987), trans. Geoffrey Bennington and Rachel Bowlby (Chicago: University of Chicago Press, 1989).

This work was published in France at the same time as the French edition of Victor Farías's book *Heidegger and Nazism* (1987) (ed. Joseph Margolis and Tom Rockmore [Philadelphia: Temple University Press, 1989]), which rekindled debate on the German philosopher's collaboration with National Socialism. Derrida discussed this work in an interview with Didier Eribon for *Le Nouvel Observateur*. "Why does the hideous archive seems so unbearable and fascinating? Precisely because no one has ever been able to reduce the whole work of Heidegger's thought to that of some Nazi ideologue. This 'record' would be of little interest otherwise. For more than half a century, no rigorous philosopher has been able to dispense with an 'explanation' with [*explication avec*] Heidegger." See Jacques Derrida, "Heidegger, the Philosophers' Hell," in *Points . . .*, p. 182. After having been suspected of not sufficiently dissociating himself from Heidegger's Nazism, Derrida was also suspected, in the United States, of not having sufficiently mistrusted his friend Paul de Man (1919–1983), a professor and literary theorist who taught at a number of American universities and who, it was discovered in 1987, had been guilty of writing a literary column, between 1940 and 1942, for a Belgian newspaper that supported the German occupation. See Jacques Derrida, *Memoires: for Paul de Man*, trans. Cecile Lindsay et al. (New York: Columbia University Press, 1986; rev. ed., 1989).

30. In *French Philosophy of the Sixties*, Ferry and Renaut also add to the list Jean-François Lyotard (see p. 123 n. 3), considered a Heideggerian since the publication of *The Differend* (1983), trans. Georges Van Den Abbeele (Minneapolis: University of Minnesota Press, 1988).

31. See Chapter 9 below, "In Praise of Psychoanalysis."

32. "Derrida's strategy," write Ferry and Renaut, "consists of attempting to be more fundamentally Heideggerian than Heidegger himself"; and in a later passage: "One would have to consider, of course, not that Derrida constitutes a species of Heideggerian (a 'French Heideggerian'), but that Heidegger was a sort of German proto-Derridean." *French Philosophy of the Sixties*, pp. 130, 131 [translation slightly modified].

33. Ibid., p. 123.

34. Jacques Derrida, *Le toucher: Jean-Luc Nancy* (Paris: Galilée, 1999).

35. Between 1984 and 1988, Jacques Derrida devoted his seminar at the Ecole des Hautes Etudes en Sciences Sociales (EHESS) to the question of nationalism and the relation to the other: (1) "Nation, Nationality, Nationalism"; (2) "*Nomos, Logos, Topos*"; (3) "The Theologico-Political"; (4) "Kant, the Jew, the German"; and (5) "Eating the Other: Rhetorics of Cannibalism." See Jacques Derrida, *Psyché: Inventions de l'autre* (Paris: Galilée, 1987); and Derrida, *Politics of Friendship*, p. vii.

36. Jacques Derrida, *The Other Heading: Reflections on Today's Europe* (1991), trans. Pascale-Anne Brault and Michael P. Naas (Bloomington: Indiana University Press, 1992), p. 29.

37. In this regard, see Carl Schorske, *Fin-de-Siècle Vienna: Politics and Culture* (New York: Vintage, 1981); and Jacques Le Rider, *Crises of Identity: Culture*

and Society in Fin-de-Siècle Vienna, trans. Rosemary Morris (New York: Continuum, 1993).

38. After active participation in the anti-Nazi resistance, Jean Beaufret (1907–1982) was the spokesman in France for one of the major currents of Heideggerian thought. He contributed to a real engagement with Heidegger's texts but also to an obfuscation of Heidegger's involvement with the Nazis.

39. An heir to the Frankfurt School, Jürgen Habermas (b. 1929) broke with the Heideggerian legacy. See Jürgen Habermas, *Philosophical-Political Profiles,* trans. Frederick Lawrence (Cambridge, Mass.: M.I.T. Press, 1983).

40. Jürgen Habermas, *Philosophical Discourse of Modernity: Twelve Lectures* (1985), trans. Frederick Lawrence (Cambridge, Mass.: M.I.T. Press, 1987).

41. Jacques Derrida, *Limited Inc.,* ed. Gerald Graff, trans. Sam Weber (Evanston, Ill.: Northwestern University Press, 1988).

42. Derrida, *Other Heading,* and Jacques Derrida, *Du droit à la philosophie* (Paris: Galilée 1990).

43. See Jacques Derrida, "Racism's Last Word" (1983), trans. Peggy Kamuf, *Critical Inquiry,* 12 (Autumn 1985), pp. 290–99; and "The Laws of Reflection: Nelson Mandela, in Admiration" (1986), trans. Mary Ann Caws and Isabelle Lorenz, in Jacques Derrida and Mustapha Tlili, eds., *For Nelson Mandela* (New York: Seaver, 1987), pp. 13–42. See Chapter 6 below, "The Spirit of the Revolution."

CHAPTER 2

1. First published in French in the journal *Tel Quel,* 20 (Winter 1965), and included in Jacques Derrida, *Writing and Difference* (1967), trans. Alan Bass (Chicago: University of Chicago Press, 1978). [The English translation retains the French title.—Trans.]

2. First published in Jacques Derrida, *Théorie d'ensemble, Tel Quel* series (Paris: Seuil, 1968), and was later included in Jacques Derrida, *Margins of Philosophy* (1972), trans. Alan Bass (Chicago: University of Chicago Press, 1982). [Here, too, the English translation retains the French title.—Trans.]

3. Inspired by the work of Marcel Mauss, Georges Bataille distinguished two structural poles in his analysis of human societies and their institutions: on one side, the homogeneous, or the domain of productive human society, and on the other, the heterogeneous (the sacred, the drives, madness, crime, the unproductive, excrement, filth, etc.), which is impossible to symbolize or to normalize within the order of reason: an "other" existence expelled from all norms. Lacan was apparently inspired by this notion when he formulated his concept of the real, as was Foucault in his conception of "divisions" (reason/unreason/madness, etc.). See Georges Bataille, *The Accursed Share* (1949), vol. 1, trans. Robert Hurley (New York: Zone, 1988). See also Elisabeth Roudinesco, *Jacques Lacan* (1993), trans. Barbara Bray (New York: Columbia University Press, 1997).

4. This idea is also developed in "Plato's Pharmacy" (1968), in Jacques Derrida, *Dissemination,* trans. Barbara Johnson (Chicago: University of Chicago Press,

1981). In this reading of Plato's *Phaedrus*, Derrida analyzes the myth of Theuth (Thoth). According to the Platonic reading, Theuth—who is simultaneously the god of writing, a drug (*pharmakon*), and a remedy for the drug—enables the invention of writing as a remedy against forgetting. But writing is also something that causes sleep, and is therefore a figure of evil, a figure it claims to eradicate. To escape from the presence of the platonic *pharmakon*, it is therefore necessary to go against Plato, to vindicate the *pharmakon* as a differance, and thus to locate Socrates, the one who does not write, behind Plato, the one who writes and who closes the pharmacy. Here, too, we find the idea, already developed above in Chapter 1, of the possibility of turning a dominant discourse against itself.

5. See Chapter 5 below, "Violence Against Animals."

6. Jacques Derrida, *Monolingualism of the Other; or, The Prosthesis of Origin* (1996), trans. Patrick Mensah (Stanford, Calif.: Stanford University Press, 1998).

7. In February 1999, the French Parliament adopted a text introducing the differences between the sexes into Article 3 of the Constitution: "The law determines the conditions for organizing equal access for women and men to electoral procedures and elected office." In this way parity, and therefore the legal obligation to represent this difference, was written into law. This modification enables the National Assembly to vote on laws that will extend parity de facto at every level of civil society. It contradicts Article 2, which stipulates the indivisibility of republican sovereignty.

8. A term created by Jacques Derrida that combines phallocentrism and logocentrism, used to designate the primacy granted, on the one hand, by Western philosophy to the Platonic logos and, on the other, by psychoanalysis to the Greco-Freudian symbolics of the phallus, according to which there exists only one libido (or sexual energy), which is in essence masculine.

9. This is the gist of an article I published in *Le Monde*, February 11, 1999, in response to one by Sylviane Agacinski, *Le Monde*, February 6, 1999. For the arguments against parity, see Elisabeth Badinter, ed., *Le Piège de la parité* (Paris Hachette, 1999).

10. Jacques Derrida, "Mes 'humanités' du dimanche," *L'Humanité*, March 4, 1999: "Go for parity, then. A stopgap that is purely French, really, not to say Parisian, and hardly something that can be universalized (so much and yet so little has been said about universality on both sides), since so many other European democracies have been able to reach or approach the desired result, without a constitutional modification of this sort. . . . The trap of the constitutional debate means that no one has any confidence in their own political strength . . . and here it is outlined, directly before us, in certain discourses, in the somnambulant form of a maternalist fantasy: woman determined in her essence, as mother—and who can choose to be such herself, all alone naturally."

11. On this question, see the position taken by John R. Searle, "Is There a Crisis in American Higher Education?," *Partisan Review*, 4 (1993), pp. 693–708.

12. The term "revisionism" was adopted by certain American researchers call-

ing for a revision of the founding concepts of Freudianism. It has nothing to do with the "negationism" that denies the existence of the Nazi gas chambers. Generally speaking, revisionism in history is an attempt to critique established dogmas, a critique that can in no way be included with the type of negationism that attempts to deny the reality of acknowledged facts. In France, it was Henry Rousso who introduced the term *négationnisme*, in *Le syndrome de Vichy* (Paris: Seuil, 1987); published in English as *The Vichy Syndrome: History and Memory in France since 1944*, trans. Arthur Goldhammer (Cambridge, Mass.: Harvard University Press, 1991) (see especially the section entitled "Negationism," pp. 151–57). See Chapter 7 below, "Of the Anti-Semitism to Come."

[The French term *négationnisme* is often rendered as "Holocaust denial"; however, I will also use "negationism," especially when the context calls for a term that is less historically specific.—Trans.]

13. The petition was published in *Les Carnets de Psychanalyse*, 8 (1997). Concerning these debates, see *Le Monde*, June 14, 1995; and Elisabeth Roudinesco, *Why Psychoanalysis?* (1999), trans. Rachel Bowlby (New York: Columbia University Press, 2001), pp. 95–97.

14. Renaud Camus, *La campagne de France* (Paris: Fayard, 2000). Appearing in bookstores in April 2000, this book, by the author of some forty works, several volumes of which consist of personal diaries, contained anti-Semitic and racist passages. In the style of the Maurassian tradition, Renaud Camus defends those who are "of French stock" against immigrants and proceeds to give a count of the number of "Jewish" journalists working at France Culture [the French national public radio station—Trans.], while also explaining how revolted he was by Nazism and the Shoah. These passages were subject to the law of 1881 as modified by the law of 1972, which makes any form of public incitement to racial hatred a criminal offense. The book was therefore pulled from the shelves, which sparked an intense debate. Some took the side of Renaud Camus, pointing to the threat of censorship and "political correctness" and invoking the right of every writer to unlimited freedom of expression; others, on the contrary, emphasized the necessity of respecting the law in question and of opposing the sale of works containing such statements. Jacques Derrida was among the signatories of the petition initiated by Claude Lanzmann, who described the racist and anti-Semitic passages of the book as "criminal" (see *Le Monde*, May 25, 2000). Later, after studying Renaud Camus's earlier works, several commentators remarked that these works are shot through with similar passages, which in some cases had escaped the notice of the author's usual editor, and in other cases had been expurgated and replaced by blank spaces (see *Le Monde*, Aug. 3, 2000). It was in this form that *La campagne de France* appeared in bookstores again in July. The polemic finally expanded into a vast public debate concerning the relations between the law, censorship, and literature. On this question, see Chapter 7 below, "Of the Anti-Semitism to Come."

15. The original reads: "à coup de langue de bois."—Trans.

16. Dinesh D'Souza, *The End of Racism* (New York: Free Press, 1995).

D'Souza's excessive claims were criticized, notably, by Denis Lacorne in "Des coups de canon dans le vide?: La 'civilisation occidentale' dans les universités américaines," in *Vingtième Siècle*, no. 43, 1994, p. 4–17. See also Eric Fassin, "Les intellectuels, la politique et l'université aux Etats-Unis," in *Annales E.S.C.*, no. 2, 1993, pp. 265–301.

17. See Chapter 8 below, "Death Penalties."

18. See Chapter 9 below, "In Praise of Psychoanalysis."

19. Derrida, "Mes 'humanités' du dimanche."

20. Roudinesco, *Why Psychoanalysis?*; Elisabeth Roudinesco, "Rapport sur la psychanalyse dans le monde," presented July 8, 2000, at the Etats généraux de la psychanalyse, Paris.

21. Founded by Freud in 1910, the International Psychoanalytic Association (IPA) has ten thousand members representing thirty-two countries.

22. The "Pacte Civil de Solidarité" (PaCS) took effect in France after a law was passed on November 15, 1999. It allows couples (homosexual or heterosexual) to legalize their unions with a specific contract.

23. See Elisabeth Roudinesco and Michel Plon, *Dictionnaire de la psychanalyse* (Paris: Fayard, 1997; rev. ed., 2000).

CHAPTER 3

1. Coparenting is a situation in which a lesbian mother or a gay father works together with partners to have and to raise a child; these partners may include the biological parents as well as the social parents who raise the child. Thus a coparent can be a legal parent, a social parent, or a biological parent. "Same-sex parenting" [*l'homoparentalité*] is a term that appeared in 1997 to designate a situation in which at least one parent identifies him- or herself as homosexual.

2. On this question see Daniel Borillo, Eric Fassin, and Marcela Iacub, *Au-delà du PaCS: L'expertise familiale à l'épreuve de l'homosexualité* (Paris: PUF, 1999); and Martine Gross, ed., *Homoparentalités, états des lieux: Parentés et différence des sexes* (Issy-les-Moulineaux: ESF éditeur, 2000).

3. In the Netherlands, where homosexual marriages have been recognized by law since September 2000, approximately 20,000 children are being raised in coparenting or same-sex parenting situations. In a report in *Le Nouvel Observateur* (June 22–29, 2000), Theo, a seven-year-old, is quoted as saying: "I live with mama and Tata. Tata is like a mom, but she's more strict. I never had a dad. He was a friend of mom's who said he'd make a baby to help us. . . . When I grow up I'm going to live with a girl; it's less complicated for making babies."

4. Elisabeth Roudinesco, *Why Psychoanalysis?* (1999), trans. Rachel Bowlby (New York: Columbia University Press, 2001).

5. In certain cases of AID [artificial insemination with a donor], a child can come from three "mothers": the first donates her eggs, the second carries the child and gives birth to it, the third adopts and raises it.

6. On the question of cloning, see Chapter 4 below, "Unforeseeable Freedom."

7. "The relation would not be a-sexual, far from it, but would be sexual otherwise: beyond the binary difference that governs the decorum of all codes, beyond
the opposition feminine/masculine, beyond bi-sexuality as well, beyond homosexuality and heterosexuality which come to the same thing. As I dream of saving
the chance that this question offers, I would like to believe in the multiplicity of
sexually marked voices. I would like to believe in the masses, this indeterminable
number of blended voices, this mobile of non-identified sexual marks whose cho-
reography can carry, divide, multiply the body of each 'individual,' whether he be
classified as 'man' or as 'woman' according to the criteria of usage." Jacques Derrida, "Voice II," trans. Verena Andermatt Conley, in *Points . . . : Interviews,
1974–1994* (1994), ed. Elisabeth Weber (Stanford, Calif.: Stanford University Press,
1995), p. 156.

8. This is Didier Eribon's argument, which uses categories from the work of
Pierre Bourdieu; see Didier Eribon, *Réflexions sur la question gay* (Paris: Fayard,
1999). For a discussion of the homosexual gene, see Roudinesco, *Why Psychoanalysis?*

9. On this question see Françoise Héritier, *Masculin féminin: La pensée de la
différence* (Paris: Odile Jacob, 1996).

10. Freud never abandoned the idea of finding a biological foundation for psychic organization, which did not prevent him from renouncing the construction of
a "biology of the mind." On the contrary, he turned toward the construction of a
metapsychology, distinct from classic psychology, which aimed at elaborating theoretical models not directly tied to clinical observation.

11. Sigmund Freud writes: "As Lichtenberg says, 'An astronomer knows
whether the moon is inhabited or not with about as much certainty as he knows
who his father was, but not with so much certainty as he knows who his mother
was.' A great advance was made in civilization when men decided to put their in-
ferences upon a level with the testimony of their senses and to make the step from
matriarchy to patriarchy." *Notes upon a Case of Obsessional Neurosis* (1910), *SE* 10,
p. 233 n. 1.

12. Jacques Derrida, "La veilleuse," preface to Jacques Trilling, *James Joyce ou
l'écriture matricide* (Belfort: Circé, 2001).

13. The reader will have noticed the presence, or intrusion, of this figure of life
also in the phrase I have chosen to translate *le psychisme*: "psychic life."—Trans.

14. On this question see Geneviève Delaisi de Parseval, "La part du père et de
la mère à l'aube de l'an 2000," in Liber amicorum Marie-Thérèse Meulders-Klein,
Droit comparé des personnes et de la famille (Brussels: Bruylant, 1998), pp. 143–60.

15. For Derrida's commentary on Lacan's famous seminar on Poe's "The Purloined Letter," see Jacques Derrida, "The Purveyor of Truth," in *The Post Card*
(1980), trans. Alan Bass (Chicago: University of Chicago Press, 1987), pp. 413–96.
For the seminar, see Jacques Lacan, *Ecrits* (Paris: Seuil, 1966). Lacan's seminar was
first published in English as "Seminar on 'The Purloined Letter,'" trans. Jeffrey
Mehlman, *Yale French Studies*, 48 (1972), pp. 39–72; it was subsequently printed,

along with Derrida's "Purveyor of Truth," in *The Purloined Poe: Lacan, Derrida and Psychoanalytic Reading*, ed. John P. Muller and William Richardson (Baltimore: Johns Hopkins University Press, 1988). See also Chapter 9 below, "In Praise of Psychoanalysis."

CHAPTER 4

1. The term "scientism" came into general use around 1911 to designate the belief that *Science* would be able to explain and resolve all human phenomena. In 1890, in *L'avenir de la science* (Paris: Calmann-Lévy, 1949), Ernest Renan had already criticized this attitude and denounced what he called "the religion of science" (published in English as *The Future of Science* [Boston: Roberts Brothers, 1891]). Scientism is thus a "discourse on science that claims to abolish philosophy by using the discourse of science itself" (from Dominique Lecourt, ed., *Dictionnaire d'histoire et de philosophie des sciences* [Paris: PUF, 1999], p. 852).

2. Lacan did in fact say to Françoise Wolf, during an interview following his lecture at the University of Louvain in 1972, that he never speaks of freedom—which doesn't mean that he didn't speak of it on numerous occasions. Most often, he associates the term with madness, claiming that man's being can be understood only "because he carries madness within himself as a limit to his freedom." He also maintains that human freedom is an illusion, a phantom, a "horrible freedom," but he associates it with desire, death, and the Revolution; see "On a Question Preliminary to Any Possible Treatment of Psychosis," in *Jacques Lacan, Ecrits: A Selection*, trans. Bruce Fink (New York: Norton, 2002), p. 215; Jacques Lacan, "Kant with Sade," trans. James B. Swenson, *October*, 51 (Winter 1989), p. 69; and Jacques Lacan, *Ecrits* (Paris: Seuil, 1966), p. 157.

3. In Husserl, the bracketing of the transcendental world (epochē) leads to a transformation of ontology (the study of abstract realities) into an egology: being is reduced to the I who thinks. See Edmund Husserl, *Cartesian Meditations: An Introduction to Phenomenology* (1929), trans. Dorion Cairns (The Hague: Martinus Nijhoff, 1960). See also Jacques Derrida, *The Problem of Genesis in Husserl's Philosophy* (1953), trans. Marian Hobson (Chicago: University of Chicago Press, 2003).

4. Jacques Derrida, "Freud and the Scene of Writing" (1966), in *Writing and Difference* (1967), trans. Alan Bass (Chicago: University of Chicago Press, 1978). In this essay, Derrida interrogates the shift in Freud's work from the neurological to the psychical. See Chapter 9 below, "In Praise of Psychoanalysis."

5. "C'est (ce) *qui arrive*": the verb *arriver* can mean both "to arrive" and "to happen." *Arrivance*: as with *différer/différance*, Derrida has forged a substantive from *arriver* by way of its present participle *arrivant* ("arriving" but also, as the noun *l'arrivant*, "the one arriving" or "the arrival"); hence the very approximate rendering as "arriving-ness," with the implication also of something like "happening-ness."—Trans.

6. Freud points out that science has inflicted three major blows on human narcissism (on the ego); a cosmological one: no longer being at the center of the uni-

verse (Copernicus); a biological one: no longer being made in the image of God, but rather being an animal (Darwin); and a psychological one (the most painful): no longer being master in one's own house (Freud). See Sigmund Freud, "A Difficulty in the Path of Psycho-Analysis" (1917), *SE* 17, pp. 137–44; and Sigmund Freud, "Fixation to Traumas—The Unconscious," in *Introductory Lectures on Psychanalysis* (1916–17), *SE* 16, pp. 284–85.

7. On this question see Elisabeth Roudinesco, *Jacques Lacan & Co.: A History of Psychoanalysis in France, 1925–1985* (1986), trans. Jeffrey Mehlman (Chicago: University of Chicago Press, 1990).

8. On September 21, 1897, in a letter to Wilhelm Fliess, Freud abandoned this first conception of the psychic apparatus, his *neurotica*, based on the so-called seduction theory, which assumes the existence of a real sexual seduction, and therefore a trauma, at the origin of all neurosis. See *The Complete Letters of Sigmund Freud to Wilhelm Fliess*, trans. and ed. Jeffrey Moussaieff Masson (Cambridge, Mass.: Belknap Press of the Harvard University Press, 1985).

9. Jean-Luc Nancy, *The Experience of Freedom* (1988), trans. Bridget McDonald (Stanford, Calif.: Stanford University Press, 1993).

10. In this paragraph "it" (for "the other") could also mean "he" or "him," as the French pronouns (*il, le*, etc.) are ambiguous.—Trans.

11. The reproductive cloning of humans is a technique used for the creation of embryos to be implanted in a uterus, leading to the birth of a baby genetically identical to an individual already born. Nonreproductive cloning consists in fabricating embryos in order to use certain cells for therapeutic ends and to treat illnesses like diabetes or Alzheimer's without the risk of tissue rejection. On this subject, see Henri Atlan, Marc Augé, Mireille Delmas-Marty, Roger-Pol Droit, Nadine Fresco, *Le clonage humain* (Paris: Seuil, 1999). In August 2000, the British government pronounced a favorable judgment on nonreproductive cloning.

12. Established in 1983 by François Mitterrand, the Comité d'éthique (Committee on Ethics; full name: le Comité consultatif national d'éthique pour les sciences de la vie et de la santé) is a paragovernmental committee set up to evaluate ethical issues in biomedical research and practice, such as cloning, genetically modified food, and euthanasia.—Trans.

13. We might recall, for example, the American biologist Hermann Joseph Muller (1890–1967), winner of the 1947 Nobel prize in medicine, who thought up the insane idea of creating a sperm bank for Nobel laureates for the purpose of reproducing intelligent children.

14. Georges Canguilhem, "Le cerveau et la pensée" (1980), in *Georges Canguilhem: Philosophe, historien des sciences* (Paris: Albin Michel, 1992), pp. 11–33.

15. The congressional consultation with Claude Vorilhon took place in March 2001. See *Libération*, March 30, 2001.

16. Dan Sperber has also written: "There is no intellectual task a brain can accomplish that would remain in principle out of reach of a computer. That, at least, is the conviction driving the cognitivists. . . . Although it is still somewhat rough

today, this model can be improved indefinitely." See Roger-Pol Droit and Dan Sperber, *Des idées qui viennent* (Paris: Odile Jacob, 1999), p. 19.

17. Michel Foucault, *L'herméneutique du sujet: Cours au Collège de France, 1981–1982* (Paris: Gallimard-Seuil, 2001).

18. Derrida has addressed the question of hospitality on numerous occasions: "Not all new arrivals are received as guests if they don't have the benefit of the right to hospitality or the right of asylum, etc. Without this right, a new arrival can only be introduced 'in my home,' in the host's 'at home,' as a parasite, a guest who is wrong, illegitimate, clandestine, liable to expulsion or arrest." Jacques Derrida and Anne Dufourmantelle, *Of Hospitality: Anne Dufourmantelle Invites Jacques Derrida to Respond*, trans. Rachel Bowlby (Stanford, Calif.: Stanford University Press, 2000), p. 61. See also Jacques Derrida, *On Cosmopolitanism and Forgiveness* (1997), trans. Mark Dooley and Michael Hughes (New York: Routledge, 2001).

19. The affair of the so-called *sans-papiers* began on March 18, 1996, when 430 Africans in irregular circumstances (no identity papers), supported by several humanitarian associations, occupied the Saint-Ambroise church in the eleventh arrondissement of Paris and began a hunger strike, in order to persuade the government to regularize their status. This event occurred at a moment when the government, supported by a rightist majority in the Parliament, was planning to enforce the "Pasqua-Debré" laws on immigration that had been adopted in December 1993. Other, similar actions were carried out later by immigrants, with the support of a number of intellectuals. The affair was prolonged when the Left took power after the legislative elections in June 1997.

20. Jacques Derrida, "Manquements du droits à la justice," an improvised intervention of December 21, 1996, at the Théâtre des Amandiers, during a demonstration in support of "undocumented" immigrants; in Jacques Derrida, Marc Guillaume, and Jean-Pierre Vincent, *Marx en jeu* (Paris: Descartes, 1997), pp. 73–91.

21. Jacques Toubon is a former minister of culture and minister of justice and a member of the Gaullist RPR party (Rassemblement pour la république [Rally for the Republic]).—Trans.

22. See Derrida, *On Cosmopolitanism and Forgiveness*, p. 16.

23. See Pierre Tévanian and Syvie Tissot, in *Mots à maux: Dictionnaire de la lepénisation des esprits* (Paris: Dagorno, 1998), p. 209: "Behind formulas like 'zero immigration' or 'not one immigrant more,' or even behind the words of the socialist demagogue Patrick Weil, one cannot help thinking of another formula: 'final solution.'" Minister of the Interior under Lionel Jospin, Jean-Pierre Chevènement approved the decision in August 1997 not to repeal the Pasqua-Debré laws but instead to modify them by following some of the recommendations made by the historian Patrick Weil in a report, commissioned from him by Chevènement, concerning the laws on nationality. In October 1997, Chevènement was taken to task by some one thousand intellectuals and artists in a petition "demanding the regularization of all the undocumented immigrants who had requested it" (see *Le*

Monde, October 2, 1997). This was the first significant rupture between the socialist government and the intellectuals who had expected Jospin to keep his campaign promises and to repeal the controversial laws.

24. See *Le Monde*, October 2, 1997. In a text supporting Jean-Pierre Chevènement, published in *Libération* on October 7, 1997, the petitioners are accused of
"manipulative provocation" and "charitable naïveté."

CHAPTER 5

1. Paola Cavalieri and Peter Singer, eds., *The Great Ape Project: Equality Beyond
Humanity* (New York: St. Martin's, 1994). See also the two issues of *Le Débat* containing articles on this subject, especially Paola Cavalieri, "Les droits de l'homme
pour les grands singes non humains?," *Le Débat*, 108 (January–February 2000),
pp. 156–62; and Elisabeth de Fontenay's response, "Pourquoi les animaux n'au-
raient-ils pas droit à un droit des animaux?," *Le Débat*, 109 (March–April 2000).
See Elisabeth de Fontenay, *Le silence des bêtes: La philosophie à l'épreuve de l'ani-
malité* (Paris: Fayard, 1998).

2. "Even before being determined as human (with all the distinctive characteristics that have always been attributed to man and the entire system of significa-
tions that they imply) or nonhuman, the *grammè*—or the *grapheme*—would thus
name the element." Jacques Derrida, *Of Grammatology*, trans. Gayatri Chakravorty Spivak, corrected ed. (Baltimore: Johns Hopkins University Press, 1998), pp.
9ff. This is also valid for the discourse on differ*a*nce. Indissociable from this concept of the gramma or the trace, and however "unthinkable" it may seem, differ-
*a*nce extends to "life/death" in general and brings the economic and the aneconomic into an alliance beyond the limits of the human. See "Différance" (1968),
in Jacques Derrida, *Margins of Philosophy* (1972), trans. Alan Bass (Chicago: University of Chicago Press, 1982).—J.D.

3. See in particular Marie-Louise Mallet, ed., *L'animal autobiographique: Au-
tour de Jacques Derrida* (Paris: Galilée, 1999), especially the chapter by Jacques
Derrida, "L'animal que je suis" (a fragment from the introduction to a series of
four seminar sessions given at Cérisy-la-Salle in 1997 on Descartes, Kant, Heidegger, Levinas, and Lacan. This is part of a book in preparation). Prior to that, the
question of the animal was addressed, most often in a direct and explicit manner,
in almost all of my books. A few examples only: "Freud and the Scene of Writing,"
in *Writing and Difference* (1967), trans. Alan Bass (Chicago: University of Chicago
Press, 1978), p. 197; *Glas*, trans. John P. Leavey, Jr., and Richard Rand (Lincoln:
University of Nebraska Press, 1986), pp. 99ff. and passim; "How to Avoid Speaking: Denials," trans. Thomas A. Carlson, in Harold Coward and Toby Foshay,
eds., *Derrida and Negative Theology* (Albany, N.Y.: SUNY Press, 1992);
"Geschlecht II: Heidegger's Hand," trans. John P. Leavey, Jr., in *Deconstruction
and Philosophy: The Texts of Jacques Derrida*, ed. John Sallis (Chicago: University of
Chicago Press, 1987), pp. 161–96, in particular the passage entitled "Of Man and
Animality"; *Of Spirit: Heidegger and the Question* (1987), trans. Geoffrey Benning-

ton and Rachel Bowlby (Chicago: University of Chicago Press, 1989), in particular pp. 11–12, 57; and "Che cos'è la poesia?," trans. Peggy Kamuf, in *Points ... : Interviews, 1974–1994* (1994), ed. Elisabeth Weber (Stanford, Calif.: Stanford University Press, 1995), pp. 288–99.

What is "massively unavoidable," henceforth, in the "question of what is becoming of so-called 'animal' life" is clearly situated in Jacques Derrida, *Specters of Marx* (1993), trans. Peggy Kamuf (New York: Routledge, 1994), p. 85. See also "A Silkworm of One's Own," trans. Geoffrey Bennington, in *Acts of Religion*, ed. Gil Anidjar (New York: Routledge, 2002), pp. 311–55. Wherever the motif of the hand or the "hand of man" reappears, the so-called "question of the animal" is opened again, from *Of Grammatology* to *Le toucher: Jean-Luc Nancy* (Paris: Galilée, 1999), where the deconstruction of what is there named *humainisme* plays a determining role throughout the book.—J.D. [By adding an "i" to *humanisme*, Derrida introduces the *main*, or hand, of which he is speaking here.—Trans.]

4. Derrida addressed the question of cruelty in a lecture given in the large amphitheater of the Sorbonne on July 10, 2000, at the invitation of René Major, who initiated the States General of Psychoanalysis. See Jacques Derrida, "Psychoanalysis Searches the States of Its Soul: The Impossible Beyond of a Sovereign Cruelty," in *Without Alibi*, ed. Peggy Kamuf (Stanford, Calif.: Stanford University Press, 2002), pp. 238–80.

5. Jacques Derrida, *Aporias* (1993), trans. Thomas Dutoit (Stanford, Calif.: Stanford University Press, 1993).

6. Paola Cavalieri writes: "We have always been aware, in our species, of the presence of non-paradigmatic individuals who are irrevocably deprived of characteristics judged to be typically human: the mentally handicapped, the half-witted, the senile" ("Les droits de l'homme pour les grands singes non humains?," p. 158).

7. See, for example, Jacques Derrida, "'Eating Well,' or The Calculus of the Subject," an interview with Jean-Luc Nancy, trans. Peter Connor and Avital Ronell, in *Points ...* , pp. 255–87.

8. Heinrich von Kleist (1777–1811) was a German writer and playwright. In *Penthesilea*, written in 1808, he adapts the ancient legend of Achilles' murder by Penthesilea, queen of the Amazons, in order to dramatize a romantic heroine divided between an intense drive to devour the other and a passion for love that leads to her self-annihilation.

9. Luc Ferry, *Le nouvel ordre écologique* (Paris: Grasset, 1992); and Claudine Germe, *Des animaux et des hommes* (Paris: LGF, 1994). See also Luc Ferry, "Des 'droits de l'homme' pour les grands singes? Non, mais des devoirs envers eux, sans nul doute," *Le Débat*, 108 (January–February 2000), pp. 163–67.

10. Derrida is using the word *zoophilia* here in its classical sense of "love of animals," and not in the sense given it by the sexologists of the late nineteenth century: sexual relations between a human and an animal.

11. Jacques Amyot (1513–1593) was an eminent translator of Plutarch.—Trans.

12. "Unfortunately for those who evoke the *summa injuria* [a reference to Nazi

zoophilia and to Hitler's vegetarianism—J.D.] only the better to mock the pity shown for mute and anonymous suffering, it happens that some very great Jewish thinkers of this century have been haunted by the animal question: Kafka, Singer, Canetti, Horkheimer, Adorno. By insistently inscribing it within their works, they will have contributed to an interrogation of rationalist humanism and of the cogency of its decision. Victims of historic catastrophes have in fact often seen animals as other victims, to a certain extent comparable to themselves and those like them." See the preface to Plutarch, *Trois traités pour les animaux* (Paris: POL, 1992), p. 71.—J.D.

13. Theodor Adorno, *Beethoven, Philosophie der Musik, Fragmente und Texte*, ed. Rolf Tiedemann (Frankfurt: Suhrkamp, 1993), pp. 123–24; published in English as *Beethoven: The Philosophy of Music*, trans. Edmund Jephcott (Stanford, Calif.: Stanford University Press, 1998), p. 80.—J.D.

14. Jean-Pierre Marguénaud, "La personnalité juridique des animaux," *Recueil Dalloz*, 20 (1998), pp. 205–11.

15. Jeremy Bentham, *An Introduction to the Principles of Morals and Legislation* (1789) (London: Athlone, 1970), p. 44.

16. President of the Confédération Paysanne [Farmer's confederation], José Bové is the leading figure in an international struggle against "bad food" connected with the globalization of agribusiness and the food industry, for which the McDonald's restaurants are a symbol throughout the world.

17. Bovine Spongiform Encephalopathy (BSE), or Creutzfeldt-Jakob disease, inflicted cows raised in Great Britain.

18. De Fontenay, "Pourquoi les animaux," p. 153. See also de Fontenay, *Le silence des bêtes*, chap. 19.

19. *Le droit* can mean either "right" (as in "the right to vote" or "human rights") or "law" (as in a body of law or a legal code). French also has *la loi*, which usually refers to a particular law, though it can also mean "the law in general."—Trans.

20. See Chapter 7 below, "Of the Anti-Semitism to Come."

CHAPTER 6

1. Elisabeth Roudinesco, *Théroigne de Méricourt: A Melancholic Woman During the French Revolution* (1989), trans. Martin Thomas (London: Verso, 1991).

2. See Elisabeth Roudinesco, *Généalogies* (Paris: Fayard, 1994).

3. The book's subtitle is *The State of the Debt, the Work of Mourning, and the New International.* The dedication reads in part: "But one should never speak of the assassination of a man as a figure, not even an exemplary figure in the logic of an emblem, a rhetoric of the flag or of martyrdom. A man's life, as unique as his death, will always be more than a paradigm and something other than a symbol. And this is precisely what a proper name should always name. . . . I recall that it is a *communist* as such, a *communist* as *communist*, whom a Polish emigrant and his accomplices, all the assassins of Chris Hani, put to death a few days ago, April 10th. The assassins themselves proclaimed that they were out to get a communist."

Jacques Derrida, *Specters of Marx* (1993), trans. Peggy Kamuf (New York: Routledge, 1994).

4. Karl Marx and Friedrich Engels, *Manifesto of the Communist Party* (1848): "A specter is haunting Europe—the specter of Communism. All the Powers of old Europe have entered into a holy alliance to exorcise this specter: Pope and Czar, Metternich and Guizot, French radicals and the German police-spies." *The Marx-Engels Reader*, ed. Robert C. Tucker, 2nd ed. (New York: Norton, 1978), p. 473.

5. Jacques Derrida and Catherine Malabou, *La contre-allée* (Paris: La Quinzaine littéraire/Louis Vuitton, 1999), p. 63.

6. Derrida and Althusser were colleagues at the Ecole Normale Supérieure on the rue d'Ulm in Paris.

7. The line is spoken by Hamlet just after he has encountered the ghost of his father, who enjoins the prince to avenge his death. Hamlet, addressing Horatio and Marcellus, curses himself for having been given the task of setting the world aright:

> With all my love I do commend me to you:
> And what so poor a man as Hamlet is
> May do, to express his love and friendship to you,
> God willing, shall not lack. Let us go in together;
> and still your fingers on your lips, I pray.
> The time is out of joint; O cursed spite,
> That ever I was born to set it right!
> (*Hamlet*, act 1, scene 5)

"The time is out of joint" has been translated into French as (1) "le temps est hors de ses gonds," time is off its hinges; (2) "le monde est à l'envers," the world is upside down; (3) "le temps est détraqué," time is broken down, unhinged, out of sorts; (4) "cette époque est déshonorée," this age is dishonored. See Derrida, *Specters of Marx*, pp. 18–19.

8. Jacques Derrida, "Force of Law: The 'Mystical Foundation of Authority,'" trans. Mary Quaintance, in *Acts of Religion*, ed. Gil Anidjar (New York: Routledge, 2002), pp. 228–98.

9. See Derrida, *Specters of Marx*, particularly pp. 23–29. "Beyond right, and still more beyond juridicism, beyond morality, and still more beyond moralism, does not justice as relation to the other suppose on the contrary the irreducible excess of a disjointure or an anachrony, some *Un-Fuge*, some 'out of joint' dislocation in Being and in time itself, a disjointure that, in always risking the evil, expropriation, and injustice (*adikia*) against which there is no calculable insurance, would alone be able to *do justice* or *render justice* to the other as other? A *doing* that would not amount only to action and a *rendering* that would not come down just to restitution? . . . Here . . . would be played out the relation of deconstruction to the possibility of justice. . . . This is where deconstruction would always begin to take shape as the thinking of the gift and of undeconstructible justice, the undeconstructible condition of any deconstruction, to be sure, but a condition that is

itself *in deconstruction* and remains, and must remain (that is the injunction) in the disjointure of the *Un-Fug*" (pp. 27–28).—J.D.

10. Ibid., p. 122.

11. Ibid., p. 195 n. 35, for example.

12. Max Stirner (1806–1856) was a German philosopher of the Hegelian Left and author of the book *The Ego and Its Own* (1844) (ed. David Leopold [Cambridge, Eng.: Cambridge University Press, 1995]), which was vehemently attacked by Marx in *The German Ideology* (1845) (in Karl Marx and Friedrich Engels, *Collected Works*, vol. 5 [New York: International Publishers, 1976]).

13. "Une Révolution ne se programme pas." I have resisted the temptation to translate this sentence, abusively, after the well-known song: "The revolution will not be televised."—Trans.

14. François Furet, *Interpreting the French Revolution* (1978), trans. Elborg Forster (Cambridge, Eng.: Cambridge University Press, 1981); Jules Michelet, *History of the French Revolution*, trans. Keith Botsford (Wynnewood, Pa.: Livingston, 1972).

15. Maurice Blanchot, *The Work of Fire* (1949), trans. Charlotte Mandell (Stanford, Calif.: Stanford University Press, 1995).

16. "This is the meaning of the Reign of Terror. Every citizen has a right to death, so to speak: death is not a sentence passed on to him, it is his most essential right; he is not suppressed as a guilty person—he needs death so that he can proclaim himself a citizen, and it is in the disappearance of death that freedom causes him to be born. Where this is concerned, the French Revolution has a clearer meaning than any other revolution. Death in the Reign of Terror is not simply a way of punishing seditionaries; rather, since it becomes the unavoidable, in some sense the desired lot of everyone, it appears as the very operation of freedom in free men. When the blade falls on Saint-Just and Robespierre, in a sense it executes no one. Robespierre's virtue, Saint-Just's relentlessness, are simply their existences already suppressed, the anticipated presence of their deaths, the decision to allow freedom to assert itself completely in them and through its universality to negate the particular reality of their lives. Granted, perhaps they caused the Reign of Terror to take place. But the Terror they personify does not come from the death they inflict on others but from the death they inflict on themselves." (ibid., pp. 319–20)—J.D.

17. "These moments are, in fact, fabulous moments: in them, fable speaks; in them, the speech of fable becomes action. That the writer should be *tempted* by them is completely appropriate. Revolutionary action is in every respect analogous to action as embodied in literature: the passage from nothing to everything, the affirmation of the absolute as event and of every event as absolute. . . . The writer sees himself in the Revolution. It attracts him because it is the time during which literature becomes history. It is his truth. Any writer who is not induced by the very fact of writing to think, 'I am the revolution, only freedom allows me to write,' is not really writing. . . . Literature contemplates itself in revolution, it finds

its justification in revolution, and if it has been called the Reign of Terror, this is because its ideal is indeed that moment in history, that moment when 'life endures death and maintains itself in it' in order to gain from death the possibility of speaking and the truth of speech." (ibid., pp. 318–22)

In this Hegelian-Mallarméan language, Blanchot here describes a *temptation*, and that is why I underline the word "tempted." Blanchot speaks here of what he calls, on the previous page, "another temptation." To be fair to the tremendously equivocal nature of this text, it is necessary to take into consideration the status and the destiny of such "temptations," those of Blanchot and those he analyzes. I will try to do this elsewhere.—J.D.

18. Ibid., p. 321 [translation slightly modified].

19. "Sade is not close enough to his own wickedness to recognize his neighbor in it. A trait which he shares with many, and notably with Freud. For such is indeed the sole motive of the recoil of beings, sometimes forewarned, before the Christian commandment.

"For Sade, we see the test of this, crucial in our eyes, in his refusal of the death penalty, whose history, if not its logic, would suffice to show that it is one of the corollaries of Charity." Jacques Lacan, "Kant with Sade," trans. James B. Swenson, *October* 51 (Winter 1989), p. 74 [translation slightly modified].—J.D.

20. See Chapter 8 below, "Death Penalties."

21. Cesare Beccaria (1738–1794) was an Italian philosopher and economist and the author of a treatise entitled *On Crimes and Punishments* (1764). He initiated the reform of penal law in Europe. See *"On Crimes and Punishments" and Other Writings*, ed. Richard Bellamy, trans. Richard Davies with Virginia Cox and Richard Bellamy (Cambridge, Eng.: Cambridge University Press, 1995).

22. During a debate in the Assembly in 1848, Victor Hugo declared, referring to the death penalty in political matters: "Abolition must be simple, pure, and definitive."

23. See in particular Victor Hugo, *Ecrits sur la peine de mort* (Arles: Actes Sud, 1979), pp. 13, 99, 247.

24. Ibid., p. 219.

25. See Chapter 8 below, "Death Penalties."

26. Sigmund Freud, *Totem and Taboo: Some Points of Agreement Between the Mental Lives of Savages and Neurotics* (1913), *SE* 13. And Theodor Reik, *The Compulsion to Confess: On the Psychoanalysis of Crime and Punishment*, trans. Katherine Jones and Norbert Rie (New York: Grove, 1961), especially "Freud's View on Capital Punishment," pp. 471–74: "Only the fact that mankind shrinks from facing facts, from acknowledging the facts of unconscious emotional life, delays the victory of the concept of capital punishment as murder sanctioned by law. My attitude concerning the problem of capital punishment originates, therefore, not in humanitarian reasons, but in the appreciation of the psychological necessity of the general human prohibition: thou shalt not kill. . . . I profess to be an opponent of murder, whether committed by the individual as a crime or by the state in its re-

taliation." See also Elisabeth Roudinesco, "Freud et le régicide: Eléments d'une réflexion," *Revue Germanique Internationale*, 14 (2000), pp. 113–26; and the preface by Rudinesco to the new edition of Theodor Reik, *Le psychologue surpris* [*Surprise and the Psychoanalyst*] (Paris: Denoël, 2001).

27. Ernst Kantorowicz, *The King's Two Bodies: A Study in Mediaeval Political Theology* (Princeton, N.J.: Princeton University Press, 1957). This feudal conception of royalty assumes that the king has two bodies, a natural body subject to the passions and to death, and a political body. The latter's members are the subjects of the kingdom, incorporated into this political body, of which the king is the head. Being immortal, this second body of the king, the political body, continues well beyond the actual death of the sovereign.

28. In France, the death penalty was abolished on September 30, 1981, thanks to the struggle led by Robert Badinter, a lawyer who became the minister of justice under president François Mitterrand. See Robert Badinter, *L'abolition* (Paris: Fayard, 2000).

29. The phrase *à la guerre comme à la guerre* is a common saying that means literally "in war as in war"; it implies taking things as you find them and doing what is necessary, given the circumstances. Derrida uses the expression more literally to say that a state might well use the notion of war or of a "public enemy" to justify killing its own citizens as though out of necessity and for the sake of survival.—Trans.

30. Jacques Derrida, *Politics of Friendship* (1994), trans. George Collins (London: Verso, 1997).

31. "What you call 'globalization' is a strategy of depoliticization enrolled in the service of particular political interests" (ibid., pp. 157–58). This statement is part of a "rejoinder" in response to some critical questions posed by Derrida, presented as though it were spoken by Schmitt himself; see ibid., pp. 156–57.

32. Jean Bodin (1530–1596), jurist and French historian, was the first to advance a theory of sovereignty as the "foundation of the being of the Republic." A supporter of monarchy, he referred to Plato's philosophy in order to undo the link between religion and politics, for the purpose of secularizing the idea of the republic. See Jean Bodin, *Les six livres de la République* (1576), vol. 1, Corpus des oeuvres de philosophie en langue française (Paris: Fayard, 1986). For an abridged English translation, see *The Six Books of the Commonwealth*, trans. M. J. Tooley (New York: Barnes and Noble, 1967).

33. This motif of sovereignty appears in particular in Georges Bataille, *Inner Experience*, trans. Leslie Anne Boldt (Albany: SUNY Press, 1988); and Georges Bataille, *Sovereignty*, in *The Accursed Share*, vol. 3, trans. Robert Hurley (New York: Zone, 1991); see also the *Conférences sur le non-savoir*, in Georges Bataille, *Oeuvres complètes*, vol. 8 (Paris: Gallimard, 1976). My analysis can be found in "From Restricted to General Economy: A Hegelianism Without Reserve," particularly in the subsection entitled "The Epoch of Meaning: Lordship and Sovereignty," in Jacques Derrida, *Writing and Difference* (1967), trans. Alan Bass

(Chicago: University of Chicago Press, 1978), pp. 254ff. [Note that in this title, "Lordship" translates *maîtrise*, "mastery" (the Hegelian concept of *Herrschaft*); I have modified the following quotations to reflect this more literal translation of the French term.—Trans.] "Simultaneously more and less than mastery, sovereignty is totally other. Bataille pulls it out of dialectics. He withdraws it from the horizon of meaning and knowledge. And does so to such a degree that, despite the characteristics that make it resemble mastery, sovereignty is no longer a figure in the continuous chain of phenomenology" (*Writing and Difference,* p. 256). This movement becomes still more complicated. Later in the same text, we read: "In *doubling* mastery, sovereignty does not escape dialectics. . . . Far from suppressing the dialectical synthesis, it inscribes this synthesis and makes it function within the sacrifice of meaning. It does not suffice to risk death if the putting at stake is not permitted to take off, as chance or accident, but is rather invested as the work of the negative. Sovereignty must still sacrifice mastery and, thus, the presentation of the meaning of death" (pp. 260–61).—J.D.

34. The Battle of Valmy, in which the revolutionary French forces defeated the Prussians, took place on September 20, 1792, the day before the proclamation of the Republic on September 21.—Trans.

35. Notably in Jacques Derrida, *The Other Heading: Reflections on Today's Europe* (1991), trans. Pascale-Anne Brault and Michael P. Naas (Bloomington: Indiana University Press, 1992), and in idem, *Monolingualism of the Other; or, The Prosthesis of Origin* (1996), trans. Patrick Mensah (Stanford, Calif.: Stanford University Press, 1998).

36. Stéphane Courtois, Nicolas Werth, Jean-Louis Panné, Andrzej Paczkowski, Karel Bartosek, and Jean-Louis Margolin, *The Black Book of Communism: Crimes, Terror, Repression* (1997), trans. Jonathan Murphy and Mark Kramer (Cambridge, Mass.: Harvard University Press, 1999). The criminalization of communism is most evident in Stéphane Courtois's preface, which led some of the authors of the book to distance themselves.

37. François Furet, *The Passing of an Illusion: The Idea of Communism in the Twentieth Century* (1995), trans. Deborah Furet (Chicago: University of Chicago Press, 1999).

38. SOS-Racisme is an association founded in France in 1984.—Trans.

39. Paul Yonnet, "Sur la crise du lien national," *Le Débat,* 75 (May–August 1993), p. 138.

40. Paul Yonnet, *Voyage au centre du malaise français* (Paris: Gallimard, 1993), p. 15. The theses of this book were sharply criticized, notably by Laurent Joffrin in "Quand l'intelligentsia soutient Le Pen," *Le Nouvel Observateur,* January 14, 1993.

41. Pierre-André Taguieff, *L'effacement de l'avenir* (Paris: Galilée, 2000).

42. Viviane Forrester, *The Economic Horror* (1998) (Cambridge, Eng.: Polity, 1999). The title is from a poem by Arthur Rimbaud.

43. Immanuel Kant, *Perpetual Peace*, Second Section, Third Definitive Article on Perpetual Peace: "Cosmopolitan Right shall be limited to Conditions of Uni-

versal Hospitality." In *Political Writings*, ed. Hans Reiss, trans. H. B. Nisbett, 2nd ed. (Cambridge, Eng.: Cambridge University Press, 1970, 1991), p. 105.

44. See Jacques Derrida, *On Cosmopolitanism and Forgiveness* (1997), trans. Mark Dooley and Michael Hughes (New York: Routledge, 2001).

45. The formulation of the original Declaration published by the National Assembly in 1789.—Trans.

46. See Chapter 9 below, "In Praise of Psychoanalysis."

47. Jacques Derrida, "Racism's Last Word" (1983), trans. Peggy Kamuf, *Critical Inquiry*, 12 (Autumn 1985), pp. 290–99; and idem, "The Laws of Reflection: Nelson Mandela, in Admiration" (1986), trans. Mary Ann Caws and Isabelle Lorenz, in Jacques Derrida and Mustapha Tlili, eds., *For Nelson Mandela* (New York: Seaver, 1987), pp. 13–42.

48. The ANC was founded in 1912.

49. Chris Hani was assassinated on April 10, 1993, by an Afrikaner, a member of a Far Right organization. The killer acted alone and was attempting to cause a breakdown in negotiations between the ANC and the government, negotiations that were to lead to the first "multiracial" elections, then to the victory of the ANC. He was denounced by a white woman of Afrikaner origins.

50. Nelson Mandela secretly wrote down his memories during his incarceration in the Robben Island penitentiary. See *Long Walk to Freedom: The Autobiography of Nelson Mandela* (Boston: Little, Brown, 1994): "I confess to being something of an Anglophile. When I thought of Western democracy and freedom, I thought of the British parliamentary system" (p. 263).

51. "Prison not only robs you of your freedom, it attempts to take away your identity. Everyone wears the same uniform, eats the same food, follows the same schedule. It is by definition a purely authoritarian state that tolerates no independence or individuality" (ibid., p. 291).

52. Apartheid was abolished in June 1991.

53. Nelson Mandela relates the death of his father when he was nine years old: "I do not remember experiencing great grief so much as feeling cut adrift. Although my mother was the center of my existence, I defined myself through my father. My father's passing changed my life in a way I did not suspect at the time. . . . My mother and I never talked very much, but we did not need to. I never doubted her love or questioned her support" (*Long Walk*, p. 13). A wealthy aristocrat from the Thembu tribe, Mandela's father lost his fortune and his title and, after a dispute, was dispossessed of most of his income. He had thirteen children by his three wives. Nelson was the eldest son of Nosekeni Fanny, the third wife, from the amaMpemvu clan. In the polygamous system of the Xhosa nation, to which Nelson Mandela's parents belonged, circumcision was practiced, and each wife had her own kraal (homestead), which allowed them to live apart from each other.

54. Accused of high treason in 1956, along with twenty-nine other militants, Mandela chose to defend himself at his trial in 1961. He received a verdict of not

guilty and then went into hiding. Arrested again, he went to prison for twenty-seven years, from 1963 to 1990.

55. Louis Althusser, *For Marx* (1965), trans. Ben Brewster (London: New Left Review Editions, 1977); idem, *The Future Lasts Forever: A Memoir* (1992), ed. Olivier Corpet and Yann Moulier Boutang, trans. Richard Veasey (New York: The New Press, 1993); idem, *Lettres à Franca* (1961–1973) (Paris: Stock/IMEC, 1998).

56. Louis Althusser died on October 22, 1990.

57. A *caïman* [a teacher with lighter duties than a professor—Trans.] and a professor at the Ecole Normale Supérieure (ENS) on the rue d'Ulm, Louis Althusser taught philosophy to generations of students. See Yann Moulier-Boutang, *Louis Althusser, une biographie* (Paris: Grasset, 1992). On Louis Althusser's teaching at the ENS and his relations with Lacan and psychoanalysis, see Elisabeth Roudinesco, *Jacques Lacan & Co.: A History of Psychoanalysis in France* (1986), trans. Jeffrey Mehlman (Chicago: University of Chicago Press, 1990); and Elisabeth Roudinesco, *Jacques Lacan* (1993), trans. Barbara Bray (New York: Columbia University Press, 1997).

58. The French translator of Hegel's *Phenomenology of Spirit* (*La phénoménologie de l'esprit*) (1939–41), Jean Hyppolite (1907–1968) played a fundamental role in the teaching of philosophy in France, as director of the ENS and as a professor at the Collège de France. He was also an important interlocutor of Lacan. See Jacques Derrida, "The Time of a Thesis: Punctuations," in *Philosophy in France Today*, ed. Alan Montefiore (Cambridge, Eng.: Cambridge University Press, 1983).

59. Louis Althusser, *Reading "Capital"* (1965), in collaboration with Etienne Balibar, Roger Establet, Pierre Macherey, and Jacques Rancière; trans. Ben Brewster, 2nd ed. (London: NLB, 1977).

60. Agrégatifs are the candidates for the *agrégation,* the highest level of certification for teachers in secondary education in France.—Trans.

61. On November 16, 1980, Louis Althusser announced to his doctor that he had strangled his wife, Hélène Rytmann. He was protected under article 64 of the penal code in effect at the time. See Althusser, *The Future Lasts Forever.*

62. See Chapter 1 above, "Choosing One's Heritage."

63. Louis Althusser, *Writings on Psychoanalysis: Freud and Lacan* (1993), ed. Olivier Corpet and François Matheron, trans. Jeffrey Mehlman (New York: Columbia University Press, 1996). On Louis Althusser's place in psychoanalysis in France, see Roudinesco's *Jacques Lacan & Co.* and *Jacques Lacan.*

64. Jacques Derrida, "Politics and Friendship: An Interview with Jacques Derrida," in *The Althusserian Legacy*, ed. E. Ann Kaplan and Michael Sprinker (London: Verso, 1993).

65. Althusser, *Lettres à Franca.*

CHAPTER 7

1. Geoffrey Bennington and Jacques Derrida, *Jacques Derrida* (1991), trans. Geoffrey Bennington (Chicago: University of Chicago Press, 1993). The section written by Derrida is entitled *Circumfession* and the one by Bennington *Derridabase.*

2. Born in El Biar, near Algiers, Jacques Derrida moved to France in 1949.

3. *Marrano* means "pig" in Spanish. This term of contempt was used in Spain and Portugal beginning in the fifteenth century to refer to converted Jews and their descendants. Forced to convert, the *marranos* led a double life, remaining secretly faithful to their religion. Whenever possible, they emigrated, and it was in Amsterdam, nicknamed the "Dutch Jerusalem," that a number of *marranos* were able to return to Judaism.

4. Sigmund Freud, *The Interpretation of Dreams* (1900), *SE* 4, p. 197.

5. On the "Hannibalian" conception of psychoanalysis and Freud's identification with the Semitic general, see Elisabeth Roudinesco, *Histoire de la psychanalyse en France*, vol. 1 (Paris: Seuil, 1986), p. 107.

6. See Carl Schorske, *Fin-de-Siècle Vienna: Politics and Culture* (New York: Vintage, 1981).

7. See Elisabeth Roudinesco, *Jacques Lacan* (1993), trans. Barbara Bray (New York: Columbia University Press, 1997).

8. See, notably, *Circumfession*, in Geoffrey Bennington and Jacques Derrida, *Jacques Derrida* (1991), trans. Geoffrey Bennington (Chicago: University of Chicago Press, 1993); Jacques Derrida, *Monolingualism of the Other; or, The Prosthesis of Origin* (1996), trans. Patrick Mensah (Stanford, Calif.: Stanford University Press, 1998); and Jacques Derrida and Catherine Malabou, *La contre-allée* (Paris: La Quinzaine littéraire/Louis Vuitton, 1999). Also see Jacques Derrida, "A Silkworm of One's Own," trans. Geoffrey Bennington, in *Acts of Religion*, ed. Gil Anidjar (New York: Routledge, 2002), pp. 311–55.

9. *Night and Fog* is a 1956 film by Alain Resnais, with a commentary by Jean Cayrol.

10. Founded by Jean-Marie Le Pen, the National Front, an extreme right wing party, represented 1 percent of the French electorate in 1981 and 15 percent in 1997. It imploded in December 1999 because of internal divisions, ceasing then to play a major role for voters in the political relations between the Right and the Left. [This note must be updated: In the first round of the French presidential elections of April 2002, Le Pen received 17 percent of the vote, unexpectedly beating out the socialist candidate, Lionel Jospin, and qualifying for the final runoff vote against incumbent president Jacques Chirac. French voters reacted with anger and shame, denouncing Le Pen in mass demonstrations and rallying around his opponent in order to ensure Le Pen's defeat. Although Chirac won the election, Le Pen received an unprecedented 18 percent of the vote in the second round.—Trans.]

11. On the Renaud Camus affair, see note 14 in Chapter 2 above, "Politics of Difference."

12. According to a survey conducted by the Commission Consultative des

Droits de l'Homme [Advisory Commission on Human Rights] and published on March 15, 1999.

13. Octave Mannoni, *Clefs pour l'imaginaire ou l'autre scène* (Paris: Seuil, 1969).

14. This question will be taken up later in this chapter and in note 28 below.

15. Jacques Derrida, "Interpretations at War: Kant, the Jew, the German," trans. Moshe Ron, in *Acts of Religion*, pp. 135–88; and Jacques Derrida, *Adieu to Emmanuel Levinas*, trans. Pascale-Anne Brault and Michael Naas (Stanford, Calif.: Stanford University Press, 1999).

16. Originally a term for noncitizen residents of ancient Greece (from *metoikos*, one who changes houses; "metic" in English), the French word *métèque* came to be a racial slur meaning "an undesirable (usually Mediterranean) foreigner."—Trans.

17. The term "Jewish self-hatred" was invented by Theodor Lessing in an essay published in 1930: *Der Jüdische Selbsthass*. See Jacques Le Rider, *Crises of Identity: Culture and Society in Fin-de-Siècle Vienna*, trans. Rosemary Morris (New York: Continuum, 1993).

18. See, notably, Jacques Derrida, "Shibboleth for Paul Celan" (1992), trans. Joshua Wilner, in *Word Traces*, ed. Aris Fioretos (Baltimore: Johns Hopkins University Press, 1994); and Derrida, *Monolingualism of the Other*.

19. The head of the Shas party, an ethno-religious party in Israel, Ovadia Yosef declared that the victims of the Shoah, a majority of whom were Ashkenazim, were in reality the reincarnation of "bad Jews."

20. Esther Benbassa and Maurice Szafran, *Libération*, September 11 and 16, 2000.

21. Edouard Drumont (1844–1917), a French journalist and pamphleteer, was in the forefront the most violent anti-Semitism of the end of the nineteenth century. In 1886, he published *La France juive* [Jewish France], which became the gospel of all the Far Right anti-Semitic authors between the wars.

22. The law of 1881, which governed freedom of expression in France, was supplemented in 1972 by a new text. It reads in part: "It is a crime to provoke discrimination, hatred, or violence with respect to a person or a group of persons by virtue of their origin or their belonging or not belonging to a determined ethnicity, nation, race, or religion" (article 24). The law also includes defamation (article 32) and insult (article 33) of the same persons.

23. On the question of "political correctness," see Chapter 2 above, "Politics of Difference."

24. We address the question of the pertinence of Freudian concepts in Chapter 9 below, "In Praise of Psychoanalysis." See also Jacques Derrida, "Psychoanalysis Searches the States of Its Soul," in *Without Alibi*, ed. Peggy Kamuf (Stanford, Calif.: Stanford University Press, 2002), pp. 238–80.

25. Sigmund Freud, *Civilization and Its Discontents* (1930), *SE* 21, pp. 59–145.

26. In several places, particularly in Jacques Derrida, "The University Without Condition," in *Without Alibi*, pp. 202–37.

27. On the Renaud Camus affair, we refer again to note 14 in Chapter 2 above, "Politics of Difference."

28. Passed on July 13, 1990, this law is named after the communist deputy Jean-Claude Gayssot, who was its initiator. It punishes all those "who will have denied . . . the existence of one or several crimes against humanity," as defined by the international tribunal of Nuremberg. This law was justly criticized by many intellectuals who rejected the idea of entrusting to lawmakers the task of telling the historical truth. It was under this law that the anti-Semitic and negationist work of Roger Garaudy (*Les mythes fondateurs de la politique israélienne* [The founding myths of Israeli politics]) was withdrawn from sale in France in 1995. The claims made in this book have a certain currency in the Arab-Muslim world, particularly in Egypt.

29. This is what I tried to show in relation to Céline. See Elisabeth Roudinesco, "Céline et Semmelweis: La médecine, le délire et la mort," in *Les psychanalystes parlent de la mort* (Paris: Tchou, 1979).

30. Jacques Derrida, "Ulysses Gramophone: Hear Say Yes in Joyce" (1987), trans. Tina Kendall, in *Acts of Literature*, ed. Derek Attridge (New York: Routledge, 1992); Jacques Derrida, *Signéponge/Signsponge* (1977), trans. Richard Rand (New York: Columbia University Press, 1984); and Derrida, "Shibboleth for Paul Celan." See also these works by Jacques Derrida: "A Hegelianism Without Reserve," in *Writing and Difference* (1967), trans. Alan Bass (Chicago: University of Chicago Press, 1978); *Dissemination*, trans. Barbara Johnson (Chicago: University of Chicago Press, 1981); "Comment nommer," in *Le poète que je cherche à être: Cahier Michel Deguy*, ed. Yves Charnet (Paris: Belin, 1990); and "HC pour la vie, c'est à dire," in *Hélène Cixous: Croisées d'une oeuvre* (Paris: Galilée, 2000).

31. Notably, these works by Louis-Ferdinand Céline: *Mea Culpa* (1936), *Bagatelles pour un massacre* (1937), *L'école des cadavres* (1938), and *Les beaux draps* (1941).

32. Louis-Ferdinand Céline, *Journey to the End of the Night* (1932), trans. Ralph Mannheim (New York: New Directions, 1980).

33. See, for example, among many other works, "The Double Session," in Derrida, *Dissemination*; or "This Strange Institution Called Literature," interview with Derek Attridge, in Derrida, *Acts of Literature.*—J.D.

34. See Jacques Derrida, "Force of Law: The 'Mystical Foundation of Authority,'" trans. Mary Quaintance," (1994), in *Acts of Religion*, ed. Gil Anidjar (New York: Routledge, 2002), pp. 228–98.

35. Jacques Derrida, "Passions," in *On the Name*, trans. Thomas Dutoit, John P. Leavey, David Wood (Stanford, Calif.: Stanford University Press, 1995), p. 28 [translation slightly modified].

36. See Elisabeth Roudinesco, *Généalogies* (Paris: Fayard, 1994); and Chapter 9 below, "In Praise of Psychoanalysis."

37. See Jacques Derrida, "*Demeure*: Fiction and Testimony," in Maurice Blanchot and Jacques Derrida, *"The Instant of My Death"; "Demeure: Fiction and Testimony,"* trans. Elizabeth Rottenberg (Stanford, Calif.: Stanford University Press, 2000).

38. In 1978, Robert Faurisson, a professor of literature in Lyon, sent articles to several newspapers denouncing the "rumor" of Auschwitz, arguing that the gas chambers did not exist, and characterizing his approach as "revisionist," whereas it was rather a form of "negationism" [see note 12 in Chapter 2 above—Trans.], according to the analysis presented ten years later by Henry Rousso, which was then accepted by virtually all historians. One of Faurisson's followers from a doctrinaire group of the Far Left called "La Vieille Taupe [The Old Mole]," Serge Thion, himself a negationist, asked his friend Noam Chomsky to help by signing a petition in support of his master. Chomsky did not share Faurisson's positions, but, in the name of free speech, he agreed in 1980 to write an article entitled "Some Elementary Comments on the Rights of Freedom of Expression," which was then used as a preface to Faurisson's book, *Mémoire en défense contre ceux qui m'accusent de falsifier l'histoire: La question des chambres à gaz* (Paris: La Vieille Taupe, 1980). Chomsky later disavowed the use that had been made of his text, in which he wrote nonetheless: "Is it true that Faurisson is an anti-Semite or a neo-Nazi? As noted earlier, I do not know his work very well. But from what I have read—largely as a result of the nature of the attacks on him—I find no evidence to support either conclusion. Nor do I find credible evidence in the material that I have read concerning him, either in the public record or in private correspondence. As far as I can determine, he is a relatively apolitical liberal of some sort." See Pierre Vidal-Naquet, *Assassins of Memory: Essays on the Denial of the Holocaust* (1987), trans. Jeffrey Mehlman (New York: Columbia University Press, 1992); and Robert F. Barsky, *Noam Chomsky: A Life of Dissent* (Cambridge, Mass.: MIT Press, 1997).

39. The expression "double bind" was invented in 1956 by the American psychiatrist and anthropologist Gregory Bateson (1904–1980) to designate the dilemma in which a schizophrenic finds himself trapped when he is unable to give a coherent response to two simultaneous and contradictory demands.

40. Regarding the Gayssot law, see note 28 for this chapter.

41. *Mr. Death: The Rise and Fall of Fred A. Leuchter, Jr.*, a documentary directed by Errol Morris, was released in 1999.—Trans.

42. On this question see Chapter 8 below, "Death Penalties." On the guillotine, see Chapter 6 above, "The Spirit of the Revolution," and note 45 of the present chapter.

43. See Nadine Fresco, "Les redresseurs de morts. Chambres à gaz: La bonne nouvelle. Comment on révise l'histoire," *Les Temps Modernes*, June 1980.

44. Derrida is conducting this seminar at the Ecole des Hautes Etudes en Sciences Sociales (EHESS), at the University of California at Irvine, and at the New School for Social Research, as part of a series of seminars entitled "Questions of Responsibility."

45. Joseph Ignace Guillotin (1738–1814), a doctor and deputy of Paris, persuaded the Constituent Assembly, in October 1789, to adopt the principle of egalitarian execution, identical for all: "The same type of crimes will be punished with the same type of penalty, whatever the rank and state of the guilty party." The ma-

chine that was developed, according to his specifications, by Doctor Louis was at first called the "Louison," then the "guillotine."

46. Cf. Jacques Derrida, *Specters of Marx* (1993), trans. Peggy Kamuf (New York: Routledge, 1994), p. 185 n. 5. This [1993] was the year when, in the *New York Times* as well as in a book by Deborah Lipstadt (*Denying the Holocaust*) and in the discussion around it, there appeared suspicions that were as odious as they were ridiculous. Deconstruction was suspected not actually of "negationism" but of opening the way for it by creating an "atmosphere of permissiveness" for the "questioning of historical facts," or of engendering "skepticism." I think the exact opposite is the case. It is this sort of dogmatism that engenders skepticism. And even the "negationist" temptation. Only someone who has not read or understood anything, who has become entrenched in this stubborn ignorance, could put forth such gratuitous and violently insulting suspicions.—J.D.

47. Theodor Adorno laid down this injunction in 1949: "To write poetry after Auschwitz is barbaric. And this corrodes even the knowledge of why it has become impossible to write poetry today." See "Cultural Criticism and Society," in Theodor Adorno, *Prisms*, trans. Samuel and Shierry Weber (Cambridge, Mass.: MIT Press, 1981), p. 34. Maurice Blanchot took up the injunction in another way: "There can be no fiction-story of Auschwitz"; and "No matter when it was written, every story from now on will be from before Auschwitz." In Maurice Blanchot, *Vicious Circles: Two Fictions and "After the Fact,"* trans. Paul Auster (Barrytown, N.Y.: Station Hill, 1985), pp. 68–69. See also Jean-Pierre Salgas, "Shoah ou la disparition," in Denis Hollier, ed., *De la littérature française* (Paris: Bordas, 1993), pp. 1005–13.

48. See 1 Kings 19:12 (the King James version reads "a still, small voice"). *Une voix de fin silence* is also the title of a work by Roger Laporte.—Trans.

CHAPTER 8

A large portion of this chapter, without Elisabeth Roudinesco's comments, was first translated by James D. Ingram. He also contributed extensively to the notes below (as indicated in one instance by his initials in parentheses). I gratefully acknowledge his work.—Trans.

1. In September 1971, Roger Bontemps, an accomplice of Claude Buffet, took part in the prisoners' revolt at the Clairvaux prison, which led to the assassination of two hostages. On November 28, 1972, although he had not committed any crime, he was executed along with Buffet. Robert Badinter was his lawyer. Buffet refused even the idea of a presidential pardon: "If I am pardoned, I will kill again. I will commit other murders in whatever prison I happen to be in." He demanded to be executed lying on his back, so that he could look death in the face [i.e., so that he could watch the blade fall—Trans.], but this request was denied. See Robert Badinter, *L'exécution* (1973) (Paris: Fayard, 1998); and Alain Monestier, *Les grandes affaires criminelles* (Paris: Bordas, 1988).

2. François Mitterrand was president of France from 1981 to 1995.

3. This law was passed on November 28, 1974. Introduced as a bill by Simone Veil, a minister in the right-wing government of Valéry Giscard d'Estaing, it abolished the law of 1920, which had outlawed abortion and made it a punishable offense.

4. Robert Badinter, *L'abolition* (Paris: Fayard, 2000).

5. Derrida has often written on the question of death, notably in *Glas* (trans. John P. Leavey, Jr., and Richard Rand [Lincoln: University of Nebraska Press, 1986], pp. 99ff. and passim), which also, like some of his seminars in the 1960's, deals with the question of the death penalty. In "*Demeure*: Fiction and Testimony" (in Maurice Blanchot and Jacques Derrida, *"The Instant of My Death"; "Demeure: Fiction and Testimony,"* trans. Elizabeth Rottenberg [Stanford: Stanford University Press, 2000]) Derrida gives a commentary on Maurice Blanchot's *The Instant of My Death* (ibid.). In *The Gift of Death* (trans. David Wills [Chicago: University of Chicago Press, 1995]) he interprets the attitude of Abraham on Mount Moriah: Abraham is the one who is obliged to keep silent before the angel interrupts the death he is preparing to give Isaac, in order to give it to God. This ordeal is one that we live every day: to choose a *wholly other* and to neglect *others*. It is emblematic of an experience of the impossible.

6. Juan Donoso Cortès, Marquis de Valdegamas (1809–1853), was a Spanish jurist and philosopher and the author of many political works on the manner of governing peoples. After having been a liberal and an admirer of the French Revolution and the spirit of the Enlightenment, Cortès evolved toward a flamboyant conservatism and a radical adherence to the Catholic religion. In his *Essay on Catholicism, Liberalism, and Socialism*, published in 1851, he maintains that the world is divided into two civilizations, which are irreducible to one another: Catholicism and "philosophism" (which includes liberalism and socialism). Cortès chooses Catholicism, scorns liberalism, and respects socialism as a mortal enemy in which he recognizes a diabolical grandeur. See the following note.

7. Juan Donoso Cortès, *Essay on Catholicism, Liberalism, and Socialism Considered in Their Fundamental Principles*, trans. Madeleine Vinton Goddard (Philadelphia: J. B. Lippincott, 1862). See especially bk. 3, chap. 6: "Dogmas correlative with the dogma of solidarity.—Bloody sacrifices. Theories of the rationalist schools respecting the death penalty": "We have shown that socialism is an incoherent combination of thesis and antithesis, which contradict and destroy one another. Catholicism, on the contrary, forms a great synthesis which includes all things in its unity, and infuses them in its sovereign harmony. It may be affirmed of Catholic dogmas, that although they are diverse they are one. . . . Only an absolute negation can be opposed to this wonderful synthesis. . . . The Catholic word is then invincible and eternal. . . . Nothing can diminish its sovereign virtue" (pp. 278–79). After having evoked the double dogma of *imputation* and *substitution* (a word and concept that one finds, differently but I think not without relation, in Massignon as well as in Levinas), the universal institution of blood sacrifice, from Cain and Abel to Oedipus, Cortès clarifies: "The blood of man cannot

expiate original sin, which is the sin of the species, the supreme human sin; but it nevertheless may, and does, expiate certain individual crimes, from which follows not only the legitimacy, but also the necessity and propriety of the penalty of death. The universality of this institution testifies to the universality of the belief of mankind in the purifying efficacy of blood, when shed under the right circumstances, and in its expiatory virtue when it is thus shed. *Sine sanguinis effusione non fit remissio* (Heb. 9, 22). Mankind could never have extinguished the common debt which it contracted in Adam without the blood shed by the Redeemer" (p. 288) [translation modified].

Cortès likewise violently condemns the abolition of the death penalty for political crimes by the provisional government of the French Republic in 1848, which "was succeeded by those frightful days of June which, with all their horrors, will live forever in the memories of men" (p. 289).—J.D.

8. The French *droit pénal* refers both to penal law and to criminal law more broadly. The broader sense is more common and is used here consistently, but its reference to punishment should be heard throughout.—Trans. (J.I.)

9. Walter Benjamin, "The Critique of Violence" (1921), trans. Edmund Jephcott, in *Selected Writings*, vol. 1: 1913–1926, eds. Marcus Bullock and Michael W. Jennings (Cambridge, Mass.: The Belknap Press of Harvard University Press, 1996), pp. 236–52. Cf. Jacques Derrida, "Force of Law: The 'Mystical Foundation of Authority,'" (1994), trans. Mary Quaintance, in *Acts of Religion*, ed. Gil Anidjar (New York: Routledge, 2002), pp. 228–98.

10. Victor Hugo, *The Last Day of a Condemned Man* (1829), trans. Geoff Woollen (Oxford: Oxford University Press, 1992), p. 32.

11. Hugo, Preface, *Last Day of a Condemned Man*, p. 17.

12. Victor Hugo, *Choses vues*, October 20, 1842, in *Écrits sur la peine de mort* (Arles: Actes Sud, 1979–92), p. 53.

13. Badinter correctly recalls this in *L'abolition*, pp. 163–64. It was in 1978 that the Social Commission of the French episcopacy published an official document, *Eléments de réflexion sur la peine de mort*, which, after expressing its regret for the Catholic Church's historic support for the death penalty, unequivocally concludes (while *committing only the signatories, and only within the borders of their country*): "After thorough reflection, the signatories judge that in France the death penalty should be abolished." Even though an analogous position had been taken by *L'Osservatore Romano* one year earlier, this does not yet constitute, it seems to me, a universal and unconditional commitment by the Catholic Church and the Vatican. Nothing comparable, certainly (and the comparison imposes itself once again), with the prescriptions or interdictions concerning sexuality, birth, and abortion.—J.D.

14. Hugo, Preface, *Last Day of a Condemned Man*, p. 15: "The scaffold is the only structure that revolutions do not demolish. For rarely are revolutions innocent of human blood, and, since they occur in order to dock, lop, and pollard society, the death penalty is one of the pruning blades they surrender most unwillingly" [translation modified].—J.D.

15. Ibid., p. 33: "But do not believe that law and order will be banished with
the executioner. . . . Civilization is nothing other than a series of successive transformations. . . . The merciful law of Christ will at last suffuse the Code, which will
glow with its radiance. Crime will be considered an illness, with its own doctors to
replace your judges, and its hospitals to replace your prisons. Liberty shall be
equated with health. Ointments and oil shall be applied to limbs that once were
shackled and branded. Infirmities that once were scourged with anger shall now
be bathed in love. The cross in place of the gallows: sublime, and yet so simple"
[translation modified].

Mutatis mutandis, and to say it again too briefly, I believe that this allusion to a
future where evil would be treated like a disease heralds, among other things, the
speculations of someone like Theodor Reik on the disappearance-to-come of punishment in general. This will happen when humanity has understood, *like* Freud
and *from* Freud, that the feeling of unconscious guilt precedes the crime. A general
(psychoanalytic) confession will thus have replaced criminal law. It is at the end of
The Compulsion to Confess: On the Psychoanalysis of Crime and Punishment (trans.
Katherine Jones and Norbert Rie [New York: Grove, 1961]) that Reik declares—
in Freud's name and with his authorization—his opposition to the death penalty:
"I profess to be an opponent of murder, whether committed by the individual as
a crime or by the state in its retaliation" (p. 474). In the seminar mentioned earlier,
I give the greatest possible attention to the status and argumentation of these texts
by Reik and Freud, as well as to the question of the relation between psychoanalysis and criminology.—J.D.

On these questions, one can also refer to Chapter 6 above, "The Spirit of the
Revolution."

16. Hugo, Preface, *Last Day of a Condemned Man,* p. 15 [translation modified].

17. First published in the *Nouvelle Revue Française* (June–July 1957), this essay
was reprinted in Albert Camus, *Réflexions sur la peine capitale,* with an essay by
Arthur Koestler (Paris: Calmann-Lévy, 1957).—J.D.

[For English translations of these essays, see Albert Camus, *Resistance, Rebellion, and Death,* ed. and trans. Justin O'Brien (New York: Vintage International,
1995); and Arthur Koestler, *Reflections on Hanging* (New York: Macmillan,
1957).—Trans.]

18. "In fact, the supreme punishment has always been, throughout the ages, a
religious penalty. . . . Only religious values, and especially belief in eternal life, can
serve as a basis for the supreme punishment because, according to their own logic,
they keep it from being definitive and irreparable. Consequently, it is justifiable
only insofar as it is not supreme. The Catholic Church, for example, has always accepted the necessity of the death penalty. . . . But what is the value of such a justification in the society we live in, which in its institutions and customs has lost all
contact with the sacred?" (Camus, *Resistance, Rebellion, and Death,* pp. 222–23,
225).—J.D.

19. See Jean-Luc Nancy, "The Deconstruction of Christianity," in Hent de
Vries and Samuel Weber, eds., *Religion and Media* (Stanford, Calif.: Stanford Uni-

versity Press, 2001); and Jacques Derrida, *Le toucher: Jean-Luc Nancy* (Paris: Galilée, 1999), p. 68 passim.—J.D.

20. Cesare Beccaria, *"On Crimes and Punishments" and Other Writings*, ed. Richard Bellamy, trans. Richard Davies with Virginia Cox and Richard Bellamy (Cambridge, Eng.: Cambridge University Press, 1995), p. 66: "By what right can men presume to slaughter their fellows? Certainly not that right which is the foundation of sovereignty and the laws."—J.D.

21. Charles Baudelaire, in "Pauvre Belgique!," comments in a parenthesis: "(Abolition of the death penalty. Victor Hugo dominates like Courbet. I hear that in Paris 30,000 are petitioning for the abolition of the death penalty. That's 30,000 people who deserve it. You tremble, therefore you are already guilty. At the least, you have a personal interest in the question. Excessive love of life is a descent into animality)" (*Oeuvres complètes* [Paris: Gallimard, Bibliothèque de la Pléiade, 1975–76], vol. 2, p. 899). One variant also turns around this word "interest," which bears a good part of the *charge* (both the accusation, Kantian in its principle or its form, and the problematic stakes around which we are systematically working in this seminar): "Abolishers of the death penalty—doubtless with a great deal of interest" (ibid., p. 1494).

With this alliance between perverse cruelty, sometimes frightful and anti-Semitic meanderings—as I recalled in *Given Time: I. Counterfeit Money* (trans. Peggy Kamuf [Chicago: University of Chicago Press, 1992], pp. 130–31 n. 14)—historical clairvoyance, and anti-Christian Christian compulsion, Baudelaire did not deceive himself, it seems to me, any more than Cortès, concerning the *sacrificial* essence of the death penalty. "The death penalty is the result of a mystical idea, totally misunderstood today. The goal of the death penalty is not *to save* society, at least materially. Its goal is *to save* society and the guilty party (spiritually). For the sacrifice to be perfect, there must be agreement [another Kantian argument!—J.D.] and joy on the victim's part. Giving chloroform to one condemned to die would be an impiety, since it would take away the consciousness of his grandeur as victim and do away with his chance of winning paradise" (Baudelaire, *Oeuvres complètes*, vol. 1, p. 683). (I thank Jennifer Bajorek for bringing these two texts by Baudelaire to my attention.)—J.D.

22. Emmanuel Levinas, "Interview with François Poirié," in *Is It Righteous to Be?: Interviews with Emmanuel Levinas*, ed. Jill Robbins (Stanford, Calif.: Stanford University Press, 2001), p. 51 [translation slightly modified].

To give this proposition its full weight, within a hypothesis that is, *all else being equal*, also mine, namely that there is an essential collusion between philosophy *as such* and the death penalty, let us bring out two features. On the one hand, Levinas's sentence is advanced as a *philosophical* demonstration not in the space of *justice* or *law* but in that of *charity*, a Christian notion (see above). Levinas in fact cites Matthew on the next page. The values of *love* or of *charity* are found at the center of Levinas's long response, which names the death penalty in passing. On the other hand, Levinas's remark rightly belongs to a discourse that tries not to inscribe itself within ontology but to move beyond philosophy as ontology in the Greek tradition. In the last of the *Quatre leçons talmudiques*, Levinas notes in passing: "Jewish law does not permit a death sentence on the basis of a majority of only one vote" (Emmanuel Levinas, *Nine Talmudic Readings*, trans. Annette Aronowicz [Bloomington: Indiana University Press, 1990], p. 74).—J.D.

23. Not only does Levinas *justify* the *lex talionis*, he recognizes in it the origin of *justice* itself. The *lex talionis* would deliver a "message of universalism," "one law for all." This would not in the least be "a way of reveling in the vengeance and cruelty in which a virile existence is steeped. Such inspirations were foreign to the Jewish Bible. They come from the pagans [as Matthew himself said of the *lex talionis*: a pagan affair—J.D.], or Machiavelli, or Nietzsche. . . . The principle stated by the Bible here, which appears to be so cruel, seeks only justice. . . . The rabbis have neither applied nor understood this text to the letter. They have interpreted it in the light of the spirit that pervades the whole of the Bible. . . . The Bible reminds us of the spirit of gentleness" ("An Eye for an Eye," in Emmanuel Levinas, *Difficult Liberty: Essays on Judaism*, trans. Seán Hand [Baltimore: Johns Hopkins University Press, 1990], pp. 146–48) [translation slightly modified].

Without being able to undertake the reading required in this connection, I content myself with a reminder: this distinction between the letter and the spirit is not only that of the rabbis but, literally, the essential argument of Kant and of Hegel in their pleading *for* the *lex talionis* and, indissociably, *for* the death penalty.—J.D.

24. The original reads: "ce qui a toujours tenu ensemble, attenants ou maintenus dans un même tenant."—Trans.

25. "There are only two grounds on which the death of a citizen might be held to be necessary. First, when it is evident that even if deprived of his freedom, he retains such connections and such power as to endanger the security of the nation, when, that is, his existence may threaten a dangerous revolution in the established form of government. The death of a citizen becomes necessary, therefore, when the nation stands to gain or lose its freedom, or in periods of anarchy, when disorder replaces the laws. But when the rule of law calmly prevails, under a form of government behind which the people are united, which is secured from without and from within, both by its strength and, perhaps more efficacious than force itself, by public opinion, in which the control of power is in the hands of the true sovereign, in which wealth buys pleasures and not influence, then I do not see any need to destroy a citizen, unless his death is the true and only brake to prevent others from committing crimes, which is the second ground for thinking the death penalty just and necessary" (Beccaria, *On Crimes and Punishments*, pp. 66–67). Can these lines not be read as one of the most effective pleas in favor of the death penalty?—J.D.

26. "But if I can go on to prove that such a death is neither necessary nor useful, I will have made the cause of humanity triumph" (ibid., p. 66; this sentence is used as an epigram by Robert Badinter in his book *L'abolition*). Two pages later,

Beccaria applies himself to demonstrating the superiority of perpetual forced labor, crueler than the death penalty and therefore more suitable "to deter even the most resolute soul": "neither fanaticism nor vanity survives in manacles and chains, under the rod and the yoke or in an iron cage; and the ills of the desperate man are not over, but are just beginning" (*On Crimes and Punishments*, p. 68).—J.D.

27. The entire sentence reads: "Il lui faudrait donner raison à la raison juridique qui a raison de lui."—Trans.

28. "Suicide," a term forged from the Latin *sui* ("of oneself") and *caedes* ("murder"), was introduced into English in 1636 and into French in 1734.

29. Allow me to refer here to the logic of autoimmunity, which I have tried to generalize elsewhere, notably in "Faith and Knowledge: The Two Sources of 'Religion' at the Limits of Reason Alone," trans. Samuel Weber, in *Acts of Religion.*—J.D.

30. Immanuel Kant, *The Metaphysics of Morals*, trans. and ed. Mary J. Gregor, in *Immanuel Kant: Practical Philosophy*, ed. Allen Wood (Cambridge, Eng.: Cambridge University Press, 1996), p. 472.

31. On July 5, 1982, at the end of a botched trial, Mumia Abu-Jamal was sentenced to death, under his former name Wesley Cook, for the murder of police officer Daniel Faulkner. Incarcerated in the state correctional institute known as Green Prison in Pennsylvania, he spent nineteen years on death row and was several times granted a stay of execution. Jacques Derrida contributed a preface to the French edition of one of his books, written in prison, denouncing the rigidity of the American justice and prison system. See Mumia Abu-Jamal, *Live from Death Row* (Reading, Mass.: Addison-Wesley, 1995); for Derrida's preface, see "For Mumia Abu-Jamal" (1996), in Jacques Derrida, *Negotiations: Interventions and Interviews, 1971–2001*, ed. and trans. Elizabeth Rottenberg (Stanford, Calif.: Stanford University Press, 2002), pp. 125–29.

32. A staunch supporter of the death penalty, George W. Bush was elected president of the United States on December 18, 2000.

33. Introduced into the penal code in 1810, article 64 stipulated that there "is neither a crime nor an infraction when the concerned party was in a state of insanity at the time of the action." In 1992, it was replaced by article 122.1: "Any person stricken, at the moment of the deed, with a psychic or neuro-psychic disturbance that has abolished his or her judgment or control over his or her acts, is not responsible for a crime."

34. I have come to insist more and more on this distinction between *specter* or *phantom* on the one hand, and *revenant* on the other. Like "phantasm," "specter" and "phantom" carry an etymological reference to visibility, to appearing in the light. To that extent, they seem to suppose a horizon on the basis of which, *seeing* what comes or comes back, one annihilates, masters, suspends, or deadens the surprise, the unforeseeability of the event. On the contrary, this latter arises where there is no horizon and where, coming to us vertically, from very high, from behind or from below, it allows itself to be dominated neither by a gaze, nor by a conscious perception in general, nor by a *performative* act of language (which is of-

ten credited with producing the event, when it does so only on the condition of "a legitimating convention" and the institutional authority of an "I can," "I am entitled to," etc.). The "revenant," however, comes and comes back (since singularity *as such* implies repetition) like the "who" or "what" of an event without a horizon. Like death itself. Thinking the event and haunting together would thus be thinking the *revenant* rather than the specter or the phantom.—J.D.

35. Take for example the film *The Sixth Sense*, in which we see a child who becomes the instrument of a terrifying duty to communicate compassion from the living to the dead, by way of a psychiatrist who can listen to him only because he himself is already dead.

36. Derrida is referring here to the opposition between the term "incorporation," advanced by Freud, and that of "introjection," invented by Sandor Ferenczi. "Incorporation" designates a process in which a subject fantasmatically takes an object into his or her body, and "introjection" describes the way in which a subject takes objects from outside into his or her sphere of interest, according to a (neurotic) mechanism contrary to that of (paranoid) projection.

37. Jacques Derrida, "'Eating Well,' or The Calculus of the Subject," interview with Jean-Luc Nancy, trans. Peter Connor and Avital Ronell, in *Points ... : Interviews, 1974–1994* (1994), ed. Elisabeth Weber (Stanford, Calif.: Stanford University Press, 1995), pp. 255–87.

38. This was the subject of Derrida's seminar at the Ecole des Hautes Etudes en Sciences Sociales (EHESS) between 1996 and 1999. See "Le siècle du pardon: Entretien avec Michel Wieviorka," in Jacques Derrida, *Foi et savoir, suivi de Le Siècle du Pardon* (Paris: Seuil, 2000).

39. See Hannah Arendt, *Eichmann in Jerusalem: A Report on the Banality of Evil* (New York: Viking, 1963).

40. Vladimir Jankélévitch, *L'imprescriptible: Pardoner? Dans l'honneur et la dignité* (Paris: Seuil, 1986).

41. "The discoverer of the role of forgiveness in the realm of *human affairs* was Jesus of Nazareth. The fact that he made this discovery in a religious context and articulated it in religious language is no reason to take it any less seriously in a strictly secular sense. . . . Certain aspects of the teaching of Jesus of Nazareth which are not primarily related to the Christian religious message but sprang from experiences in the small and closely knit community of his followers, bent on challenging the public authorities in Israel, certainly belong among [these authentic political experiences], even though they have been neglected because of their allegedly exclusively religious nature." Hannah Arendt, *The Human Condition* (1961) (Chicago: University of Chicago Press, 1998), pp. 238–39, my emphasis. I believe that, with regard to the gospels she cites (Matthew, Mark, Luke), one can draw a conclusion that is exactly the opposite of hers, when she writes: "In all these instances, the power to forgive is primarily a human power: God forgives 'us our debts *as* we forgive our debtors'" (my emphasis). As always, the "as," the "as such" of an "as," bears the entire burden of the interpretation.—J.D.

42. "The alternative to forgiveness, but by no means its opposite, is punishment, and both have in common that they attempt to put an end to something that without interference could go on endlessly. It is therefore quite significant, *a structural element in the realm of human affairs,* that men are unable to forgive what they cannot punish and that they are unable to punish what has turned out to be unforgivable" (ibid., p. 241; my emphasis). Arendt, like Jankélévitch when he says similar things, is no doubt thinking of the Shoah: unforgivable, to the extent that it exceeds the dimensions of any possible punishment.—J.D.

43. On this question, see Chapter 9 below, "In Praise of Psychoanalysis."

44. "Let us never forget the Christian, in truth Lutheran, memory of Heideggerian deconstruction (*Destruktion* was first the *destructio* of a Luther concerned to reactivate the originary sense of the Gospels by deconstructing the theological sediments). Let us never forget this, if we do not want to mix together all the 'deconstructions' of this time and this world. . . . A 'deconstruction of Christianity,' if it is ever possible, would therefore have to begin by letting go of a Christian tradition of the *destructio.*" Derrida, *Le toucher,* p. 74.

CHAPTER 9

1. *The Correspondence of Sigmund Freud and Sandor Ferenczi,* vol. 3, 1920–33, ed. Eva Brabant, Ernst Falzeder, and Patrizia Giampieri-Deutsch; trans. Peter T. Hoffer (Cambridge, Mass.: The Belknap Press of Harvard University Press, 1993–2000).

2. See Elisabeth Roudinesco, *Généalogies* (Paris: Fayard, 1994).

3. See Nicolas Abraham and Maria Torok, *The Wolf Man's Magic Word: A Cryptonomy* (1976), with a foreword by Jacques Derrida, trans. Richard Rand (Minneapolis: University of Minnesota Press, 1986).

4. René Major is a prominent French psychoanalyst and author.—Trans.

5. René Major was the first to make known in France the work done by German scholars on the relations that psychoanalysis had maintained with Nazism. See especially *Les années brunes: La psychanalyse sous le IIIe Reich,* ed. Jean-Luc Evard (Paris: Confrontation, 1984). In 1997, he arranged for the translation into French of a book by Helena Besserman Vianna, who publicized the collaboration of certain Brazilian psychoanalysts with the dictatorship in 1973, as well as the ambiguous role of the French psychoanalyst Serge Lebovici (1915–2000), the president of the International Psychoanalytic Association (IPA) at the time. See Helena Besserman Vianna, *Politique de la psychanalyse face à la dictature et à la torture: N'en parlez à personne,* with a preface by René Major ("Préface et lettre ouverte") (Paris: L'Harmattan, 1997). [The original Portuguese title is *Não conte a ninguém: Contribução à historia das sociedades psicanalíticas do Rio de Janeiro* (Rio de Janeiro: Imago, 1994).—Trans.]

6. René Major, *Au commencement: La vie la mort* (Paris: Galilée, 1999); and René Major, *Lacan avec Derrida: L'analyse désistentielle* (1991) (Paris: Flammarion, collection "Champs," 2001).

7. The States General brought together a thousand participants from thirty-three countries in the large amphitheater of the Sorbonne in Paris. Jacques Derrida and the Chilean jurist Armando Uribe each gave a lecture on this occasion. [See Jacques Derrida, "Psychoanalysis Searches the States of Its Soul: The Impossible Beyond of a Sovereign Cruelty," in *Without Alibi*, ed. Peggy Kamuf (Stanford, Calif.: Stanford University Press, 2002), pp. 238–80.—Trans.]

8. Jacques Derrida, *Politics of Friendship* (1994), trans. George Collins (London: Verso, 1997). In the chapter we are referring to ("For the First Time in the History of Humanity," words taken from a letter from Ferenczi to Freud), one reads, for example: " . . . an address to the father that we shall take seriously, despite the outburst of laughter—terminable interminable—which will rock us to the end. To the end—that is, as long as we will be saying, in reading such a letter (for example), that really, if something has not happened to psychoanalysis *up until now*, this is indeed typical of psychoanalysis; and that undoubtedly nothing will ever happen to it, especially not in the chain of generations of its founding fathers, unless it has already happened in this non-event, and unless it is precisely this, the event of this non-event, that we must perhaps attempt to think, to live, and finally to admit" (p. 280 [translation slightly modified]).—J.D.

In a letter to Freud dated December 26, 1912, Ferenczi excoriates Jung's behavior. He reproaches him for not being able to tolerate a "paternal" authority over him, for neglecting the father and giving too large a place to the "Christian community of brothers": "If you had the strength to overcome in yourself, without a leader (*for the first time in the history of humanity*), the resistances which all humanity brings to bear on the results of analysis, then we must expect of you the strength to dispense with your lesser symptoms" (Ferenczi's emphasis). Cited in Derrida, *Politics of Friendship*, p. 280. (*Correspondence of Freud and Ferenczi*, vol. 1, 1908–1914, pp. 449–51.)

9. Jacques Derrida, *Les chemins de la connaissance*, radio interview with Jean Birnbaum, France Culture, March 24, 2000. Jacques Derrida, "Freud and the Scene of Writing," in *Writing and Difference* (1967), trans. Alan Bass (Chicago: University of Chicago Press, 1978). The latter was a lecture given in 1966 at the Société Psychanalytique de Paris, at the invitation of André Green.

10. See Elisabeth Roudinesco, *Jacques Lacan* (1993), trans. Barbara Bray (New York: Columbia University Press, 1997).

11. See Jacques Derrida, "For the Love of Lacan," in *Resistances of Psychoanalysis*, trans. Peggy Kamuf, Pascale-Anne Brault, and Michael P. Naas (Stanford, Calif.: Stanford University Press, 1998). The conference "Lacan avec les philosophes" will be discussed later in this chapter.

12. Both of these are included in *Jacques Lacan, Ecrits: A Selection*, trans. Bruce Fink (New York: Norton, 2002).

13. Derrida, "Freud and the Scene of Writing." In this lecture, Derrida comments on a 1925 article by Freud, "A Note on the 'Mystic Writing-Pad,'" in which Freud compares the block of celluloid that had just come on the market under the

name "Mystic Writing-Pad (Wunderblock)" to the psychic apparatus. On this block, writing can be erased, but the trace of the writing remains imprinted. See *SE* 19, pp. 227–32.

14. On this history, see in particular Elisabeth Roudinesco, *Jacques Lacan & Co.: A History of Psychoanalysis* (1986), trans. Jeffrey Mehlman (Chicago: University of Chicago Press, 1990).

15. Jacques Derrida, *The Post Card* (1980), trans. Alan Bass (Chicago: University of Chicago Press, 1987), pp. 413–96. It is in this well-known article that Derrida critiques the Lacanian conception of the signifier, according to which a letter always arrives at its destination. Lacan's seminar on Edgar Allan Poe's story "The Purloined Letter" opens the French edition of the *Ecrits*. See Roudinesco, *Jacques Lacan & Co.*, and "Du tout," an interview with Jacques Derrida and René Major (1978), in *The Post Card*, pp. 497–521. The problematic of the purloined letter was taken up in a number of texts published in France and the United States. See in particular *The Purloined Poe: Lacan, Derrida and Psychoanalytic Reading*, ed. John P. Muller and William Richardson (Baltimore: Johns Hopkins University Press, 1988).

16. Jacques Derrida, "Telepathy," trans. Nicholas Royle, *Oxford Literary Review*, 10 (1988), pp. 3–41.

17. Included today under the term "metapsychology" are writings such as "Project for a Scientific Psychology" (1895; *SE* 1), chap. 7 of *The Interpretation of Dreams* (1900; *SE* 5), "On Narcissism: An Introduction" (1914; *SE* 14, pp. 67–107), *Beyond the Pleasure Principle* (1920; *SE* 18, pp. 7–64), *The Ego and the Id* (1923; *SE* 19, pp. 12–59), and *An Outline of Psychoanalysis* (1938; *SE* 23, pp. 141–207). To these are added the five essays on metapsychology written between 1915 and 1917: "Instincts and Their Vicissitudes " (*SE* 14, pp. 111–40), "Repression" (*SE* 14, pp. 143–58), "The Unconscious" (*SE* 14, pp. 161–215), "Metapsychological Supplement to the Theory of Dreams" (*SE* 14, pp. 219–35), and "Mourning and Melancholia" (*SE* 14, pp. 239–58). For an analysis of these works and terms, see Elisabeth Roudinesco and Michel Plon, *Dictionnaire de la psychanalyse* (Paris: Fayard, 1997; rev. ed., 2000).

18. Sigmund Freud, *Moses and Monotheism, SE* 23, pp. 7–137.

19. On reason and psychoanalysis, on the reason of psychoanalysis, see Jacques Derrida, "Let Us Not Forget Psychoanalysis," trans. Geoffrey Bennington and Rachel Bowlby, *Oxford Literary Review*, 12, nos. 1–2 (1990). This text is the introduction to a lecture by René Major given at the Sorbonne, "La raison depuis l'inconscient" (December 16, 1988). See René Major, *Lacan avec Derrida*, p. 11. It was a question of responding in protest to the accusation of irrationalism aimed at a psychoanalyst who was said to be unfaithful to the Enlightenment: " . . . as though, finally, it were again legitimate to accuse of obscurity or irrationalism anyone who complicates things a little by wondering about the reason of reason, about the history of the principle of reason or about the event—perhaps a traumatic one—constituted by something like psychoanalysis in reason's relation to itself" (Derrida, "Let Us Not Forget," p. 4).—J.D.

20. See Derrida, "Psychoanalysis Searches the States of Its Soul."

21. On the "autoimmune function" at work everywhere, and particularly in psychoanalysis, see Jacques Derrida, "Faith and Knowledge: The Two Sources of 'Religion' at the Limits of Reason Alone," trans. Samuel Weber, in *Acts of Religion*, ed. Gil Anidjar (New York: Routledge, 2002); and Derrida, "Psychoanalysis Searches the States of Its Soul," p. 244. This page is preceded by a few reservations: "As a result, I am not sure, at this point, that I am altogether one of you even if, in part, I remain proud to claim to be by sharing your worry" (p. 243).—J.D.

22. "The only discourse that can today claim the thing of psychical suffering as its own affair would indeed be what has been called, for about a century, psychoanalysis. . . . But 'psychoanalysis' would be the name of that which, without theological or other alibi, would be turned toward what is most *proper* to psychical cruelty. Psychoanalysis, for me, if I may be permitted yet another confidential remark, would be another name for the 'without alibi.' The confession of a 'without alibi.' If that were possible" (Derrida, "Psychoanalysis Searches the States of Its Soul," p. 240).—J.D.

23. See in particular the conclusions of Derrida, "Psychoanalysis Searches the States of Its Soul," concerning "an unconditional without sovereignty," "beyond the economy of the possible" (p. 276). See also Derrida, *The Post Card*.

24. See Elisabeth Roudinesco, *Why Psychoanalysis?* (1999), trans. Rachel Bowlby (New York: Columbia University Press, 2002).

25. On the definition of the major concepts of the second topography, see Jean Laplanche and Jean-Bertrand Pontalis, *The Language of Psychoanalysis*, trans. Donald Nicholson-Smith (New York: Norton, 1973); and Roudinesco and Plon, *Dictionnaire de la psychanalyse*.

26. On the question of the responsibility of an author, see Chapter 7 above, "Of the Anti-Semitism to Come."

27. See Jacques Derrida, "Géopsychanalyse" (1981), in *Psyché: Inventions de l'autre* (Paris: Galilée, 1987), pp. 327–52; and René Major, *De l'élection: Freud face aux idéologies américaine, allemande et soviétique* (Paris: Aubier, 1986).

28. The IPA is made up of four types of groups: study groups, provisional societies, constituent societies, and regional societies. See Roudinesco and Plon, *Dictionnaire de la psychanalyse*.

29. Here I am drawing on my introductory lecture for the States General of Psychoanalysis (publication forthcoming).

30. "*Master without commandment*" is the phrase I used to describe Freud's position in the IPA after 1910. See Elisabeth Roudinesco, *Histoire de la psychanalyse en France*, vol. 1 (Paris: Seuil, 1986).

31. The conference "Lacan avec les philosophes" was organized by René Major, Patrick Guyomard, and Philippe Lacoue-Labarthe at the Collège Internationale de Philosophie. It took place May 24–27, 1990, and brought together many scholars and researchers from France and elsewhere who had engaged with Lacan's work, among them Alain Badiou, Christian Jambet, Etienne Balibar, Pierre Macherey,

and Nicole Loraux. See *Lacan avec les philosophes* (Paris: Albin Michel, 1991). Also see Derrida, "For the Love of Lacan."

32. Roudinesco, *Jacques Lacan.*

33. That is, only a few blocks from Lacan's former office, on the rue de Lille.—Trans.

34. Among the speakers at this conference of the Société Internationale d'Histoire de la Psychiatrie et de la Psychanalyse (SIHPP) were Patrick Mahoney, Ilse Grubrich-Simitis, Riccardo Steiner, Malcolm Bowie, and Per Magnus Johansson.

35. Yosef Hayim Yerushalmi, "Series Z: An Archival Fantasy," *Journal of European Psychoanalysis*, no. 3–4 (Spring 1996–Winter 1997). [This article can found on-line: see www.psychomedia.it/jep/number3–4/yerushalmi.htm.—Trans.]

36. Yosef Hayim Yerushalmi, *Freud's Moses: Judaism Terminable and Interminable* (New Haven, Conn.: Yale University Press, 1991); Jacques Derrida, *Archive Fever* (1995), trans. Eric Prenowitz (Chicago: Chicago University Press, 1996).

37. See Elisabeth Roudinesco, *L'analyse, l'archive* (Paris: Editions de la BNF [Bibliothèque Nationale de France], Seuil diffusion, 2001).

38. See *Télévision*, a film on Lacan made by Benoît Jacquot in 1974 for the Institut National de l'Audiovisuel (INA) in collaboration with Jacques-Alain Miller. The text of the interview was published the same year and reprinted in *Autres écrits* (Paris: Seuil, 2001); it appeared in English in *Television*, trans. Denis Hollier, Rosalind Krauss, and Annette Michelson (New York: W. W. Norton, 1990). Also see *La conférence de Louvain*, a film on Lacan made by Françoise Wolf in 1972 for Radio Télévision Belge de la Communauté Francophone (RTBF). Using images from this conference, Elisabeth Kapnist and I made a documentary entitled *Jacques Lacan: La psychanalyse réinventée*, with the participation of Maria Belo, Jacques Derrida, Christian Jambet, Juliet Mitchell, Jean-Bertrand Pontalis. It was produced by the INA and broadcast by Arte in 2001.

39. An archon was an Athenian magistrate possessing not only the power to rule over the city but also the power to interpret the texts of the law and the archives (*arkheion*).

40. David Bakan, *Freud and the Jewish Mystical Tradition* (Princeton, N.J.: D. Van Nostrand, 1958); Peter Gay, *A Godless Jew: Freud, Atheism and the Making of Psychoanalysis* (New Haven, Conn.: Yale University Press, 1987).

41. Anna Freud, "Inaugural Lecture for the Sigmund Freud Chair at the Hebrew University, Jerusalem," *International Journal of Psycho-Analysis*, 59 (1978), pp. 145–48. In this paper, read on her behalf in 1977, Anna Freud recalled the fact that the enemies of psychoanalysis had characterized it as a "Jewish science." In reference to this, she added: "However the other derogatory comments may be evaluated, it is, I believe, the last-mentioned connotation which, under the circumstances, can serve as a title of honor."

42. "Everything happens here as if Yerushalmi had decided in turn to circumcise Freud, as if he felt the obligation to come and re-circumcise him figuratively

by confirming the covenant, as if he felt the duty, in truth, to repeat Jakob Freud's gesture" (Derrida, *Archive Fever*, p. 42) [translation slightly modified].

43. "If Moses had actually been killed by our forefathers," writes Yerushalmi, "not only would the murder not have been repressed but—on the contrary—it would have been remembered and recorded" (*Freud's Moses*, p. 85). To which Jacques Derrida replies: "Whether one goes along with him or not in his demonstration, Freud claimed that the murder of Moses *effectively* left archives, documents, symptoms in Jewish memory and even in the memory of humanity" (*Archive Fever*, pp. 64–65).

44. For these texts and their discussion, I must refer to Derrida, *Archive Fever* (pp. 63–67). At issue is also what I call, beyond this particular debate, the "problematic field of an *archive of the virtual*" (p. 66).—J.D.

45. Cf. Derrida, *Archive Fever*, p. 59.

46. The word "Judaism" [*le judaïsme*] designates the monotheistic religion of the Jews as well as Jewish doctrine and institutions. "Jewishness" [*la judéité*] refers to the fact of being Jewish and to the feeling one has of being Jewish independently of Judaism, in other words, to the way in which one continues to feel and to think of oneself as Jewish in the modern world, even if one is a nonbeliever, agnostic, secular, or atheist.

47. Cf. Derrida, *Archive Fever*, pp. 68–81.

48. See Elisabeth Roudinesco, "Carl Gustav Jung: De l'archétype au nazisme: Dérives d'une psychologie de la différence," *L'Infini*, 63 (Spring 1998), pp. 73–94.

49. Michel Foucault, *The History of Sexuality, Volume I, An Introduction*, trans. Robert Hurley (New York: Random House, 1978), p. 150.

50. Thomas Mann, "A Brother," in *Order of the Day: Political Essays and Speeches of Two Decades*, trans. H. T. Lowe-Porter (New York: Alfred A. Knopf, 1942), p. 159 [translation much modified]. For the German text see "Bruder Hitler," in Thomas Mann, *Gesammelte Werke*, vol. 12 (Frankfurt: S. Fischer Verlag, 1960), pp. 850–51.

51. From a letter to Arnold Zweig from Freud, cited in Yerushalmi, *Freud's Moses*, p. 15. See *The Letters of Sigmund Freud and Arnold Zweig*, ed. Ernst L. Freud (New York: Harcourt, Brace and World, 1970).—Trans.

52. Zhdanovism was an ideology named after Andrei Zhdanov, a leading functionary under Stalin who was largely responsible for the extreme nationalism and strict political control of intellectuals and the arts after the Second World War.—Trans.

53. See Derrida, *Archive Fever*, p. 50 and passim.

54. The Haskalah is the Jewish Enlightenment of the late eighteenth and nineteenth centuries.—Trans.

55. Jean-Paul Sartre, *Réflexions sur la question juive* (1946) (Paris: Gallimard, 1954); published in English as *Anti-Semite and Jew*, trans. George J. Becker (New York: Schocken, 1995). I have recently discussed this book and the decisive history of my relations to it in a lecture, "Abraham, l'autre," presented in December 2000

at the conference "Judéités: Questions pour Jacques Derrida" (proceedings forthcoming with Galilée), held at the Centre Communautaire de Paris. See also Jacques Derrida, "Avouer l'impossible: 'Retours,' Repentir et Réconciliation," in *Comment vivre ensemble?: Actes du XXXVIIIe Colloque des Intellectuels Juifs de Langue Française* (Paris: Albin Michel, 2001).—J.D.

56. *D'ailleurs Derrida* (Paris: Arte-Gloria, 2000), a documentary film on Jacques Derrida by Safaa Fathy; released in English as *Derrida's Elsewhere* (1999). See also Jacques Derrida and Safaa Fathy, *Tourner les mots* (Paris: Arte-Galilée, 2000).

57. Derrida points out that among the Jews in Algeria, one almost never spoke of "circumcision" but rather of "baptism," and rather than "bar mitzvah" one said "communion." See Derrida's *Circumfession*, in Geoffrey Bennington and Jacques Derrida, *Jacques Derrida* (1991), trans. Geoffrey Bennington (Chicago: University of Chicago Press, 1993).

58. In *Circumfession*, Derrida continually associates the memory of circumcision with the memory of the suffering and death of his mother, Esther Georgette Safar Derrida.

59. See in particular Derrida, "Faith and Knowledge." I would like to point in this context to Gil Anidjar's remarkable introduction—entitled "'Once More, Once More': Derrida, the Arab, the Jew"—to Derrida, *Acts of Religion*. In the first section of "Faith and Knowledge," which is the text of a lecture given at Capri, Derrida remarks: "We represent and speak four different languages [German, French, Spanish, Italian—E.R.], but our common 'culture,' let's be frank, is more manifestly Christian, barely even Judeo-Christian. No Muslim is among us, alas, even for this preliminary discussion, just at the moment when it is toward Islam, perhaps, that we ought to begin by turning our attention. No representative of other cults either. Not a single woman!" (ibid. p. 45).

60. "Islam is not Islamism and we should never forget it, but the latter operates *in the name of* the former, and thus emerges the grave question of the name" (Derrida, "Faith and Knowledge," p. 46. Islamism is a political version of Islam. It is necessary therefore to distinguish spiritual Islam (Islam) from political Islam.

61. In the "mythic" history of psychoanalysis, the invention of psychoanalysis as a "talking cure" is attributed to Anna O. (whose real name was Bertha Pappenheim). See Josef Breuer and Sigmund Freud, *Studies on Hysteria* (1895), *SE* 2. One can imagine that psychoanalysis, if it manages to take root in the Muslim world, might serve to defeat, undo, or deconstruct this system, and particularly the repression of the feminine that it establishes. This is Fethi Benslama's hypothesis in her article "La répudiation originaire," in *Idiomes, Nationalités, Déconstructions: Rencontre de Rabat avec Jacques Derrida* (Casablanca: Editions Toubkal, 1998).

Cultural Memory | in the Present

Talal Asad, *Formations of the Secular: Christianity, Islam, Modernity*

Dorothea von Mücke, *The Rise of the Fantastic Tale*

Marc Redfield, *The Politics of Aesthetics: Nationalism, Gender, Romanticism*

Emmanuel Levinas, *On Escape*

Dan Zahavi, *Husserl's Phenomenology*

Rodolphe Gasché, *The Idea of Form: Rethinking Kant's Aesthetics*

Michael Naas, *Taking on the Tradition: Jacques Derrida and the Legacies of Deconstruction*

Herlinde Pauer-Studer, ed., *Constructions of Practical Reason: Interviews on Moral and Political Philosophy*

Jean-Luc Marion, *Being Given: Toward a Phenomenology of Givenness*

Theodor W. Adorno and Max Horkheimer, *Dialectic of Enlightenment*

Ian Balfour, *The Rhetoric of Romantic Prophecy*

Martin Stokhof, *World and Life as One: Ethics and Ontology in Wittgenstein's Early Thought*

Gianni Vattimo, *Nietzsche: An Introduction*

Jacques Derrida, *Negotiations: Interventions and Interviews, 1971–1998*, ed. Elizabeth Rottenberg

Brett Levinson, *The Ends of Literature: Post-transition and Neoliberalism in the Wake of the "Boom"*

Timothy J. Reiss, *Against Autonomy: Global Dialectics of Cultural Exchange*

Hent de Vries and Samuel Weber, eds., *Religion and Media*

Niklas Luhmann, *Theories of Distinction: Redescribing the Descriptions of Modernity*, ed. and introd. William Rasch

Johannes Fabian, *Anthropology with an Attitude: Critical Essays*

Michel Henry, *I Am the Truth: Toward a Philosophy of Christianity*

Gil Anidjar, *"Our Place in Al-Andalus": Kabbalah, Philosophy, Literature in Arab-Jewish Letters*

Hélène Cixous and Jacques Derrida, *Veils*

F. R. Ankersmit, *Historical Representation*

F. R. Ankersmit, *Political Representation*

Elissa Marder, *Dead Time: Temporal Disorders in the Wake of Modernity (Baudelaire and Flaubert)*

Reinhart Koselleck, *The Practice of Conceptual History: Timing History, Spacing Concepts*

Niklas Luhmann, *The Reality of the Mass Media*

Hubert Damisch, *A Childhood Memory by Piero della Francesca*

Hubert Damisch, *A Theory of /Cloud/: Toward a History of Painting*

Jean-Luc Nancy, *The Speculative Remark (One of Hegel's Bons Mots)*

Jean-François Lyotard, *Soundproof Room: Malraux's Anti-Aesthetics*

Jan Patočka, *Plato and Europe*

Hubert Damisch, *Skyline: The Narcissistic City*

Isabel Hoving, *In Praise of New Travelers: Reading Caribbean Migrant Women Writers*

Richard Rand, ed., *Futures: Of Derrida*

William Rasch, *Niklas Luhmann's Modernity: The Paradox of System Differentiation*

Jacques Derrida and Anne Dufourmantelle, *Of Hospitality*

Jean-François Lyotard, *The Confession of Augustine*

Kaja Silverman, *World Spectators*

Samuel Weber, *Institution and Interpretation: Expanded Edition*

Jeffrey S. Librett, *The Rhetoric of Cultural Dialogue: Jews and Germans in the Epoch of Emancipation*

Ulrich Baer, *Remnants of Song: Trauma and the Experience of Modernity in Charles Baudelaire and Paul Celan*

Samuel C. Wheeler III, *Deconstruction as Analytic Philosophy*

David S. Ferris, *Silent Urns: Romanticism, Hellenism, Modernity*

Rodolphe Gasché, *Of Minimal Things: Studies on the Notion of Relation*

Sarah Winter, *Freud and the Institution of Psychoanalytic Knowledge*

Samuel Weber, *The Legend of Freud: Expanded Edition*

Aris Fioretos, ed., *The Solid Letter: Readings of Friedrich Hölderlin*

J. Hillis Miller / Manuel Asensi, *Black Holes / J. Hillis Miller; or, Boustrophedonic Reading*

Miryam Sas, *Fault Lines: Cultural Memory and Japanese Surrealism*

Peter Schwenger, *Fantasm and Fiction: On Textual Envisioning*

Didier Maleuvre, *Museum Memories: History, Technology, Art*

Jacques Derrida, *Monolingualism of the Other; or, The Prosthesis of Origin*

Andrew Baruch Wachtel, *Making a Nation, Breaking a Nation: Literature and Cultural Politics in Yugoslavia*

Niklas Luhmann, *Love as Passion: The Codification of Intimacy*

Mieke Bal, ed., *The Practice of Cultural Analysis: Exposing Interdisciplinary Interpretation*

Jacques Derrida and Gianni Vattimo, eds., *Religion*